Monastery Without Walls

This collection of John Main's letters, revised and edited by Laurence Freeman, was first published as two volumes: *Letters from the Heart* (Crossroad, 1982) and *The Present Christ* (Darton, Longman & Todd, 1985). The present edition has been edited to better represent John Main's thought for contemporary readers in gender inclusive language.

John Main became a Benedictine Monk after diplomatic service in the Far East and teaching law at Trinity College, Dublin. He founded a new style of community in Montreal, which was open to all and from this sprang The World Community for Christian Meditation, a worldwide spiritual family with 100,000 members in 114 countries.

Laurence Freeman OSB is a Benedictine monk of the Olivetan Congregation and director of The World Community for Christian Meditation.

personal

church - institution

interesting; explanation etc

Other books by John Main available from Canterbury Press

Word Into Silence: A manual for Christian meditation
– a spiritual classic on the art of contemplation

Door to Silence: An anthology for meditation
A new collection of quotations from the writings of John Main
– a rich spiritual treasury and a springboard for meditation

Monastery Without Walls

The Spiritual Letters of John Main OSB

THE COMPLETE EDITION

Edited by
Laurence Freeman

CANTERBURY
PRESS
Norwich

© The World Community for Christian Meditation 2006

First published in 2006 by the Canterbury Press Norwich
(a publishing imprint of Hymns Ancient & Modern Limited,
a registered charity)
9–17 St Alban's Place, London N1 0NX

www.scm-canterburypress.co.uk

British Library Cataloguing in Publication data

A catalogue record for this book is available
from the British Library

ISBN 1-85311-737-4/978-1-85311-737-4

Typeset by Regent Typesetting, London
Printed and bound by
MPG Books Ltd. Bodmin, Cornwall

CONTENTS

Part 1

A NEW MONASTICISM

John Main OSB

In 1974 I returned to my own monastery in London, England, after serving for five years as headmaster of the school at St Anselm's Abbey in Washington, DC. Each of these years, as I spoke to the graduating class, I wondered how well we Western Benedictine monks had prepared these young students for their lives in the world. Would they know life in the dimension of Spirit, as a mystery rooted in the joy of being or would their lives be restricted to a struggle for material success, in relation to which the fading memory of their monastic schooling would become increasingly remote and irrelevant?

The Lay Community

All through these years in the most success-orientated of cultures, I had been thinking of a more truly spiritual contribution that Western monasticism could make to our world. How could we open our heritage of meditation and spiritual discipline to our contemporaries and share it with them in the confidence that it was real and present? Now, with my return to London, the opportunity to do this arose.

With the support of the abbot and the community at Ealing Abbey, we started a spiritual centre in a large house on the edge of the property alongside the monastery. Our aim was simple and modest – we were not running eclectic courses on spirituality or going for numbers and success. Instead, we would invite a small group of young men (we were not allowed to accommodate women) to come and live our life with us for a short time and, during their stay, we would try to teach them to meditate. The tradition from which we would teach was that of Western monasticism from its origin: the teaching of John Cassian, invoked as a spiritual guide in the Rule, St Benedict's 'teacher of prayer'. Like both these founders of the Benedictine tradition, we were convinced that the best way to teach others to pray is to pray with them.

We began with six young laymen who had heard what we were planning and asked if they could come in order to learn to meditate with us. As often happens with enterprises that begin like this, we were led in unexpected directions. The development of our initial plan revealed an inner logic that we had not at first fully understood. Following it led us into an unexpected terrain full of potential for radical monastic self-renewal and contemporary Christian self-knowledge.

One of the first things that the presence of these spiritually committed members of the lay community in our monastery made us consider was the significance of our own monastic life and practice. Like many monasteries, we were deeply involved, due to our own history, in external works – especially those relating to a large school and parish. Despite our being overstretched numerically, the works were flourishing, enriched by great generosity in terms of time and energy being given by the monks. As a result, the Divine Office had come to occupy the central place in the community's life of monastic prayer. The relationship between our ministries – what St Benedict called labour or the work of the monks and the Office – was often strained because time was short and the demands were many. The Office can easily become the central spirituality of the monk's life. Without radical self-evaluation, the ongoing conversion of life that St Benedict urges us to achieve does not happen as it is easy for a disruption in the monastic balance between prayer, work and study to establish itself without us being aware of it and for this then to be transmitted from one monastic generation to another.

The laymen meditating in the new centre were a stimulus for such monastic self-evaluation. It soon became evident that the spiritual growth the laymen were experiencing did not derive primarily from the recitation of the Divine Office, but from the practice of silence, the interiorized work of their meditation. Indeed, it seemed to them that the Office, which they attended faithfully, could only be properly appreciated when it nurtured and led to silence. This silence was not the result of institutional rules, it was the silence that they were discovering as a living presence in their own hearts. It was with them throughout the day at all times and places, in all activities, in community or alone. It was the expanding inner atmosphere in which they saw reality in a new depth-dimension that showed how wonder is an essential part of life. It was also the silence that they were beginning to understand was the worship of God in 'spirit and truth'.

Those of us meditating regularly with the lay community and in our own practice became aware of the power of this silence as an interior dimension and a medium of being with others. We also sensed its fragility. The satellite lay community, for example, had no television or radios in its house – distractions that we take for granted but which can so insidiously disrupt the spiritual dimension of life today. The community conventions according to which the house operated were specifically directed towards prayer. In the early days, we prepared for meditation by listening to some music together, but soon we came to feel that the best preparation for the silence of meditation and the best response to the immediate period after it was silence itself. Thus, our silence deepened and grew.

The Call to Share

The spirit of this small community grew quietly. It was not its intention to recruit members or promote meditation; its essence was to be open to the mystery of its own being. This mystery – predictably, as we saw later – was soon called on to share itself. Word of what we were doing began to spread. This led to another unexpected development – the arrival of many laypeople of all ages, walks of life and religious backgrounds. They wrote or telephoned or came to the door to ask if they could share in the instruction on meditation we were giving and join us for our times of meditation.

It seems curious now to remember that at first we were hesitant about responding. This was not what we had thought would happen, nor was it clear that it was what we should do. The questions of space and timetabling were manageable, but the shift in the new community from being resident and self-contained to hosting transient groups might threaten the 'purity' of our monastic spirit – so we feared. A number of things soon led us to see that this perceived danger was illusory and a product of fear. There was, above all, the essential principle of our life based on meditation. It was the principle of openness to reality – a reality not seen in terms of our own limitations, but known as a mystery greater than ourselves and containing us. We could not, then, lay down preconditions for being open. This would be

5

treating the monastic pilgrimage as a package tour made for our own benefit. Many who could not leave their family or work responsibilities to live with us for six months nevertheless seriously wanted to learn to pray. They were seeking a contemplative journey, so surely it fell to us to give whatever we had received to help them. The seriousness and perseverance of all those who had sought us out and who kept returning to ask when we would be starting groups for non-residents was the deciding factor in the next phase of our evolution. We let go of our fears and immediately felt ourselves carried forward on the stream of the Spirit.

The speed of the current surprised us all. In a short time, there were nine separate groups coming to the house weekly. In size they ranged from 5 to 30 people and in age from teenagers to octogenarians. For each group meeting we had essentially the same message. The simple practical instruction on how to meditate was given at the first meeting. Because of its unfamiliarity, it needed to be repeated frequently in the early stages of learning to meditate. It is so difficult for us to believe that anything so simple could be so effective. Holding to its simplicity and not yielding to the temptation to complicate the teaching for the sake of cleverness or novelty was the main reason people returned each week. They did so not to hear something new, but to better understand its meaning and apply it more deeply in their daily lives. We urged everyone, between sessions, to meditate every day of the week, twice daily, morning and evening, for about half an hour. We repeated this message week after week – to be simple, to be faithful.

As the members of the groups deepened their personal commitment, we gradually developed the theology of the introductory talks. It was a scriptural theology of meditation based on the 'secret' of St Paul's letters, the indwelling Spirit of God in the human heart, 'the secret of Christ in you'. Even this developing theology – wonderful as it was to feel it evolve as the groups matured – was not the reason for meeting, however. As anyone in the groups would say, they came, above all, simply to meditate together. The half hour of silence had a greater influence than the talk beforehand or the discussion period afterwards. Quite often, in fact, with the more experienced groups, there would be no discussion or sharing after the meditation and, in relaxed friendship, people would simply leave in silence.

Experience is the Teacher

In this early development period of the first Christian Meditation Centre it seemed that we had stumbled on – or been led to – discoveries that could point the way to a monasticism of the future. The first was the incredible richness of the Christian monastic tradition of contemplative prayer. It lay latent before us, but effectively closed until we stepped into the experience itself, which then disclosed its treasures.

Experientia magistra, a phrase from Cassian's *Conferences,* kept coming to my mind – 'experience is the teacher'. Perhaps only the powerful confidence of the New Testament itself would help those Christians trained to distrust 'spiritual experience' to see that the silence and stillness of meditation opens us in faith to deeper knowledge of the person of Christ. It is an experience in which the one who is experiencing also becomes, in full consciousness, the one who is experienced. In the Christian understanding of meditation – of all prayer – this experience is a union of love. The familiar pages of the New Testament put this before us in words that we often misunderstand on the very level at which they must be heard. What else does the New Testament mean when it says that 'we possess the mind of Christ' but that the experience is already within us?

The richness of the monastic tradition of meditation grew directly out of the paradox of the 'rich poverty' of the gospel. The connection with individual experience, we said to the groups, is poverty of spirit. The poor in spirit find that the reign of God is not a place but an experience – an experience of the whole person who is in love. Meditation as a spiritual practice is at the heart of the monastic tradition because it is the direct way of becoming poor in spirit. The message was and is universal. The monk exists, separated from people but in harmony with everyone, to prove that it is also personal and unique. The journey into the kingdom of God is daily perseverance in deepening poverty. The early days of beginning to meditate can be full of great enthusiasm as one explores a new world of spiritual richness previously undreamed of, but this can be the 'first fervour of conversion', as St Benedict called it, the romantic stage of love. The hinge on which we swing into self-transcendence is faithful, regular practice. When spiritual commitment moves into this phase, it is no longer concerned with 'good' or 'bad' meditations. Instead, there is only one meditation – the one where we are faithful to the deepening of our poverty. This was the heart of the ancient monastic wisdom and the people coming to the meditation centre seemed grateful for being reminded of it.

We were beginning to see that a commitment to the daily practice of meditation awakens us to an experiential theology that is written on our own hearts. We understood what Evagrius meant when he said, 'A theologian is one who prays and one who prays is a theologian.' As I talked to the groups from this wisdom, it sometimes seemed strange to me that they did not find it stranger. What we were teaching was just what John Cassian had taught at the beginning, 1500 years before. The tradition had passed on from one monastic generation to another, but the teaching had now become experientially weak, even for many monks and scholars of the texts. Yet, here were growing numbers of laypeople, with busy lives and heavy responsibilities, building a transcendent commitment to poverty of spirit, mind and heart into their daily lives. They were finding from their own faith journey that the purpose of prayer is not 'to experience the experience', but to be one with the *experience-in-itself*. The discipline of the silence we shared each week and each day in our own places of meditation led into realms of faith and gnosis that cannot be understood in terms of self-conscious or merely intellectual ways. This experiential knowledge, born of faith, is one of the great gifts that monasticism still has to offer the world through the Church.

This experience underpins the whole self-communication of Christ in his body. It was with wonder – not novelty, but a deepening maturity in their daily practice – that the new meditators in the groups began to *see* what previously they had just looked at. Insight into the meaning of the gospel stories, the words of St Paul, grew. This was a re-evangelization for many of them. Later it extended to the Eucharist, incorporating a half hour of meditation after Communion, which we then held weekly in the meditation room. People did not come to these insights dramatically – their way had begun in faith and they were prepared to trust that it would end in faith. Our emphasis on experience did not mean encouraging people to be on the lookout for new experiences in their meditation times, but wonder at the journey had stirred and was growing. The faith-based experience was getting deeper. As it deepened, through 'times of prosperity and adversity' (as Cassian puts it), it brought forth that knowledge we call wisdom.

A New Monasticism

The latent richness of our own tradition was the first thing that made me think of a new monasticism – one that could regain its necessary role in the world through the teaching of prayer. In the contemplative equation, self-discovery leads into other-centredness. A renewed monasticism would be called forth by responding to the spiritual crisis of our time.

We were familiar enough with this crisis. What I began to see now, more sharply, was that it was not only a crisis of materialism or even of a loss of spiritual values – it was more painful even than that. The crisis was that people with deep, hungry spiritual seriousness were being blocked from what they needed and had, naturally, begun by looking for it in their own tradition. Their confusion and crisis has affected our entire Western society, which has become alienated from spiritual knowledge, and this alienation has affected even the Church, the traditional spiritual authority of the West. So, it is the blind leading the blind. The Church has seemed unable to deliver the goods people have been looking for.

These seekers were the real apostles on whom the Church depended. They were the catalyst that would break the spell of materialism and restore the spirit of wisdom to the institutions of society. If these people, living and working in the world, lacked the deeper interiority of spiritual experience, how could they redeem and transform the world in compassionate love? They came to our small centre in Ealing because they felt the lack of this interiority and depth. They had come to accept that merely going to church or even practising personal devotions would not be enough. Even if, as many were, they were practising their religion faithfully, they felt a spiritual void and they could no longer be content to try and fill it with just more religious activity. They knew that the way to transform emptiness into plenitude is to enter it in person. I sensed that we were witnessing the birth of a contemplative Christianity

At our centre, many found a source for the faith necessary for this journey into poverty of spirit. It seemed to me that, in our faith-deficient society, it is a monastery's pre-eminent service to be a place where faith is lived, honoured and nurtured. It is a place where very ordinary people, not spiritual heroes, prove that faith is possible. Perhaps what I have been saying seems to underemphasize the ordinariness of everyone involved in our centre, but it was an ordinariness touched by sublimity – the sublimity of the knowledge of Christ.

This sublimity fed the creative spirit that all those involved in the centre felt was at work. It came from a wonderful and liberating paradox. We were ordinary people becoming aware of the universal human call to sublimity that the gospel declares. This awareness grew from the personal discovery of the paradox of Christ's teaching – that we must lose our life in order to find it. What harmonizes the many facets of life's mystery is at root not words, thoughts or images, but the simple and simplifying experience of prayer itself. This is the meaning of the daily practice of meditation.

So, very early on, it became clear that only a monasticism vitalized by a return to its essential task of 'seeking God' in pure prayer can re-establish a useful relationship with the modern world. This relationship is a release and transmission of spiritual energy if monasticism is true to itself and monks are true to their personal vocation. Our discoveries in the meditation centre suggested what this relationship might be. The laypeople who came were searching for a way to enter into a more direct, personal experience of God. If they were Christians, as most were, they believed that this meant the way of prayer, but prayer could no longer be satisfactorily defined as talking to God or thinking about God – it needed to be an experience of prayer best described as the awareness of God in Jesus. They came to learn how they could enter this experience within their own tradition and as that tradition teaches. They came to receive the support of monks whom they felt had made this the priority of their lives and those who, in the world like themselves, were beginning to live the contemplative dimension of life.

The new monasticism, in its relationship with the world, must include this role of contemplative teacher. The people who came to us to learn to meditate had the humility, the realistic self-knowledge, to *want* to learn. They were very teachable. However, to say that we were their teachers of prayer needs to be qualified in a Christian context. We were talking to people whose hunger and humility had already brought them to know what St Paul meant when he said that 'we do not even know how to pray'. They were people with some spiritual maturity. As Cassian put it, 'You are on the brink of knowledge if you attentively recognize what you should ask about and you are not far from knowledge if you begin to understand how much you do not know' (*Conferences* X: ix). Not surprisingly, therefore, our meditation groups shared the awareness that even the best oral teaching is limited. Anything that can be said is a preparation for the silence in which the experience, teaching and teacher are one. Our oft-repeated message was that the way to the experience is faithful practice. We had the grace to learn from the beginning that to teach others how to meditate means to meditate with them.

The Call to Move On

It was an intense time of growth, but none of these insights was instantaneous. They arose and were tested by events during the first two years of the existence of the centre. After this, we were presented with another opportunity and difficult challenge.

It was more demanding than had been the first arrival of people knocking at the door asking to learn to meditate. Word of the centre was spreading widely, through personal contact and our first publications. By a peculiar series of connections, it reached Montreal and led to an invitation from its archbishop to make a monastic foundation there in the spirit of the London meditation centre. Bishop Leonard Crowley, the Auxiliary Bishop in charge of English language affairs, described the kind of contemplative monastic centre that he felt the diocese needed. I placed the proposal before the Ealing community and they unanimously declined it.

The community naturally felt honoured by the invitation and wanted to make a contribution to the universal Church, but it felt unable to respond to the Montreal invitation because of our own shortage of monks. No one could be spared. Far from deterring Bishop Crowley, this seemed to increase his own faith in the idea. He persistently put his vision to us and in the end his determination won through. At the beginning of 1977, the community bravely accepted his proposal for a two-year trial period. The catalyst for change was the lay community, four of whom offered to support the foundation by coming to help. Brother Laurence Freeman, who had joined the monastery after six months in the lay community was in simple vows and had started his theological studies, also volunteered to come. So, the founding members were formed: two monks leaving familiar ground to start what we knew would be a new kind of monastery and four laypeople, risking their security, leaving jobs and families.

We were starting our monastery in Montreal from scratch. Bishop Crowley had found a house for us, but we had few of the resources most monasteries depend on for their 'monastic identity'. This, though, gave us a unique opportunity. We could re-engage with the essentials of monasticism. In an unexpected way, we found ourselves transported from a monastic life in which the means of livelihood and service, the daily structure of work and worship, were all established and well-worn.

Overnight, we were thrown back from familiar custom and on to the bedrock of tradition. We were rediscovering primitive, archetypal monasticism. Now we had only this tradition as a present reality coming alive in the experience of prayer. I felt as if I was discovering in quite new ways how 'tradition' has life and meaning. Tradition becomes just historical memory when it is separated from personal experience. To show that tradition and experience are one in the moment of love – this seemed to be the important contemporary message of monasticism. This experience of prayer, which the new community shared, and the formation in the Rule of St Benedict that the monastic members knew, were the basic elements of change. We lived and watched and felt it grow within us in the first few months. This was a crucial time for the refining of our monastic spirit. It led us into a clearer understanding of the Rule as the great spiritual document it is. The Rule, with its human gentleness, flexibility and tolerance is also marked by a tough commitment to the centrality and priority of prayer. It is this unifying vision of life that allows the Rule to integrate everything in life as part of its 'seeking God', 'preferring nothing to the love of Christ' and 'never despairing of the mercy of God'.

Our relationship with the city, the Church and our new continent grew from this renewal of the Rule of Benedict in the new chemistry of pure tradition and experience. We did not have a school or parish or any external apostolate, so our new kind of monastic life would work if our prayer opened up a direct communication with the complexities of modern society. This communication would be our monastic *word*. In communication with such a complex and mobile world, our word would have to be simple and steady and emanate from a growing but stable tradition. Then, contact with the reality of modern urban life, far from threatening our life as a city monastery, would be the opportunity to deepen it even more than is usually possible in a traditional cloister. Having a relationship with the world would help the monastic spirit develop because the world was coming to us with the gift of its spiritual hunger. Through this hunger, the unstable world of modernity and the traditional stability of the Rule would form a new kind of monastery.

Our communication with the city generated a spiritual teaching. It reflected what the desert fathers and mothers called the *word* – an interpersonal experience of the wisdom of the spirit. The world expected this of us as people whose archetypal form of life was supposed to recall a spiritual reality deeper than the world's restlessness. This expectation was a challenge. It asked us to prove that what we had come to Montreal to teach was as relevant as the word that drew the inhabitants of fourth-century Alexandria out to the desert to meet the first Christian monks and hermits. The word, the message, was the same – we were not trying to be original. The challenge was to find the way to make it glow and grow today.

The Spoken Word

Shortly before leaving England I had made three cassettes on prayer.[1] They were a response to the need to help people beginning their contemplative practice to understand and better integrate meditation into daily life. This meant persuading people of the simplicity of meditation.

Nearly everyone asked what they should read on prayer. Few were content to be told to read nothing much until they had begun to meditate. An essential part of Christian life that we did recommend, however, was an attentive reading, a 'chewing', of scripture alongside the twice-daily meditation practice. This is the *lectio divina* of the Rule. There were a few books (usually not bestsellers) that we recommended as companions for the daily pilgrimage, such as Abhishiktananda's *Prayer* and *Saccidananda*.[2] My own set of tapes were made for ongoing use – not to define prayer or reveal anything esoteric, but to point away from too much concern with what was or was not happening in

---

1 Now published as the CD and tape sets *The Essential Teaching* (Medio Media, 1991) and as the book *Word into Silence* (Canterbury Press 2006).

2 Abhishiktananda, *Saccidananda: A Christian Approach to Advaitic Experience* (ISPCK, Delhi, 1974).

meditation to the faith and knowledge that were growing in life through practice and perseverance.

The first cassette, 'An Introduction to Christian Meditation', was a response to people who wanted a summary of the practice that they could share with others, as well as support their own beginning in meditation. The four talks on this first tape demanded a certain effort of concentration. They were the substance of the introductory talks at the Monday night groups. What is meditation? Why should we meditate? How can we begin this journey today? Is it really prayer? How does it fit in the Christian tradition? How to do it and how to keep it simple?

It seems to me still that the spoken word is the essential medium for the communication of the gospel. The gospel experience is the fullest personal experience of communion. It communicates itself between people who are alive to themselves and each other. One can pour one's personal truth into a book, but it will only rarely happen that a reader will be able to truly receive and absorb it. We cannot tell how the printed word carries meaning to the reader. Together, face to face, words are part of a much deeper and richer use of language – the language of the whole person. Barriers to full communication are lowered through the spoken word, where the demand for attention, essential to any communication in any medium, is continuously being adapted and personalized. Sharing the gospel through the spoken word makes it possible to re-present the absolute, simple call of Christ. One can be continually surprised by it as something that is not idealistic but eminently practical in *my* life. Not '*people* must lose their life', but '*I* must lose *my* life'.

Listening to a tape is not the same as being with the person speaking, but it helps to retain the personal nature of what is being communicated and maintain the discipline of attentive listening that opens the heart. I said at the beginning of the first talk, 'if you can listen to this tape carefully you are taking your first step in learning to meditate'. To meditate is to listen to the word. In the early days of our literate culture, the link between the book and the spoken word had not been severed. St Benedict told monks not to read too loudly in the cloister while at their private *lectio*. St Augustine was reading his Bible aloud when his great awakening occurred. Reading aloud deepens the personal incorporation of the words' meaning. Today, reading books is a silent and private experience that we rarely communicate to others.

We tend to be intensely introverted when we read, as we are now trained to do. There are advantages in the privatized reading of books: systems of thought that it would be impossible to communicate orally can be lucidly rendered in silent print and can be revisited and reread. Prayer, though, is not a system of thought. Using the spoken word as the principal medium for teaching meditation was an attempt to communicate the message of the tradition as a living word, not just ideas, as the *logos,* which is the original principle of all communication. Thought, imagination and language are reflections of the primary experience of the mystery of God that happens in the transcendence of all limited ways of knowing. To know God, we have to abandon all our habits of knowing and enter into the divine self-knowledge. This is the work of unknowing and of silence.

The spoken word on tape does seem capable of leading people into this work of silence. So, if, in reading this book, you feel drawn to explore the way of meditation, I would suggest that you also *listen* to the original cassettes.[3] Books and tapes are no substitute for a fully personal communication, however. This is only fully realized in Christ, the teacher within, and in the community in which he is present. This is the heart of the monastic tradition. It is my experience that each person discovers this when the logic of personal growth demands it, when the time is ripe. So, all we have to do is begin where we are.

The Theology of Perseverance

The first cassette encouraged people to begin. The second tape, made a year later, addressed those who had begun and were trying to persevere. As a theology of meditation grew from our experience within the community of the weekly groups, it seemed natural to communicate this as well.

It was not meant to be abstract theology, but nor was it anti-intellectual. Some people complain about meditation that it is not 'incarnational': it seems to reject the physical-psychological-intellectual-spiritual unity of our humanity. Others complain that it denies the gifts of the mind, imagination, memory, reason. I feel that these complaints can only be made before the experience of meditation is

---

3 Since this was written, more than 200 of John Main's talks on meditation have been published.

known. The experience *is* the integration, through silence, of body and mind in the heart beyond self-reflective consciousness. This integration then begins to pervade the mysterious *wholeness* of the meditator's life. When people ask how they can tell if they are making progress in meditation, since they are not supposed to analyse or evaluate the actual time of meditation, the answer is: your life. You can tell you are on a real journey because of a greater personal peace and rootedness in the self, more emotional stability, a greater capacity to love and pay attention to others. These are the signs of spiritual growth. It can be put even more simply: it is becoming more loving and more aware of love as the essential energy of life. These are the real signs of making the inner journey authentically. Physical benefits result from greater mental and emotional simplicity.

What before may have seemed understandable only in complicated ideas and self-qualifying terminology is increasingly seen as being really quite simple, self-evident and immediate. Reality, one realizes, is not an idea but, well, reality – everything that is. Knowing experientially what before was speculation develops new forms and ways of expression. A new language for spirituality is born for the communication of the truth. For many meditators, the starting point of this new clarity is a fresh experience of the Word communicated in the New Testament or a new 'reading' of one's own situation in the light shed by God's Word. Scripture comes alive through the experience of meditation. In the diminishing of self-consciousness we undergo our greatest detachment. What is gained in this loss is beyond anything we can expect or explain. Liberty of spirit, healings of the broken heart and expansion of the mind all lead the meditator further into that integration of consciousness, holiness, in which our response is simple thankfulness and wonder.

'The Christian Experience', the second tape, tried to communicate something of this wonder that overwhelms the mind as we enter the Trinitarian dimension of prayer. All human experience is limited, but we felt, in these early days of the new community, that we were experiencing something that should be communicated. We moved to and fro between experience and tradition, always grounded in the rhythm of our regular return to meditation. This led to a sense of what kind of community was appearing through the meditation. This taught me what seems to me to be the deepest dynamic of monastic life as well as its essential witness: that to know God we have first to know ourselves and that we fully know ourselves in the moment of prayer. This is the moment of the evaporation of all multiplicity and division, the transcendence of the idea of consecutive states of knowledge (as if we knew ourselves and *then* knew God), and the revelation that all knowing is known within the self-knowing of God, which *is* God's love. This second of the tapes tried to describe this as the supreme mystery that motivates the absolute simplicity and poverty of meditation. We leave self behind in order to find our enduring reality, to find ourselves one with the one with whom Jesus was one.

The first tape, as I mentioned, tried to get people to begin to meditate. The second tried to deepen their understanding of what they had started. The concluding tape of the set, 'Twelve Talks for Meditators', was made in response to the needs of missionaries. The Medical Missionaries of Mary had invited me to take part in their renewal programme at their mother house in Drogheda. I said how we had to work not for a merely *religious* renewal, on the levels of community structures and self-image. There is no renewal of the Church despite all the energy expended on courses, meetings and reorganization if there is not also a radical renewal in spirit. Because of its depth and the nature of its mystery, this radical renewal is not in our own power to make happen. What we can do is prepare for the power that will do it. Our preparation is deepening openness and vulnerability to the power of God dwelling in us. This is prayer. Religious renewal boils down to a renewal in prayer.

Talking to these wonderful sisters, I was greatly moved by their sincerity and enthusiasm – they really *wanted* this inner renewal – but I was equally struck by the challenge I was proposing. Their lives in the mission field were demanding and unpredictable. Frequently, just when it seemed possible to find time and space for prayer, their daily schedule was overturned. They also spoke of the loneliness of the missionary life, its many emotional detachments. It was hard, they said, to maintain any life of prayer far away from spiritual direction or the other supports of religious life. However, they did not think that meditation was irrelevant to them, that this was a 'contemplative' form of prayer unsuitable for their 'active' lives. They knew perfectly well, maybe better than most 'contemplatives', how universal is the gospel call to the loss and rediscovery of self. They understood how meditation is a response to this call. This was not the problem. The problem lay in personal discipline and lifestyle.

It was with these good sisters in mind that I made the 'Twelve Talks for Meditators'. They are short boosters meant to encourage solitary meditators, who lack an immediate support group, to grow in fidelity to the twice-daily times of prayer. They can be as useful to family groups or city workers as they are to missionaries in the Third World. They locate meditation in the challenge to grow in the actual life we are living. For many today this involves instability, insecurity, loneliness or isolation, so the talks stress the vital connection between prayer and community. For those praying alone each day, it helps to know that, even without a visible community, the commitment to pray leads into a spiritual community. In subtle but perceptible ways this can give us the strength and encouragement we all need, saints and sinners alike, to persevere. Community is more than a place or a habit; it *happens* among those who are faithful and whose faith allows them moments of grace to recognize each other.

From Tapes to Newsletter

These three tapes, with a short book of monastic conferences introducing meditation that found a good response from laypeople too,[4] were soon in wide circulation. Because of these publications and the growing numbers of meditators in London, several weekly groups of meditators had started in other places. They offered a form of community to beginners and those persevering. The groups continue to meet weekly.[5] It was to keep in touch with these groups and the many who were meditating without that support that we began to send out a newsletter from Montreal.

It was designed to give more than local news and domestic details of our community, but, even the minutiae of community life are part of the deeper teaching that is being lived in prayer and community. As with our other ventures, we found that the newsletters were developing into something more than we had expected. Before long, our mailing list in North America grew to the size of the European list. People with whom we had had contact only through the tapes or book asked

---

4 *Christian Meditation: The Gethsemane Talks* (Medio Media). Three groundbreaking conferences John Main gave at Thomas Merton's monastery of Gethsemane in 1976.

5 In the past 25 years, the meditation groups have spread to more than 100 countries and formed The World Community for Christian Meditation.

to be put on the mailing list. One consequence of this was that the newsletter was being read by people who had not met us or even begun to meditate. We started to receive letters from people who were curious or confused by what we were doing.

Sometimes this confusion was about the word meditation itself. We were using it in its original, monastic sense of a simple practice leading into 'pure' or imageless prayer. *Meditare* has the sense of chewing or repeating a *word*. This original meaning clashes with other meanings that developed later in other schools of spirituality – especially meditation seen as discursive prayer with emphasis on the use of imagination. On the other hand, most people today, especially the younger generation, understood meditation in the original sense because of their acquaintance with Eastern traditions. We also continued to use the word meditation, despite the confusion, because, through the confusion, a person might come to a clearer understanding of prayer. The surprise of discovering its traditional meaning might be the opportunity to rethink their ideas about prayer itself. The pity for so many Christians is that their received ideas about prayer are so incomplete and connect so little to the contemplative dimension of the gospel and their own faith.

Christians often think of prayer too much in terms of 'methods'. They have inherited systems with which to analyse and categorize prayer. The result of this is an intensifying of the very self-consciousness and self-obsession that is the enemy of prayer. People often make genuine attempts to deepen their prayer, only to be misled by their inadequate training and the manuals of prayer. They are thrown off course by self-objectification: is this the prayer of quiet, of simple regard, of infused contemplation? These are traditional categories of prayer states, but even more modern terms can also keep the person trying to pray stuck in self-centred self-analysis. Through our widening contact with different expressions of the Christian tradition I realized how important it was to emphasize the original simplicity of meditation and its radical other-centredness.

Confusion About Prayer

There is much confusion about the real simplicity of prayer.

For some people, what we teach seems so contrary to the theory of prayer that they may have followed faithfully for a lifetime they even react to meditation with hostility. Others are more open but can be equally confused. Christian meditation, to some whom we met in these early days, was a new, syncretistic technique – a bit of the East, a bit of the West, another thing to try. Sometimes the worst confusion about prayer that we encountered came from clergy and religious. For them, meditation seemed impractical, impossible, unbalanced. It was platonic, abstract, narcissistic and an escape from the real world. It was not 'truly Christian' because it was not truly incarnational.

This distinction between 'spiritual' and 'incarnational' prayer is often a cause of confusion. I have never found that this confusion (of logic and theology) can be cleared just by talking. We all become so attached to our own terms and definitions. If these are themselves confused, the discussion that revolves around them will be fruitless. Our approach, therefore, to people who wanted only to argue about meditation might have sometimes seemed arrogant. We said 'try it'. Discussion *about* meditation only helps understanding when it is orientated towards a time of silence, when we stop talking and begin to pray together. Of course, there are genuine questions to raise and ideas to explore, but, if there is no common acceptance of the priority of experience, of silence, words produce more words.

The present confusion about Christian prayer has to be addressed, but it can only be clarified if we are willing to be open to the contemplative dimension and the different perspective that others see. Ultimately we must let go of everything. We begin by relaxing our attachment to our own opinions. All discussion about prayer should cultivate the act of faith by which we pass beyond all thinking of who God is and enter the living mystery. Even this letting go, if misunderstood, could become an ideology, merely another fixed way of thinking. Some people respond enthusiastically to meditation at first sight because they think that they have found a quick and easy way to escape from the diminishing returns of other kinds of prayer, but their initial excitement wanes when the simplicity of the practice shows how absolute it is in the discipline of meditation and fidelity to the poverty.

So, while some people misunderstand meditation, thinking that it is unchristian, others embrace it but find it too demanding. In the early days of the community, we were often asked to dilute the absolute simplicity of the teaching. People might say, for example, that they had reached a stage where the discipline of the mantra was no longer necessary. The mantra had 'become a distraction' or it was 'blocking the Spirit'. I don't condemn any way of prayer, but I do not think that we should misrepresent the challenge of the tradition in this particular way of prayer. Discussion about meditation can often substitute for meditation. After a while there is only one thing to say: 'Just do it.' The act of faith that meditation demands is ever deepening. It is a journey that begins and ends in faith. It must be an entirely free choice to follow it or not, free of inner or outer compulsion. I do not say that meditation is the only way. I simply say that if this is the way you freely choose, then the teaching is to recite the mantra – 'without ceasing' and 'in prosperity and in adversity', as John Cassian, the *Cloud of Unknowing* and the hesychast tradition of the Jesus Prayer all teach – until you can no longer say it. If, during the meditation, we can ask ourselves the question 'Is it time I stopped saying it?' this is a sure sign that we must continue to say it.

People who disagree with this have complained that meditation is only one method of prayer and we were making too exclusive a claim for it. I hope this is not so. It would not be true to the catholic tradition, which is naturally inclusive. Rather, because there is such ignorance about the contemplative dimension of Christian prayer, it is necessary to emphasize it strongly. The aim of our community is to do this and, as far as we are able, to prove by our lifestyle that there are, in fact, no 'methods of prayer'. It is the discipline of faith, not techniques, that leads to personal transformation. There is only prayer, the prayer of Jesus; not words or intentions he addresses to the Father, but the overflowing plenitude of his relationship with the Father. Even to speak about 'my prayer' too individualistically is to miss the essential Christian meaning of prayer: 'We do not know how to pray.' We learn how to by following the Master who takes us into the creative and liberating mystery of his prayer, the stream of love that flows between him and his Father, which is the Spirit. 'My prayer', then, means going beyond our selves and entering into this stream of divine love. This realizes our incorporation with Jesus – not because we read or think about it, but because we know and *experience* it. Peace, joy and freedom of spirit in daily life are signs that this mystical union is happening. These 'fruits of meditation' grow by discovering that the stream of love we have been plunged into is the ground of all reality: being itself.

The moment of pure prayer is not when a technique begins to work, but transcendence that involves us totally in the mystery of God and reveals God's mystery as our own mystery: not something solved but life fulfilled. The *ecstasies* of prayer is being taken out of ourselves and inserted into the self-knowledge of the divine mystery. The self we have lost is also found in God, no longer alienated from itself and from God by self-consciousness. Loss of self is ceasing to think about one's self. What we turn to (though we don't know this *until* we turn) is the one who is the source of our self. The intimate otherness of God is revealed in transcendent other-centredness.

The letters collected here try to reflect this mystery of Christian prayer through the story of an imperfect experiment in Christian contemplative community. They try to show that all human renewal – whether personal renewal in Christ or monastic renewal in community – happens through self-transcendence in the present moment. The point of departure in each letter is the call to be wholly real in the *now*. This is contemplative living in the nowness of the true God. Our stressful relationship with time and our distracted desire for the next consolation or amusement makes it difficult to see meditation in this spiritual perspective. Only too easily we see meditation as a technique of stress-reduction, self-therapy or mental hygiene. Seeing it like that means the Christian experience gets indefinitely postponed into a disincarnate future.

Never before in history has it been more important to listen to a tradition that says prayer is an ever-deepening penetration of the present moment. It is a journey into a union of love. The progressive shedding of self-consciousness leads into that union. However, such is the nature of the risk that makes the human being free, even this great tradition can teach us little if we don't have some light born of our own experience to recognize it by. It is this experience that saves the tradition from becoming merely a memory reproduced in print. Experience revitalizes tradition for every generation. In the personal act of faith that opens us to this experience, the tradition is invested with human relevance for all. Meditation is for all. It is universally relevant because it restores us to that present moment in which we are propelled into the presence of God.

The Present Christ

Monastic renewal is mere nostalgia or scholarship if it is only a return to historical origins. History, however, shows that the founders of

Christian monasticism did not see their goal as a return to the historical Jesus. For them, the monastic life was the wonder of a present encounter with the risen and fully alive Jesus.

In this encounter they knew – in time – the freedom from time and history that the life of Jesus throws open to all. It is freedom from the individual bondages of our personal histories as well as from the collective enslavement to sin, fear, ignorance and weakness. By knowing this freedom of Jesus as the deepest human reality, the monastic founders ignited a living tradition. The spirit of their tradition, rather than the letter, conveys the mystery to us today. The tradition has to be as alive for us as it was for them. It has to be extracted from the raw material of modern living because the 'new creation' to which Jesus is the door is as fresh and liberating for us as it was for his first disciples.

What our Montreal letters try to communicate is that knowledge of the presentness of Christ comes from our personal encounter with the living teacher who dwells in our hearts. Christian monasticism will be renewed to meet the spiritual needs of our day only when its monks return to their primary responsibility – seeking God who is present now. Monastic renewal, then, works like a lever in the spiritual machinery of the Christian community, teaching and inspiring others to seek God in the here and now. Today, monasticism needs to realize that it is not the only way to live the contemplative life (being in the present moment), but it has a special responsibility to teach what the contemplative life means. The body of Christ is a chain of inter-dependent events, the influence of which radiates beyond its visible boundaries. Experience of its boundless life depends on personal commitment and the contagion of personal example. There is no shortage of books and talks on prayer and meditation, even summer courses on advanced spirituality. In our new monastery our aim was not so much to talk about prayer but pray in a deep simplicity with daily fidelity and thus help others into their own experience of contemplation.

The difficulty that this kind of monasticism poses to modern people is that the interior silence necessary for deep prayer is so foreign to contemporary culture. We are accustomed to regarding prayer as talking *to* God, thinking *about* God or *imagining* God or the historical Jesus – with many variations on these mental activities. It has become hard for us to see prayer as *being with God*. With so much mental activity, we forget that the essence of prayer is silence, stillness and awe in the presence of God.

The pressures and distractions of modern life have made silence seem an attractive idea. Often, though, it is the idea of a silence as only turning down the volume, listening to soft music in the background, or of an introverted consciousness, listening to the chatter of our own minds. True silence is the absence of thought. When we come to it – and hear nothing – we may panic and make noise by resuming self-consciousness. The monastic word is that silence is the medium of transcendence and it is natural and possible for people in every walk of life. Monasteries can offer companionship for the journey into silence, but each person has to follow it for themselves. In the solitude of this personal integrity we find that we are in communion with all.

Our message in these letters is therefore a simple one. In our experience of silence, to which our repeated act of faith leads us, we know prayer not as observing God or setting a trap for God, but total absorption in God. To pray means to leave self behind and find our self absorbed in God. It means that the journey from self is a penetration into the infinite mystery of God. We can never say 'we have arrived, we have made it'. Absorption in God means sharing in the infinite expansion of consciousness that is God's essential nature, God's love. In the Christian revelation, we are united with this mystery personally, not as in a notional way but ontologically. The ground of our being and consciousness are pervaded by the mind of Christ, whose love unites us to himself. In its boundlessness, the mystery of God has always been beyond us, even though it has contained us. Now, in person, it is dwelling within us.

Beyond Word, Thoughts and Images

It takes only a little experience of meditation to convince us that awakening to this nature of being is the essential logic and meaning of life. Not all the secrets of the Kingdom are revealed to us in a flash. It means we have entered into a real relationship with the mystery. We have begun to turn from self in order to be divinized. We have begun to 'put on Christ'. The great challenge of our time is to get to the threshold of this experience, this initiatory moment of truth.

It is a difficult challenge because, in our time, the familiar ways of prayer have been so weakened. Most people today have little religious preparation to lead them from one level of prayer to a deeper one. Prayer is usually taught as a mental or vocal way of placing ourselves at the centre. When we think about God, for example, we tend to think of God only in relationship to ourselves – as if we were the sun around which everything orbits. All the qualities and even the will we attribute to God then become emanations of our own desires and self-consciousness, in direct or inverse proportion to reality. Even when we see prayer as praise and adoration, we do so assuming that the praise and adoration offered are 'mine'. God is meant to be grateful, to respond in kind. In both these approaches, thinking of or praising God, we can be controlled by pre-Christian conceptions of God as separate from us and objectified by us; unpredictable, yet omnipotent; God must be placated or his attention held. As St Paul told the first Christians, we are no longer obliged to remain subject to these religious patterns with their preconceptions of fear, reward and punishment. The God who cannot be thought of or imagined can, however, be known in love because we have been brought into the inner kingdom of love through the human experience of Jesus. This is why it is not our praise or adoration that is ultimately significant. True praise of God rises from the mind and heart of Christ and we are included in it. With even a little experience of the silence of meditation we begin to know ourselves *being found* in him.

So often when we talk to God we are talking about ourselves – help me to do this, to be that. However altruistic the basic intention behind this may be, the very structure of the language keeps us as the centre of our own consciousness. This is also true for those who may have no religious frame of reference but whose spiritual practice is self-referential. Even if they use no words or hold any image of God and are not asking for favours, the danger of self-fixation is as great. It is this we must let go of in order to move deeper. There is no standing still on the journey, no drifting. If we become spiritually complacent, we fall back into our own centre of gravity. We are drawn back into the orbit of the self-reflecting ego. It is to avoid this collapse into ourselves and stay alert and awake that we meditate. In meditation, God the mystery is always at the centre. As we move into union with that centre, we come to know God by the divine light. The name of this movement is love and the experience of it is a progressive loss of self and self-consciousness. This does not mean that it is all our own work. The mystery of absorption in God is not just the sum total of our efforts. It originates in a reality that is prior to the birth of self-consciousness – namely, our eternal incorporation in Christ. That is why our movement into God is the mystery of Jesus himself as he takes us with him to the Father in the Spirit.

The attempt to imagine God or Jesus at the time of prayer is as limited as talking to him or theologizing about him. We imagine only those who are absent. Christian tradition proclaims that faith received as grace helps us to see that God is not absent. God is present to us fully in the Jesus whose life flows in our heart. Our prayer, as I have said, is our awareness of God in Jesus. So, our time of prayer must be committed to the fullest openness that we are capable of – openness to this reality of presence, not to 'vain imaginings'. All ideas and images, and the phantasmagoria of mental consciousness where thought and image are combined, are dropped in meditation because they derive from our own limited consciousness. All images link back to a central image of self and the great illusion of independent permanence we call the ego. Its primary forces are desire and fear, the inversion of love and truth, and so it is the 'father of lies'. It is an illusion because the true self has no image. It is full, undifferentiated consciousness. Human consciousness is limited and fractured by the false image, the shadow of the ego. It is made whole by the light of Christ in whom there is no darkness, no objectification of separateness of being that can cast a shadow. In Christ, but not of ourselves separately, we can say that he is the image of God, the supreme self, because of his pre-existent oneness with the Father.

This message of Christian revelation has to be addressed to a modern world acutely self-conscious of its modernity. Our world is built on the cult of the ephemeral yet longs for permanence. For this very reason, the modern mind could be fertile soil for the paradox of Christianity – an historical religion rooted in the physical reality of the incarnation of the logos. Its claim that it is still able to engage people today is the promise of Jesus to be with us for all time, even to the end of the world. This promise is verified in deep prayer. When it is verified in our own experience, we are made more real and authentic. It is the living Christ who is the centre of our prayer and invites the attention of the world. When we know him in prayer, his promise rings true in our experience and the Gospels change our worldview. As Kierkegaard said, 'Only that past which can become present is worth remembering.'

A life centred in the present Christ who reveals the divine nature of love is rooted in prayer and lived in the present moment. The present moment has its own dynamic. Living in the present moment does not mean drifting aimlessly from moment to moment. An uncompromising simplicity resists the tendency towards complexity and distraction. One exemplary and universal model for living in the present moment of Christ is the monastic life, which is ordinary life revealed in Christian depth and simplicity.

Benedictine Synthesis

In community, our life is built on the simple threefold synthesis of St Benedict – *oratio* (prayer), *lectio* (reading) and labour (work).

Four times a day we meditate together for half an hour – the 'short time' of prayer suggested in the Rule. Each meditation period follows the appropriate hour of the Divine Office, except for the first meditation of the morning, which stands alone. The Office, which we see as a form of community *lectio,* is our way of preparing for the silence of meditation by an attentive listening to the Word in scripture.

The Benedictine synthesis of prayer, study and work is foundational to the whole Christian life. Each element is necessary, but the greatest of them is prayer. The centre of gravity of our life is the *oratio pura,* or, pure prayer. At the outset of the Western monastic tradition, Cassian saw 'pure prayer' – what he called the state of 'purity of heart' – as the end and goal of monastic life that determined its means. So for us, too, in so far as we can achieve it, every aspect of our lives is aligned on it.

Lectio teaches us the essential prayerfulness of concentrating away from ourselves and from our private thoughts and compulsions. Essentially monastic study is sapiential, wisdom-based, rather than discursive.

Just as in *lectio* our centre of attention is the word of God, so in our daily work our attention is drawn to whatever occupies us at the moment. Whenever we use our activity, whatever it may be, as an opportunity to deepen our attention and when we concentrate on the act rather than its fruits, we are strengthening that single-mindedness which is the condition of unceasing prayer.

Work and *lectio* are integral to a spiritual life. The interpersonal chemistry of community life itself is also a vital preparation for prayer. In the moment of prayer our centre of attention is fully focused in the transcendent and immanent other who is God who is love, but in community relationships the focus is the same. It is maintained because we seek to be open to the otherness of those we live with in kindness and considerate love. Our prayer is therefore a preparation for our life in common and our community life prepares us for prayer. When we begin to experience life in this rhythm, it becomes a process of healing and growth. Then we begin to know the wonder that fraternal love is the sacrament of the divine love in which we are all loved into reality.

The life of a contemplative monastic community is rooted and founded in otherness. This day-to-day altruism is the great contribution monasticism can offer modern people and, in our psychologically isolated and hyperindividualistic culture, it is one of the greatest challenges we face. Although one of our profoundest needs is to rediscover community by experiencing otherness, we are so conditioned by the compulsive materialism and distractedness of our society that we instinctively protect our lives from shifting our centre of consciousness. We are so threatened by the *reality* of others that we close in on ourselves in fear that, if we were to lose ourselves in a relationship with a person whose otherness is free to express itself, we might cease to exist. The psychological isolation that one can even find in monasteries grows out of the ego's fear of recentring consciousness in the other, of losing self. This is sometimes expressed as a fear of being exploited or overworked and it causes many monks to retire into a private, sealed world of their own. In monasteries, this failure of transcendence is particularly painful to witness because it is the aim of monastic life to prove that isolation, fear and illusion are not inevitable. One *can* live differently and monasteries are meant to show how differently. If anywhere, it is in a monastery that we should expect to meet people who are joyful, self-transcending, discovering the fullness of life together. Their lives should overflow the limits set by fear and desire. In our community, as in all monasteries, we also try to love the guests who visit us with that same love, the source of which we touch in both our prayer and our life together. By loving them we hope to lead them to that point of confidence, that sense of their own reality, that will teach them to plunge into the mystery the centre of which is beyond themselves.

The monastic life, and especially its spirit of hospitality, is meant to build up the human self-confidence necessary to let go of the ego. The experience of prayer, entering the silence of Jesus, is an invitation that it takes courage to accept. There are always reasons at hand for declining or postponing the invitation. Even when we have accepted it, all the subsequent steps demand an ever-deepening faith. God's eternal silence, which seems so attractive in poetry or theology, can at any point break on us with such unfamiliar otherness that it takes much love, and much being loved, to continue on deeper into the silence. Our reassurance is this: whatever degree of faith we have is sufficient to begin and, once we have begun, the additional love we need floods our inmost hearts. If we remain open, we are always given what we need to go the whole way.

A Sign for the World

The journey of prayer is both sublime and ordinary. The ordinariness of regular daily practice and community encouragement become the context for God's sublime revelation. An important part of this ordinariness is meditation in common.

Each of our four sessions of meditation is in community. It is difficult to overestimate the importance of this physical and spiritual being together. Shared silence is a self-authenticating faith in God's presence among us. Learning to meditate in common is the greatest of our exercises of communal love. In these moments we hold open with and to others the most precious part of ourselves – the heart where our treasure also is, our faith in the presence of Jesus.

Sharing this faith with an open heart day by day needs personal discipline. We learn to sit absolutely still and then bring the inner and outer silence together into a real presence. Stillness purifies us of restlessness and distraction by making us aware that we are not isolated. Meditation creates community. Our true nature revealed in stillness is being in relationship. Stillness together shows that we are members of one body, and that body is Christ. That so much can be communicated in and by silence is an endless source of amazement and hope. The aspect of our life that our guests seem to find most inspiring (and also sometimes most demanding) is the community's silence. It is the collective reverence in which God's presence is known.

Our experience of being a new kind of Benedictine community based on meditation is still experimental. It may not work in just this form. It is, of course, limited and incomplete. However, it has suggested to me something of powerful relevance to the future of

Christian religious community life. The Second Vatican Council called religious life a 'sign for the world'. It understood that the sight of men and women leaving all things to follow God in *this* particular way of life was of great value to people in *all* walks of life. The value of a monastery is not to witness to the private experience of God, but the universality of the experience.

The Christian monastery is a sign of Jesus as a living presence in the world. Monks and nuns are not born in the cloister – they were in the world and knew the world. It was through the world that they found a hidden treasure, a pearl of great price, the Kingdom that demands everything they are. Once they have learned the skills of the spiritual life, to the world again they return to give and to receive, teach and learn. They do not return and witness to the Kingdom only through their acts of service. These are real signs of love, but there is something deeper that the modern monk has to offer. The deepening of their own experience of God is their real gift to the world. It has always been the Church's tradition that the spiritual life of a monastic community is its first priority. Frequently the reality is different. The good works in which the religious have engaged have taken on a disproportionate emphasis. When work is given the wrong priority, one of the 'sacrifices' monks make is their contemplative practice, even though the other forms of prayer may be faithfully observed. The balance has been lost today and needs urgently to be regained.

It seems ever clearer to me that the contemplative renewal of monastic life is of real importance for the Church and the world. There are some things that must be witnessed to in faith and prophetic courage that perhaps monks are best positioned to say persuasively. If they are left unsaid, society forgets them. If they are to be said again, not as platitudes but as words of a living tradition, it will require a radical re-evaluation of the monastic way of life. St Benedict saw clearly the connection between these two foundations of the gospel – prayer and work. This connection affects all of modern life and has to be rediscovered because the way that we pray shapes the way we live and work. What is at stake for Christianity is the authenticity of the witness we make to the presence of Christ. If our prayer is not deeply centred in that love and if our lives are not centred in our prayer, how can our lives and work be rooted in him?

My own thoughts on this challenge have been enriched by the responses we receive to the quarterly newsletters. I know that they are a drop in the ocean and the currents of the ocean are unpredictable, but the rising and falling tides of monastic life are indicators of the spiritual health of the Church in any period of history. They rise with a deepening of the contemplative life and they fall when that life becomes thin and shallow again. Today, in the spreading of contemplation through the practice of meditation among men and women in the world, a new kind of monasticism is visible on the horizon.

In my own experience, it has often not been from monks that my faith in the monastic life of the future has been awakened but from contemplative laypeople. They have recognized and embraced something in our tradition that we as monks have forgotten or undervalued. This is leading to a new kind of monastic community, different from the past and yet in harmony with its most fundamental principles.

Not everyone will agree, but I offer these letters as a contribution to the work of our renewal. They have grown from a sincere attempt in community and in solitude to reconnect to the core experience of the gospel and our humanity, so at least the words are related to experience – and the words come from the heart. They are a small part of a long tradition of Christians writing to each other, trying to share their joy and struggles. Hopefully, they are means of mutual encouragement to persevere in the way of prayer and service.

The letters of St Paul that started and still crown this tradition had a mixed style and varied content, but they were an urgent attempt to communicate to the first Christians what we have always tried to recommunicate to each other. If his letters convey to us the ineffable richness of Christ, it is because they speak from his own lived response to that mystery. They have become a model for all Christian witness, showing that authority is grounded in the Spirit, tradition and personal experience. If I may seem at times to be so focused on the experience of meditation as a way to renew Christian community that I neglect other ways, it is not to dismiss other paths. It is only because the faith I have in this way of radical simplicity and in the joyfulness of the monastic life is a loving and urgent one.

HOW TO MEDITATE

Sit down. Sit still and upright. Close your eyes lightly. Sit relaxed but alert. Silently, interiorly begin to say a single word. We recommend the prayer-phrase 'maranatha'. Recite it as four syllables of equal length. Listen to the mantra as you say it gently but continuously. Do not think or imagine anything – spiritual or otherwise. When thoughts and images come, these are distractions at the time of meditation, so keep returning to simply saying the word. Meditate each morning and evening for between 20 and 30 minutes.

Part 2

THE LETTERS

One · From the Heart – Planting the Seed

I

CALLED TO HOLINESS

My Dearest Friends,

Greetings in the Lord. This letter is to wish you every happiness and blessing for Christmas and in the New Year.

Please forgive the delay in sending you this first newsletter from Montreal. On our arrival here on September 27th we discovered that a difficulty had arisen over the purchase of our house as the court had to agree to the contract of sale. But now that we are in the house, we can meet regularly for our meditation and the Office. Since arriving, I have given weekends of retreat to various groups expressing interest in the new Benedictine Community. In addressing a meeting of university chaplains, I tried to share my conviction that the preeminent need our world has is for men and women who can speak about and communicate Christianity out of their own inner experience. And I said that there is no authoritative way to meet this need that is not the way of personal commitment and personal fidelity to the path of prayer.

The Chaplains were from all Christian denominations and they shared the same concern over their role in the university: were they to be counsellors or spiritual leaders? I thought that their dilemma was in many ways typical of the choice facing all Christians today. Every one of us is called to be a full person, fully realized in the light of the power of the Spirit continuously springing up into life eternal in our heart, fully mature, fully human. When the Spirit is set free in us, free of the constricting bonds of ego and self-fixation, it pervades every faculty and fibre of our being. Then we become the witnesses we are called to be. We can witness with our own quality of life and our own fearless power to love. We witness to the essential, Christian and truly human experience of the transcendent Spirit of Jesus living in the centre of our being, where he holds us and all things in being. In that experience we find our own inner coherence, our harmony with others and with the forces within us and outside us. The sense of our own coherence

35

creates the confidence we need to leave thoughts of self, self-consciousness behind: to live no longer for ourselves but for Him. There is only
one Teacher and that is the Lord Jesus, the Teacher within. But in our
union with him we are summoned to mediate his teaching, which is only
his love – to make his union with all people fully conscious, fully alive.

You do not need me to remind you that in order to realize this we
must have seriously undertaken the pilgrimage of prayer. This is not
an abstract, theoretical undertaking. To make this pilgrimage we have
to put our prayer first, and do this in a very practical way. In planning
our day we must see to it that we leave a time and space for our meditation. It will become a time and space that is more and more what
holds our day and indeed our whole life in shape and keeps it on
course. We must come to see this time for meditation not as our own
time but as God's time.

The night before last I addressed a meeting of sisters from the
Diocese of Montreal on the eve of the Feast of the Immaculate
Conception. I spoke to them on what I think is the essential meaning
of Mary and indeed of all those men and women whom God has raised
up as signs of the holiness to which all men and women are called. The
meaning is, above all, in her being a model of simplicity: a simplicity
of consciousness, simplicity of heart, simplicity of faith. With this
condition of simplicity – 'a condition that demands not less than
everything', as Mother Julian of Norwich puts it – there comes that
directness of encounter with the power of God within us that deepens
and fulfils us. The process is continuous because there is no end to the
power of God. And no end to our capacity for love.

Our task is to persevere – not grudgingly or self-importantly, but
with simple faith and self-renewing love. The figure of Mary is a central one in our understanding of Christmas.[1] Above all, she is a great
example of interiority with a direct meaning for each of us. Just as she
carried the human Christ within her, so we must bear and worship
Christ in our own hearts, remembering that he is just as truly present
within us as he was bodily present in his mother.

Mary in the gospels has another meaning for us: her silence is both
the medium and the response to the presence of Jesus within us. The
true silence of our meditation is creative and fertile. As it deepens and
grows, so does the presence and power of the risen Christ expand the

---

1 See 'The OtherCentredness of Mary' in John Main, *Community of Love*.

kingdom of love in our heart. Our task is to be silent, to be still, and to allow his transforming presence to emerge within us, out of the living, creative centre of our being.

Please keep all of us here in our first days in Montreal in your hearts. We shall remember you all as we offer our Midnight Mass together: In Him, Through Him and With Him.

With much love,

John Main OSB

(December 1977)

On 28 September, 1977, John Main and Laurence Freeman flew from London to Montreal. On a rainy evening at Mirabel Airport, they were met by Bishop Leonard Crowley, whose initiative had brought them to make the first monastic foundation in the city. For the first six weeks they stayed in the rectory of a parish church waiting for the house that they had been given to become available. It was an old French-Canadian farmhouse situated in Notre Dame de Grâce, a quiet residential district about 15 minutes from the centre of the city. The house had grown with the increasing prosperity of succeeding generations of the Decarie family – one of the families who had first settled in Quebec 300 years ago – but, when they walked into it the day after their arrival, the old grandeur of the house had yielded to loose windows, peeling wallpaper and falling ceilings. For several months, its restoration was a labour of love that occupied the whole community and many of our first guests. As a result of John Main's tapes and the people who had visited our centre in London, we found that a weekly meditation group had already formed. After we finally moved into the house on 6 December, this group began to meet there and formed the nucleus of all the groups that were started later. We kept the structure of these meetings like the one that had evolved in London: an introductory talk, music, half an hour meditating in silence together, questions or discussion. In these early days John Main accepted a few invitations to talk about our work. In Boston and Montreal he spoke to religious communities and in Kingston, Ontario, to a meeting of university chaplains. The people who came to meditate with us were, from the beginning, of every age and type and included non-Christians.

2

BEING ON THE WAY

My Dearest Friends,

Greetings in the Lord.

First, I must thank you for all the letters we received in response to our first newsletter. Forgive us for not yet answering them all personally. We were delighted to hear news of you and encouraged, above all, to learn that you remain faithful to your meditation.

We started our first group here with just six people. As you can imagine, it was a memorable evening for us. As the text for the first talk, I took the words of Jesus in the Gospel of Mark: 'Anyone who wishes to be a follower of mine must leave self behind; he must take up his cross and come with me' (Mark 8.34). They are the words that really sum up all we have to say at any time and in any place about what it means to follow Jesus, to be on the pilgrimage.

Yesterday evening we had the third meeting of the group and the first session in our new meditation room. At this point I am about halfway through a series of talks here. What I have been trying to say so far is that Christianity is, above all, the communication to us of the power of God. And it is an *act* of communication, not a hypothesis or just an inspiring, nice idea. It is a real and continuous act that reveals a real and personal relationship at the very centre of our life and being. Every act of communication in which we participate must have its own medium. There must be a means by which we can receive what is being communicated to us. The means of God's communication of his power to us is, everywhere and always, the person of Jesus. Jesus, who is the image of the invisible God, is also the Son of Man, our brother. Because he incorporates us – all men and women equally – into his person, we are able to receive that communication from God. It is the communication of the power of the experience, the knowledge, and the receiving of his love. Receiving this communication *is* prayer. By receiving it we are brought to knowledge of ourselves because we are brought to the knowledge of God as the *source* of our being. Our incorporation in Jesus also reveals the *goal* of life. In my end is my beginning.

Another way of saying this is that Christianity is the *experience* of the power – what the Gospel calls the *dynamos* – of God. But it is *experience* in a special sense. It is something greater than the ordinary three dimensional experience of pleasure. It is the transcendent experience of joy. Anyone who loves another person for his or her own sake and delights in that person's unique being knows what this experience of God's *dynamos* entails. And, indeed, only those who love like this can understand because 'the person who does not love is still in the realm of death'.[1] The experience of the love of God in Jesus is a transcendent experience, and so an experience of joy. This does not mean that it is not also a present reality, rooted in us as we are here and now. The whole Christian mystery proclaims the meeting of our world with the world of God in the person of Jesus: the same person of Jesus who calls us into himself through the Spirit he has given us. And so, the power of God is a power *within* us – in our inmost hearts. And yet it is also a power utterly beyond us – the transcendent power of the God whom the eye cannot see or the mind imagine. This is the difference that the coming of Jesus has made for all humanity: his redemptive love is a continuous, insuperable power that makes it possible for us all to enter the experience of the power of God. Through him because he is the Way. *not any other way ?*

This faith reveals the nature of true Christian community. A group of Christians who meet together to meditate, to pray, to worship is not just a social gathering. It is a group aware of its power: a power that arises from the transcendent reality of the presence of the Lord Jesus in its midst. The purpose of their meeting is, above all, to attend to the reality of this presence, to deepen their silent receptivity to it, to make it (what it already is) the supreme reality of their lives. So, each member of the group is other-centred, turned away from himself or herself toward the living Lord. A group like this then becomes truly a community on the model of that described at the end of the second chapter of Acts: 'A sense of awe was everywhere ... all whose faith had

---

1 1 John 3.15.

drawn them together held everything in common ... with unaffected joy.'[2] A Christian community is aware of its ultimate meaning as being beyond itself. Then the social, cultural, or ceremonial form of the group is not something to be jealously preserved or possessed. It can even be risked.

All truly Christian response requires detachment, the letting-go of self. Detachment helps us to enjoy the transient gifts of life without being distracted from the essential reality. This reality is the power of the risen Jesus. This detachment is obvious to the believer who finds liberty in the paradox of detached commitment. But it was Jesus' teaching on liberty of spirit that threatened the Pharisees. Our own tendency, like theirs, is to opt for the security of established order in what we know and feel safe with. The danger of choosing this is that it does not allow us to remain even where we are. We begin to regress when we opt to evade the only real security there is – the 'glorious liberty of the children of God', the 'rock of Christ', the Spirit who is the *dynamos* of God. The liberty of a Christ-centred life is to have been empowered to make another option. We can then turn from the ego and its anxiety. What enables us to do so is that we have been turned around by Jesus.

This *metanoia* or 'turning around' is the subject of a talk I am giving at McGill University on Shrove Tuesday. What I will be saying then is that by becoming human God has turned toward us in Jesus. Jesus showed himself to us and thus revealed the Father to us: 'Anyone who has seen me has seen the Father,' as John's Gospel tells us.[3] But this is the beginning of the Christian mystery, not the end of it. It is here we enter the mystery because in turning toward us, and in revealing the true nature of God to us, Jesus presents us with the opportunity, and indeed the responsibility, of turning toward him. We can now open our hearts to him, and uncover the power of love when our hearts engage him.

This is our daily way. Jesus is the medium of God's revelation to humanity. We, as his Body, the Church, are the medium of his revelation to the world. I have so often said before that Christianity depends for its authenticity upon our personal witness. We have to proclaim the Good News from our own experience. In the first chapter of his

---

2 Acts 2.43.
3 John 14.9.

gospel, St Luke speaks of basing the 'authentic knowledge' of his book on 'the original eyewitnesses and servants of the gospel'. To understand the meaning of this remark we should listen to what St Paul says: 'Am I not an apostle? Did I not see Jesus our Lord?'[4] Neither Paul nor Luke had known the historical Jesus. But they both proclaim the profound Christian reality that the Way is more than an historical tradition. It is our own lived experience of the presence of the risen Lord Jesus, the Christ.

The wonder is that this is *our* Way. In Luke's Gospel Jesus' ministry is framed as his progress toward the holy city of Jerusalem. His life is his being *en route* to his priestly destiny, that culminating moment when he burst the bonds of every limitation accepted in his incarnation. He thus became, as St Paul tells us, 'life-giving spirit'.[5] In Luke's stories of Jesus encountering disciples on his journey the test of a person's response was whether they turned around, changed direction, and followed him.

During his ministry, the way was the journey that Jesus followed, his pilgrimage through love and suffering to his Father. But after the perfection of his love in the suffering of the Cross, he reached the goal of his pilgrimage and was glorified in his return to the 'Father's right hand'. Then in chapter 14 of his Gospel St John tells us that the Way is now the person of Jesus himself. The one who finishes the way becomes the Way.

Christian prayer has the dynamic quality of the mystery of Jesus himself. It is a way we follow. It is also an encounter with the person of Jesus, who is the way to the Father. The Christian pilgrimage is a turning, a conversion, a following of Christ and a journey with Christ. With such a sense of pilgrimage the Christian life can never fall into complacency or self-satisfaction. Its essential insight is that full human meaning lies beyond ourselves. Salvation is not a possession. It means being on the Way continuously, being turned toward the dynamic power of Jesus and being taken up in him to the Father. Salvation is entering the kingdom of heaven within us.

One of the perils of the pilgrimage is that we talk so much about it and so cleverly *imagine* ourselves on it that we actually fail to tread it, to put one foot in front of the other. It is the *pax perniciosa*, self-

---

4 1 Corinthians 9.1.
5 1 Corinthians 15.45.

indulgent religiosity, false piety, holy floating. To avoid it we need that virtue that St Paul speaks of in 1 Thessalonians as *hippomone*. It is sometimes translated as patience, sometimes as endurance, or fortitude. For the Christian meditator, in process of uniting mind and heart, inner and outer, faith and experience, it is a particular kind of fortitude. It is the courage to keep to the way of our twice-daily meditation. These are times each day when we explicitly put everything aside so that we may join the journey of the Lord with full attention. A discipline of prayer is necessary. Of course, we are always on the way, always journeying with him. It is the condition of all creatures and all creation. But we are called to a full, personal consciousness of it. This is what requires a daily commitment. Just as Jesus stood aside at specific times from his ministry of healing, teaching, and preaching to be alone with his Father, wholly turned toward the presence at the centre of his being, so we too must stop at particular times of the day and simply *be*. The gospels testify to Jesus' habit of withdrawing from his active life among the crowds that followed him, to pray in silence and solitude. This practice was in addition to the normal religious observance of his time that he would have followed, the three regular periods of Jewish daily prayer.

So, too, our life. The dynamic structure of a spiritually awakened life is based on regular, silent times of attention to the source. This is the discipline needed to accept that fullness of life Jesus offers. The bottom line is fidelity to our twice-daily meditation and, within the time of meditation, complete fidelity to the word. The way of the mantra leads us into the way and keeps us on the way. The spiritual beauty of the truth of the Gospels, the delights of creation, the problems of our life – everything must be placed on the altar of the living sacrifice of praise we offer by saying our mantra. By saying it to the exclusion of all thought and imagination we are led into a depth of silence, on the other side of all distraction. In this silence, Jesus, the Word made flesh, is rooted in our human heart. In this faith-filled silence we are made one with him. We journey with him beyond Jerusalem to the Father.

I will end the talk at McGill, as I must end this letter, by reminding you that for a full and balanced life we must be open to every dimension of the Christ-event. Its fullness is found in the mystery of the death and Resurrection of Jesus. It is to be found in the community of those who accept him as Lord and Saviour. This is the Church. It is an experience found in our hearts: in the presence of his living and life-giving spirit within us.

So let us live our lives to the full as followers of the Way bringing his fullness of life to all humanity.

Peace in the Lord,

With much love,

John Main OSB
(February 1978)

Our first Christmas in Montreal had required much improvisation but the simplicity of it all made us happy. The house took shape week by week. Most of our decorating efforts were devoted to the meditation room – formerly the two large music rooms of the house, light-filled and high-ceilinged. We were able to meditate in it for the third meeting of our weekly group in February. The group was growing steadily, with serious newcomers, and represented a good cross-section of Montreal society. At any one meeting there would be middle-aged people who had started to meditate a year or two before with TM, students returning from a yoga retreat, businessmen and housewives and, often, our most open and welcoming parish priest. The group had grown to about 20 by the time we sent out our second newsletter and we were already thinking of starting a second group that would be as large as our space made comfortable. We had always thought that the ideal size of a group is about 12, but the number of free evenings in a week made this difficult to realize either here or in London. People joined us, too, for the regular meditation sessions of the community. At this stage, there were three sessions: at 6.30 am with the Morning Office and Eucharist, at noon with the Midday Office and after vespers at 5.15 pm. There was little time to think of new publications, although our experience was shaping a new theology and that found some expression in these newsletters. John Main's tapes, which had grown out of our work in London, found good distributors in North America and England. Encouraging news arrived of the English meditation groups we had left behind. The Grail had started a small group of about three regular members and this was soon to flourish and produce other groups. Some individuals of the hundreds who had visited the London centre started their own groups. Small or large, these groups had begun to meet regularly to support one another in their fidelity to their twice-daily meditations. Our letters to these groups, like our talks in Montreal, continued to put the message in as simple and direct a way as we could. To meditate required fidelity each morning and evening and our life in Montreal aimed to be a witness to this. Our priority was a life based firmly on our regular periods of meditation together. Whatever developed in the way of groups or the opportunity to share our faith in monasticism with others, we would respond to as generously as we could. Meanwhile, we received constant support and encouragement from Bishop Crowley, who always prayed with us when he came to see us. On Shrove Tuesday, John Main spoke to the Faculty of Religious Studies at McGill University and met there some who would become great supporters of our community and its work. Laurence Freeman resumed his theological studies at the University of Montreal, managing to schedule them so as to allow his full participation in our community life. Another regular participant in our life was an elderly and recently widowed German-Canadian who came to us in our earliest days and greeted us as fellow Benedictines. He and his wife had been Oblates of Mount Saviour for 20 years and were close friends of its founder.

3

ACCEPT THE GIFT

My Dearest Friends,

Greetings in the Lord!

I am hoping that this will reach you in time for your celebration of the great Feast of Pentecost. This is the time when the whole Easter mystery really find its completion. From Christmas onward, through Lent and the three days of Easter itself, it is as if we are reliving the past, participating in the life and growth of Jesus up to the moment of his human fulfilment; as if we are learning how to identify our lives with his. We, too, have to lay down our lives and turn away from self to God. But after the Ascension there is that strange liturgical interval when it seems as if our identification, our union with Jesus, can go no further – until the day of Pentecost. Then the fire of the Holy Spirit touched the hearts of the Apostles as it touches ours. Then we know why Jesus said he had to leave in order to send the Spirit – to bring the Father's plan, the work of union, to completion. Pentecost gathers together all of the mystery of Easter and realizes it in us in the present moment. From now on there is only one thing to do: to fully awaken to this living mystery within us as a present reality. This is the work, the pilgrimage of our meditation.

Holy Week was a time of much grace and happiness for us here. The culmination of the week was the baptism of Gert Wolf, a friend of ours who has been meditating with us since we arrived in Montreal. On Easter night, before as many people as we could accommodate, he was baptized and confirmed at our Vigil service. And then, as at all our ceremonies, we were able to meditate together in silence. During the last weeks I have been talking to various groups about our community and our work. This really comes down to the practical way we try to live the Christian tradition of prayer as a monastic community: to follow the Way, to pursue the pilgrimage. I had, in particular, a very rewarding evening with about twenty directors of the Ignatian Spiritual Exercises. I was asked to share something of the Benedictine monastic understanding of the role of the spiritual director.

I began by saying that the very idea of a 'director' originates in that of the monastic 'spiritual father'. The way this ancient Christian tradition developed tells us something of the needs of the Church today. The communication of the Gospel and the Christian experience has always had to be a personal communication because the mystery itself is personal: the person of Jesus whose fulfilled personhood already now involves and contains ours. The monastery, in particular, has always been a place where the wonder of this personal mystery is realized and incarnated in a special way through fraternal love and what St Benedict called the 'mutual obedience' of the community. The monastery is a kind of microcosm of the Christian community at large and a place where the essential priorities of the Christian response are so arranged that they stand out in clear relief. Cassian, from whom Benedict derived much of his vision of the monastic life, also knew that the handing on of the tradition of prayer within the community was necessarily a personal communication. 'Apart from the fact', he wrote in the Institutes, 'that a life which is tested, refined, and purified is only found in a few people there is also the advantage that a person is more thoroughly instructed and formed by the example of one other person ... rather than from too many.' His point here is not that the teacher *gives* an experience or assumes the individual's personal responsibility for commitment to the pilgrimage and perseverance on it. But the teacher helps to concentrate the novice's resources, to bring unity and focus to his quest, to save him from dispersing himself among 'many and strange doctrines'. The monastic tradition, like the Christian tradition in which it is a central stream, is passed on through books and institutions, but it does not come alive until it is regenerated in the communication of a personal encounter. This encounter must be fully personal, fully conscious. Where we have often lost the vitality of the tradition is in thinking of the teacher or 'spiritual director' as someone who is there to relieve us of our personal commitment to mature growth in spirit. If a teacher is there to lead, encourage, and simplify, it is only in order that the disciple may as quickly as possible come to that self-transcendence that will enable him, in his turn, to be a channel of the love and power of the Lord for others. The teacher is a stepping stone.

Two essential points to remember about this commitment are: that 'we do not even know how to pray' and that to enter the Kingdom we must become 'as little children'. These are essential Christian, practical truths. Taking them seriously is the challenge. We have to realize that when we talk about 'our prayer' we are really talking about our disposing ourselves for the full liberation of the life of the Spirit within us, which is the prayer of Jesus and his vital connection with the Father. This is why we pray to the degree that we turn away from ourselves, from the possessive self-consciousness and trivial distractedness of everything we sum up in the word *ego*. That this really does mean everything is the demand it makes. It is summed up in the old monastic saying, 'A monk is only truly praying when he does not know that he is praying.' *Everything* includes self-consciousness. If this sounds like annihilation, it is because it describes the unified consciousness of transcendence – 'a condition of complete simplicity that demands not less than everything', as Mother Julian puts it. The difference between childlikeness and childishness is the challenge. We also have to realize that the 'kingdom' that the childlike enter demands the ascesis of deepening simplicity in which, far from being annihilated, we are fully restored to ourselves. For the first time we know the full wonder of our being, the beauty of life, the centrality of love.

The call of Jesus to 'leave self behind' is easily muted or compromised. Most often it is just postponed. We are 'too busy', or the work we are doing is just at this moment too important. It is also easier to drift in reverie rather than to 'stay awake and pray'. It is easier to sink into the restless complexity of self-conscious reflection rather than opt for the still, alert simplicity of being who and where we are. This is where the encouragement and confidence-building of a teacher and community are needed. Both are intimately connected in the life of the novice, just as Jesus and the Church are intertwined in the life of the Christian. What teacher and community together give is the religious quality of steadiness and rootedness. The word guru means 'one who is steady'. The pilgrimage demands a constant rebalancing and re-insertion into the reality of our existence and a deepening core commitment. The teacher within community points to this with constancy and directness. He does not talk for Jesus. Jesus talks for himself. But the teacher can help us to the essential prerequisite of listening, which is silence. To do this we have to be truly disciples of the Lord, that is, to have discipline; and the teacher's role is to lead people to a mature choice to pursue their pilgrimage with discipline. The teacher is not there to communicate an experience. That is in the Lord's disposal. Rather, he or she is one who can help us to remain serious, to be faithful and to avoid the self-centredness that delays or stifles growth in wholeness. It is Jesus who is the exemplar of this, and his authority as a teacher was rooted in his humility. Humility is easily mistaken for pride. The humblest of all his sayings was not, as the Pharisees and High Priest thought, an expression of blasphemous egoism but a testimony to his complete other-centredness: the Father and I are one.

Just as the centre of Jesus' consciousness is the Father, so our centre of consciousness is Jesus. When we have turned wholly towards him as the central reality of our life to which everything else relates then his unified consciousness dawns within us. In our loving union with him at the centre and, consequently, at all levels of our being, we know him as the Teacher. We know it (though it is beyond merely mental knowing) because, as St Paul says, 'we have the mind of Christ'. There is the one Lord and he is the teacher, the *sadguru*, the root guru and teacher of teachers. 'You need no other teacher, but learn all you need to know from his initiation, which is real and no illusion. As he taught you, then, dwell in him' (1 John 2.27).

One of the great insights of St Benedict is that of the *via media*, the middle way. The Rule could be summed up in one of its major phrases and themes – *ne quid nimis* (Chapter 64), 'nothing in excess'. This entails the renunciation of all fanaticism, social or religious. Benedict's insight was a very deep one, though expressed very simply. The essence of fanaticism is the ego's terror of losing itself in the other and its desperate attempt to defend itself against the intrusion of what R.D. Laing calls the 'implosion of reality'. Instead, Benedict put before his monks in simple and ordinary examples a way to become fully open to that reality: commitment to fidelity in prayer as the source of daily renewal. The words he uses suggest the essence of his vision: *via media*, like *meditation*, is linked to the word *medius*, middle or centre. It is there that we have to be rooted. It is there that our pilgrimage leads us and it is there we most truly are ourselves. *Meditare*, our word 'meditate', also expresses the way to follow this path of centrality. Its original meaning is to turn something over again and again, to repeat. The faithful repetition of the mantra roots us in the deep centre of being. As in 'medicine', the prefix med- carries the sense of care and attention.

Until you have started this pilgrimage and made the first of many re-commitments, this may sound like an unlikely doctrine despite the authority of the tradition behind it. It is, of course, a tough paradox that 'inward renewal' depends on stillness and that our vitality and creativity require steadiness. Contemporary culture flatly denies this. But this is only one facet of the multifaceted diamond, one aspect of the main paradox of Christian experience, the Paschal mystery itself. So, although it is a hard saying, it still strikes a deep chord in us today. Whoever wants to meditate has probably already discovered that what is ultimately enervating and dissatisfying is distraction and restlessness. Forever running from inner stillness is escaping reality. This reality is grounded in the abiding personal presence of Jesus in our true self. To evade or try to escape it creates anxiety where there should be delight and liberty. It creates the prison of our false personas where there should be the expanse of real identity. This evasion is the result of fear: a fear of otherness and of ourselves that causes both violence toward others and rejection of ourselves.

The wonder of the Christian revelation is the unity of being: the union of Jesus with his Father and of ourselves with Jesus. When in our meditation we turn away from the fears, desires, and concerns of the restless ego and turn other-wards, we find ourselves in Jesus. This then opens us to the source of being which is the love of the Father. This pilgrimage demands the courage to turn away from self. But there is no discovery, no arrival, unless, in Paul Tillich's phrase, we cross the 'frontier of our own identity'. This is true for you and me and for the whole Church today. Until, individually and in community, we have transferred our centre of consciousness from ourselves, we have not found ourselves. So, you see that the *via media*, the middle way of meditation, is no compromise, no easy option!

The depth of commitment we are called to is absolute and meditation is the committed prayer of pure faith. If there is one concept we should get more clearly in focus today, it is the meaning of 'faith'. I have spoken to many of you before about the importance of our personal response to the summons of Jesus, of turning with an unfragmented consciousness toward the mystery of the indwelling Spirit. I have said that real and powerful as that presence is in our hearts, and wonderful as is the transformation it works, it will not impose itself on us by force – because it is Love. It will not break through the doors of our hearts. We must open our hearts to it. The wonderful beauty of prayer is that the opening of our hearts is as natural as the opening of a flower. Just as a flower opens and blooms when we let it be, so if we simply are, if we become and stay silent, then our hearts cannot but open: the Spirit cannot but pour through into our whole being. It is this we have been created for. It is what the Spirit has been given to us to bring about.

This then is the real meaning of faith: openness, perseverance, wakefulness, commitment to the pilgrimage. The Greek word for faith (*pistis*) is common in the gospel sayings of Jesus. It can nowhere be limited to meaning 'belief' or 'conviction'. It carries instead the sense of trust, faithfulness and personal loyalty. To follow Jesus is not merely to have an intellectual understanding about him. It is to experience his self-revelation and the dimension of spirit that he has opened for us – and to experience this at the centre of our lives to the degree of union with him and, ultimately, with the Father. 'He who believes [has *pistis*] in me, believes not in me but in the One who sent me' (John 13.44). The openness and steadiness of this faith in Jesus leads us to transcend every human limitation separating us from the Father's love, the source and goal of our being. Everyone approaches the Father through Jesus. As the incarnate Word he is the Way. We enter the way through faith. Once we have entered upon it, it draws more and more of our being into itself. It will seem as if it is integrating and unifying us simply in order to possess us and fill us more perfectly. Out of this central Christian experience flows the abundance of joy and hope proclaimed by the gospel, a rootedness in ourselves and the awareness of the redemptive power of love in all human life. It demands not merely our emotional or our intellectual faculties but the whole person offered as a living sacrifice in the praise of heart and mind. Through the wonder of this wholeness a complete revolution is effected in us: 'When anyone is united to Christ there is a new world; the old order has gone and a new order has already begun.'[1]

As this new world order reveals itself we begin to see the mystery as truly personal. Once we have entered upon this pilgrimage we become a vital personal centre through which the self-communication of Jesus is made. Each one of us is summoned to participate in this work of union. If we say, 'This is too much for me' or 'I don't know what to do', we evade the call. All we have to do is to accept the gift we have

---

1 2 Corinthians 5.17.

been given: the gift of the life of the risen Lord. This life transforms and renews us by our turning towards him with our whole consciousness. The courage we need for this is the courage to become truly silent, deeply unified. Our mantra, taking us beyond the constrictions of language and imagination, leads into the unbounded reality of Jesus. Our twice-daily meditations and during these our absolute fidelity to the mantra as the one occupation of our mind and heart – this is our lifeline with the centre to which we are travelling and from which flows the abundant power of love to remain steady on the way of centrality. The centre where all lines converge is Jesus.

The wonderful quality about the relationship we now have between our community here and all the groups and friends in America, Europe and Africa is that it is renewed daily in meditation, in the pilgrimage we share daily to the centre. Its freshness does not depend on novelty but on our ever deeper penetration into the reality of the Kingdom into which the pilgrimage of the one word leads us more completely. This reality manifests itself with greater and greater generosity.

This letter has been quite long and elaborate. Let me end by reminding you that nothing can be said about prayer that can at the same time describe its utter fullness and its utter simplicity. I suggest that you now forget most of what I have said to you except the two words 'simplicity' and 'faith'. Both of these are summed up in the practice of the mantra, which allows the Spirit to guide you. I do not suggest that the simplicity is easy to reach or that the faith is easy to maintain. But let me remind you again that our wholehearted openness to love is the condition to which you and I and every human being is called. It is the meaning and purpose of our lives. It demands a great deal, but in the end we will find that all we have lost are our limitations.

We keep you all in our heart every day and wish you every blessing and the full joy in the Lord to which we are all called.

With much love,

John Main OSB
(April 1978)

As regards the weather, the first winter in Montreal was a very pleasant surprise. Instead of the predicted blizzards and frostbite, we delighted in crisp, blue skies and bright, cold sunlight week after week. The work on the inside of the house was nearing completion and we looked ahead to being able to start on the roof and front gallery. Our liturgy developed in tune with our experience that grew week by week. Having a clear priority in meditation made this development more natural and flexible and it found a real place for children in the liturgy, too. All this was made easier by the small numbers. Guests from Canada, the USA and overseas ensured that we remained open to outside forces, which also conditioned our growth. We were hampered here by lack of space, to remedy which we rented an apartment for the lay community a few minutes' walk from the house. We were then able to take two or three guests at a time. Our work was centred on teaching the tradition of meditation that we were following. The weekly groups continued to grow and we set aside Monday night for an introductory session, with the same structure as before, and Tuesday night for those who had been coming to us for some time and who had begun to meditate regularly. We started a group for priests. The response to this was small but a committed core of about seven priests met faithfully each week. Bishop Crowley continued to support and encourage us in these days of enracinement *and visited regularly to pray with us and meet the new members of the community. We invited a group of local businessmen and academics to advise us on plans we had for finding a larger property. It was to prove a long search for the right place. The delay, however, gave us time to consider more deeply what were the implications of our work for a vision of the monastic life in the modern world. We were living a very different contemplative life than that of the English Benedictine congregation, with its emphasis on the apostolates of school teaching and parochial work. Yet, even as we nurtured the specifically monastic growth of the community, the demand to share our experience with a widening range of people also grew. We asked ourselves: what really is the monastic witness to the modern world? How is the prayer of monks to find its full meaning for others? Everywhere we heard complaints about the Church's failure to teach spiritually with authority. A truly alive, contemporary monasticism could find its meaning in proving that this teaching could be given.*

4

FULLY OPEN AND ALIVE

My Dearest Friends,

This letter is quite overdue. But its delay does not betoken any neglect. Since we last wrote, life has been so full that it seemed good to postpone writing until we could give you a complete report of how we have developed here in the last few months.

The week of the visit of the Abbot of Ealing to Montreal was a busy programme and yet it was a moving sign for us in our community here that he joined us each day at Eucharist and for our three sessions of meditation preceded by the Divine Office. The way this was combined with his round of meetings and engagements symbolized how our life of prayer here has led to a deepening openness to all around us. This was a theme taken up by Bishop Crowley when he joined us to preside at our Friday evening Mass. This is part of the Bishop's address to the community on May 26:

> As you all well know, the monastic tradition within the Church has been the source of great riches, spiritually, theologically, artistically, and culturally. Benedict had the great wisdom to recognize that when men or women of singular vision are united in a common life, a common rule, a common purpose, and a common prayer life, great things are possible. The work of the Spirit is greatly facilitated and the life of the Church is immeasurably invigorated. You know better than I the many periods in history when the monastic orders proved to be the mainstay of truly human life and spiritual growth.
>
> However, what we may all be hesitant to recognize, because of the unflagging energy such a recognition demands, is the fact that our own day is calling desperately for a renewal of the monastic spirit and the deepening of the monastic commitment to cultural development ...

Without men and women of contemplative vision and spiritual depth, our hopes for building up the kingdom of God's love are destined to be based in the shifting sands of passing fads and momentary movements. What will last must be founded in the vision of the past and must look to the dreams of the future. Only the contemplative spirit of the old and the young together can provide such a pathway for contemporary people.

Benedict also had a clear sense of the early Christian community in the hospitality that he enjoined upon all his brothers and sisters in following Christ. This sense of warmth and welcome is so important for all who would come to you seeking the compassion, the understanding, the solicitude of the Good Shepherd. Let this place always be a haven of hope and a citadel of charity for any who come to you – for as has been given to you, so must you give to others ...

I invited you to come to Montreal because I know all too well how deeply the clergy, the religious, and the laity of our diocese need a strong centre of prayerful hospitality wherein they can drink deep of the timeless values of the Holy Spirit, rendered timely by men of contemplative vision. I am delighted that you have come; I hope and pray sincerely that you prosper – for your prosperity bespeaks rich and succulent fruit for my priests and people. And, after all, that is what I am here for, too.

The Abbot was the first of many visitors who made our summer a time of sharing our life of prayer with others in the way the Bishop described. A long-term guest was an Irish Capuchin, with us for six weeks, during which we spent an hour or so in conversation each day, and I want to share with you some of the insights that arose in the course of our conversations.

A basic insight growing among us is to see how important meditation is to the living tradition of the faith. All of us, at least in the West and especially those brought up in Christian homes, receive the tradition as part of a general cultural heritage. It is often just a part of the whole system of values and ways of seeing that we take for granted. The basic Christian values, at least in name, have become an essential part of cultural formation. It is easy to identify them with a particular type of westernized society and then lose sight of their meaning as society and culture evolve. When the Christian tradition loses contact with its inner dynamic, its spiritual depth, it fails to help build a new society on these basic values. It even loses its own self-confidence – that authority it derives from living, mystical contact with its source. The faith tradition we receive when we enter the Christian community depends on personal experience for its authenticity and influence. It is a rich and meaningful tradition that is never stale when it is part of an evolving pattern.

Each generation, like every individual, has a different past. The pattern and perspective of history are thus in constant change. But all the world's resourcefulness and energy is only potential until it is realized by a personal faith-decision. This must be made by each individual as a maturing member of the Christian family. This decision is a commitment of faith. It is not merely intellectual or dialectical. It is not just that we decide to 'believe' in the ideas of the Christian tradition. Much more, we need the courage, even the recklessness, to open ourselves to the unknown, the unfathomable and truly mysterious dimension of the tradition. We allow ourselves, in the full biblical sense, to 'know' the mystery or, even better, to be known by it. To allow ourselves to do this is to follow the fundamental gospel precepts of becoming simple, childlike and awake. Despite the fact that the tradition has been influencing society for so long it, is easily forgotten by those in its mainstream that these are indeed the fundamental tenets of the teaching of Jesus.

Faith is not a matter of exertion of will but of openness. We need to see faith as openness, an affirmative, creative, sensitive way of being. It is not rigid but nor is it passivity or quietism. The effectiveness of all *doing* depends on the quality of *being* we enjoy. To be open implies other qualities too: such as *being still*, because we cannot be open to what is here if we are always running after what we think is there; such as *being silent*, because we cannot listen or receive unless we give our whole attention; such as *being simple*, because what we are being open to is the wholeness, the integrity of God. This condition of openness as the blend of stillness, silence, and simplicity is the condition of prayer. It is our humanity in wholesome harmony with the being of God in Jesus.

Meditation is our way to this condition of being fully human, fully alive. It is the condition we are all called to. To meditate is to stand in the middle – *stare in medio* – and to be conscious that the centre is not ourselves but God. In meditation, therefore, we enter the living stream of faith that gives meaning to the tradition that has formed us. We are also responsible for transmitting this tradition to those not yet born.

We do so, firstly, by entering the state of faith where we are solely and exclusively open to the personal presence of the living Christ within us, knowing that it lies beyond the limitations of language and thought. We know it 'though it is beyond knowledge'. This sort of knowledge is of a different order from what we acquire and store by studying history, by scientific research, or in reading poetry. It is not knowledge of God as an object. It can never be that, because God can never be known as an object. This truth has been proclaimed by the Christian tradition since St Irenaeus, who told us that 'without God you cannot know God'. Only God can know God. We are called to participate in the divine self-knowledge and this calling is made possible because of our union with Jesus. This 'knowledge' is not mere intellectual comprehension of God's greatness, absoluteness or compassion. God's self-knowledge is love, the love that is the Trinity. That is the basic energy and prototype of all creation. God is Love, St John tells us. We are called by Love into love.

The immediacy and the urgency of the Christian revelation is that all this is a present reality, established in the centre of the human condition. It asks only that we realize it. This is why meditation is neither a backward glance nor a timorous projection forward but combines the old and the new in the glory of the eternal present – the perpetual now. It is this that makes the meditator truly contemporary, fully open and alive to the ever-present creative power of God who sustains the universe in being from moment to moment. The liberty to move with the times, to recognize the changing needs and circumstances of society is the fruit of stability at the centre of our being.

To many people it often seems that this inner stillness is an introspective state and that the meditator is going inwards to the exclusion of the people and creation around. The meditator is at best socially irrelevant, at worst purely selfish. Nothing could be further from the truth. As the Bishop said in his talk, the contemplative vision is the necessary basis for all contemporary action. It is also the essential condition for a fully human response to the richness, the unpredictability, the sheer giftedness of life. The temptation, to which we have to be constantly alert, is to opt for a half-life that denies the present reality of the Incarnation. We might then seek all value either in the world or all value in the spiritual realm. Because of Christ who is alive and active in the human heart and in all human social relationships, matter, world and spirit are gloriously interfused. From his experience of this truth, a monk of such deep wakefulness as Abhishiktananda could write these words:

> The soul tastes the supreme joy of being not only in the cave of the heart, but also in the endless multiplicity of her contacts with the world of humanity and nature of which she is part. Every moment is a sacrament of eternity; every event a sign and sacrament of the perfect Bliss; for nothing in the universe can escape being transformed by the divine Eschaton – and by its sign in the Eucharist – at every moment of time.[1]

Abhishiktananda describes how the inmost centre of the human soul opens up from within, in the power of Christ's love dwelling there. It opens towards the reality in which it knows it forever belongs – neither 'inward' nor 'outward' but simply 'with'. By entering this essential experience in faith modern people will be able to avoid the danger of a modern Gnosticism that attempts to reduce the divine infinity to something knowable within the limitations of finite minds. This is the hubris against which theology must be guarded. Meditation is so important because it leads us beyond the images and concepts that so easily try to control the divine presence. It leads indeed beyond all egotistic desire for God. At the other end of the scale is the danger for the modern religious mind of a new sort of quietism or passive sentimentality. Prayer, above all, is not nostalgia for God. Prayer is the summons to a full experience of the living Christ whose purpose, as St Paul tells us, 'is everywhere at work'. Paul's emphasis is not on religion as anaesthesia. It is not thinking about the absent God. It is not absenting ourselves from the present moment to be lost in a kind of pietistic dalliance. For Paul, authentic religion summons human beings to enter fully and courageously into the present moment. There we are filled with life by the living Christ. The call of prayer is to be fully alive in the present, without regret for the past or fear of the future.

And so, we have to accept the responsibility of being alive. We must understand the full significance and depth of the mystery contained in the Christian experience. This experience is in essence being fully open to our own humanity and the gift of our creation. It is nothing less than conscious participation in the self-knowledge of God. This is the direct message of St Paul:

---

1 Abhishiktananda, *Saccidananda* (ISPCK, Delhi, 1974), p. 186.

For the same God who said, 'Out of darkness let light shine' has caused his light to shine within us, to give the light of revelation, the revelation of the glory of God in the face of Jesus.[2]

What becomes clear is that God is never an object that we know. The truth is so much greater than merely objective knowledge. Our potential for wholeness is that God knows us and in that complete knowledge – of knowing and being known – we awaken. We have to remember that we know God, not just speculatively in our minds but existentially, lovingly in our hearts. We know and are known in the fullness and richness of prayer that leaves self entirely behind and plunges into the depths of God. We do this with no thought for self but entirely 'living for him who for our sake died and was raised to life'.[3]

We keep you in our hearts and send you all much love.

Every blessing,

John Main OSB
(September 1978)

In May, John Main gave retreats in California. He saw it as a part of the world where talks on meditation are no novelty but also one that finds the essential qualities of meditation, seriousness and fidelity very challenging. This society of entertainment and spiritual eclecticism is marked also by a genuine search for a true experience of absolute value. It seemed to him that the monastic witness of the kind we were making in Montreal was of importance for this search. It could prove to a culture built to such an extent on conditional discipleship that only absolute commitment can bring the liberation we seek but so often do not find. While he was there, he heard that the Abbot of Ealing, our founding monastery in London, was planning to visit us in Montreal that month. On his return, Laurence Freeman prepared a programme for the visit that would introduce him to the broad spectrum of our work and acquaintances, while also allowing him to participate in our round of prayer and worship. With us he visited our neighbouring Benedictine and Cistercian brethren of the city and he

---

2 2 Corinthians 4.6.
3 2 Corinthians 5.16.

spoke with the Archbishop and Bishop Crowley. All his engagements confirmed the impression he took back to share with Ealing that our foundation was truly finding its roots here – more surely than any had anticipated. It seemed evident that we would have to reconsider our original three-year trial period, as this could unnecessarily delay our growth. It was important for it to be seen that our commitment here, despite the uncertain political situation and our small numbers, was serious. His visit gave us the chance to discuss the way we would best follow the line of monastic development we had begun. The deepening contemplative orientation (we had by now built a fourth meditation period into the day after compline), was leading us into a monasticism very different from that of our founding community. Starting a novitiate or moving our location would also be tiresomely complicated if we had to wait for the approval of the London community at each step. We all agreed that, as soon as the right moment came, we would transfer our monastic stability from England. The momentum and the enthusiasm made this a friendly mutual decision. We had other monastic guests that summer, from Ealing and from Washington, DC, and a six-week visit from an Irish Capuchin, who was Spiritual Director of a seminary. He came to meditate with us, having found one of our books in a Dublin bookshop. He was taken with the need to communicate the way of meditation to his students, for whose spiritual formation he was responsible. Each afternoon, behind the thick walls of the old house that kept out the summer heat, he and John Main talked of meditation and its contemporary importance for the renewal of our religious orders. It was from out of these discussions that much of the next newsletter was derived. In September an American Benedictine joined us for six months and began work on a thesis that he would later continue in Paris. Summer days kept us out in the garden or finding corners of the exterior that needed paint or repair. The groups that had been suspended for July and August resumed and we were soon back to our former schedule. Many from the groups who could do so joined us during the summer months for our regular community sessions of meditation or the Friday Eucharist. This reinforced our sense of our primary task – to be there to meditate with whoever came. The summer had given us all the space to relax together and consider the next step we now seemed ready to take.

5

BEYOND OURSELVES

My Dearest Friends,

Greetings in the Lord! Firstly, on behalf of everyone here let me wish you all a most happy and joyful celebration of the Lord's birth.

We are very conscious just now of what it means to celebrate an anniversary as it was exactly a year ago today that we moved into this house. It is with a sense of wonder and gratitude that we look back over the last year to see how we have begun our work as a monastery in the city, grateful for the new members who have joined the community as well as hopeful for the future that opens up ahead of us.

As we have watched the community grow and develop during the last year, it has reminded us of the generosity of spirit that still makes the Rule of St Benedict an inspiration of the monastic life after fifteen hundred years. Although Benedict wrote for a particular time and for a particular type of monk, his experience of the liberty of spirit proclaimed by the gospel meant that his Rule would not be a rigid rule book. Benedict's broad vision sees the Rule as mainly concerned with the first stage of the monastic vocation – 'a little rule for beginners', as he puts it. Importantly for his modern disciples, he urges discretion and flexibility in living the Rule in different contexts. He saw that the details and the form of monastic life would be conditioned by the place and people that live it. Precisely because it is inserted into its own time and place a monastery is relevant to its social and cultural context. Because it is relevant it can relate to its contemporaries in contemporary terms. Because it can relate it can also serve. It serves by showing society that the ultimate meaning of men and women is found beyond themselves, beyond their cultural tradition. It does not do this by denouncing the secular. Monks have passed through the same formative experiences in society as everyone else. Their life interweaves with the world. Benedict testifies to relevance but arranges the priorities of living to show that the end of the human search is found in the way of transcendence. Its great Christian proclamation is that the seeds of this transcendent experience are planted in the soil of our humanity. The spiritual journey does not call for a rupture with our humanity but the fulfilment of it. It is the natural continuation of it.

The experience of transcendence cannot, therefore, be engineered to fit our own timetable of priorities. Firstly, transcendence is pure gift. Secondly, by its nature it involves our whole person. There is no curious, objective, self-reflecting ego left to stand outside the experience. So the experience of transcendence occurs within the nature of things – our human nature. Jesus' parables of the Kingdom show that the basis of this experience is natural growth. A small mustard seed grows into a tree big enough for the birds to come and roost in its branches.[1] To try to make it grow faster or slower would be absurd and counterproductive. The growth of the Kingdom in our hearts is the meaning of the journey of meditation. Day by day we let the husk of the ego drop away and like a seed we die to self so that we can fulfil the destiny, our true meaning, in which the potential of life within us comes to full fruition. It is the same when a monastic community, or any Christian community, takes root and allows the love of God to fill and expand it. The Christian vision has always respected the processes of natural growth. Grace builds on nature. Christian faith has always seen that redemption means that all human growth is now incorporate in Christ and shares the limitless achievement he has won. The mystery of the fully mature Christ is infinite growth. The mystery, as St Paul wrote, is 'Christ in you'.

The natural process of the Christian experience explains why Christianity both transcends the world and is fully incarnational. A Christian community can realize and manifest an experience of transcendence while at the same time being fully human. Indeed, because it is incarnate, a Christian community is less concerned with ideals than with reality. In its full revelation we know this reality – which is the reality of love – as divine. It is the mystery of the Being of God made visible. But we first begin to experience it in its human revelation, by the love we have for others and the love they show us. There is nothing abstract about this. It means realizing that *this* brother or *this* sister is a temple of the love of God. He or she is to be loved and

---

1 Matthew 13.31–33.

reverenced both for this universal characteristic of the mystery of creation that they embody and also for his or her frailty of temperament
or weakness of faith. Seeing this we know the mystery of what it is to
be a person: to be unique and of infinite importance in the love of God.

Perhaps the greatest social service a monastery can contribute is to
be a place where this fundamental truth of human life – the truth upon
which any sane society must rest – can be experienced. The first step
is to know that each of us has an infinite importance and value. The
second, and greater, is to know that this value empowers us to turn
away from self to another in love. A monastery can reveal that these
two steps are actually one reality. We find ourselves by loving. Finding
ourselves means knowing ourselves to be loved. St Benedict puts this
very vividly:

> This zeal, therefore, monks should practice with the most burning
> love so as to be the first in showing honor to each other. Let them
> bear with weaknesses whether of body or of character with the most
> tolerant patience. Let them vie with one another in showing mutual
> obedience. Let no one follow what he thinks is useful to himself but
> what is of use to another.[2]

Medieval monastic writers liked to emphasize that the monastic life
in Benedict's vision was essentially the Christian life 'writ large'. It is
not only the monastic community today that is called to be a beacon
of love in the Church and world. But the monastery is special. It is a
stable, hospitable sign that living this way is practical and possible.
People may be encouraged and inspired by reading the Gospels. They
are doubly inspired by seeing ordinary people trying to live the gospel
in single-minded generosity of spirit. A monastery makes this witness
in many different ways but it will do so less by theory than by practice.
Its call is not to talk about the Christian experience so much as to live
it, to communicate it, to *be* it.

Visitors to a monastery often come with unclear or mixed motives.
They may not know how to begin the next phase of their journey. Yet
they have felt its call and cannot evade or shake it off. So, what they
first experience in the monastery often surprises them. They think they
will find God as they have been imagining Him till then. But instead

---

2 Rule of St Benedict, Chapter 72.

they find themselves recognized, known, and inexplicably loved. This experience changes their expectations. They no longer seek a God of their own imagining. Instead, they begin to expand in the presence of the God they discover to be incarnate and yet beyond thought or image. They begin to realize that their earlier seeking of God often locked them blindly into themselves and locked them into the limitations of images and desires. Feeling known, they now realize that God is seeking them. They need simply to be still and allow themselves to be more fully found. All this is something only experience can teach yet a loving community provides the context for the discovery. The monk is one who follows through this discovery in such a context. He or she is one who, by their own commitment to the journey, helps create and strengthen the community in which others, maybe even by a very brief contact with it, can find their way.

Every Christian knows at some level that the central mystery of faith is the experience of love. We know it and yet our hearts can be so insecure and inconstant that we need to hear this Word of love spoken anew day after day. We hear it in the word spoken to us by our brothers and sisters as well as in the silence of our meditation. We hear it spoken in the community, which is the locus, the context where the Word of God is in ceaseless utterance. We hear it also in solitude. The silence that is integral to a monastic community helps us hear the reverberations of the Word in all circumstances and know the utterance of the Word as the mystery of Christ's presence among us. To hear it even once is to be reassured and fortified in the depth of our being. To hear it continually is to live a life impregnated with a 'joy too great for words'[3] and to realize ever more fully that we are 'incorporate with Christ'. So profound is this incorporation that we have shared his death and rising – we are his in life and death. We are bidden to enter just as profound a union with one another. Paul called his communities 'brethren in the Lord' and my sister or brother is precisely that because of what Jesus has achieved for both of us.

Dietrich Bonhoeffer once said that 'God hates visionary dreaming'. The monastic community is a place where the truth is being lived, not just dreamed. The gospel is not about ideals but reality, not about delay but beginning. The Rule of St Benedict realistically illustrates how a Christian community consists in loving people as they are. 'The

---

3 1 Peter 1.9.

man who fashions a visionary ideal of community', Bonhoeffer continued, 'demands that it be realized by God, by others, by himself. ... He acts as if he is the creator of Christian community – as if his dream binds men together.' And when this egotistic ideal goes wrong, the dreamer accuses his brethren, his God, and, finally, in despair, himself.

This shows what I was saying at the beginning of this letter. The process of Christian growth, whether for individual or for community, is natural, fully human. Its ultimate meaning is always a mystery because of this. The real contribution of a monastic community to secular society is far more profound than it may seem to be.

The touchstone of a monastic community is its seriousness. Its seriousness keeps it developing in harmony with the mystery that contains its secret meaning. But to be serious is the opposite of being solemn. To be serious is to accept the fact that we are created for ultimate happiness, that being and joy are intertwined. A monastery is a place of joy – better able than many are of having fun without being distracted from its serious purpose. It is a joy that permeates every aspect of the community. I notice it sometimes in the way we enter the meditation room together, in the way we experience each other's joy in painting a room, making a picture, publishing an article, or creating a successful boeuf bourguignon. In such ways a loving community communicates a unique experience of the unity of our lives. In this I realize that I am not many people living different lives but one person involved in the mystery of communion with my own destiny, with others, with God. The condition for this experience is a joy-filled seriousness that is the fruit of simplicity and commitment. The monastic life is not set over and against ordinary life. It is simply a special arrangement of priorities that constitute the spiritual life anywhere. It is this arrangement that the monk comes to understand then freely chooses and generously undertakes. These priorities are not rules to be imposed. They form a life-style growing out of a shared vision that is authenticated both by tradition and by personal experience.

This seriousness is lived in an expansive, hospitable spirit of love. Then the monastery fulfils a prophetic role. It points to the ultimate sadness of a life built on mere fun-seeking; to the destructiveness of distraction; to the insecurity and isolation created by triviality. It does not expose all this by denouncing it. It incarnates an actual alternative way of living into the fullness of life. It shows that this is a real possibility. Few people would deny at this point in the twentieth century that monasticism has serious thinking to do about its future. What is becoming clearer every year is that a modern monasticism is more than ever aware of itself as a community of love on the way to transcendence. The modern monastery is thus conscious of its historical roots and inspiration. It knows how central meditation is to the tradition of monastic prayer. It sees how meditation unveils the universality of its values by helping it be fully human, fully loving.

More and more monasticism will fulfil its prophetic role in society by living in the cities where the experience of community and of daily spiritual practice are all but lost. In the modern deserts of our cities the new monastery will bloom and prove how the power of faith and generosity of heart can achieve the impossible in liberty of spirit. 'Let the wilderness and thirsty land be glad; Let the desert rejoice and burst into flower.'[4] The proof of this fertile liberty and flexibility of spirit is the broad spectrum and diversity of the self-expression of the new monastic life. Some communities will pray in the city and lead people into the way of silence. Others may witness far from the city in a life more explicitly rooted in the cycle of nature. And others will engage the contemporary challenge of reconciling these two dimensions within the same community experience – service and solitude, city and village, cloister and marketplace.

The link between these two dimensions is unbreakable. To try to break it is to pursue a dream. It is to build a self-centred rather than the other-centred community. So let me stress again that what we are talking about is not an abstract, ideal world, but reality as it is a fallen, damaged world but a world redeemed. The paradoxes of monasticism reveal the contradictions of the world: the world of sin and heroism, suffering and joy, madness and sanity, pain and consolation, all redeemed by love. It is in this self-contradictory world that we build our experience of community. The power of this experience turns self-contradiction into paradox. Paradox is then the way to mystery and transcendence.

The community Christians share is not an ideal we have to create. It is the reality created by God in Christ in whom we have our being and meaning. It is a communion that reveals greater and greater depths of identity, deeper and deeper centres of consciousness. As we

---

4 Isaiah 35.1.

understand this, the more serene and the more liberating will be our community.

Thankfulness is an essential part of this communion in community: being thankful to God for the Word spoken to us, to the community for the opportunities of love it offers. Real thankfulness is the basis of all authentic celebration. But it is a sadly rare phenomenon in a world geared to acquisition rather than thanksgiving. Because of the daily pilgrimage of meditation we share, it is not a platitude to say how thankful we are for the community we know we have with you. Conceptually we have to talk of different dimensions of community, different stages of the journey. But through the communion of meditation we know the mystery that there is only one process of growth in which we all share. It is the building up in love of the one Body of Christ. 'Let us speak the truth in love; so shall we fully grow up into Christ.'[5]

The source of Christian joy is knowing how this transcendent mystery is humanly rooted in our daily lives and our loving relationships with each other. It is also the source of the power of the Christian presence in the world. What St Benedict says of monks in the last chapter of the Rule expresses the generosity of the whole Christian family through the ages as it finds its unity and vitality in the presence of Jesus: 'Let them put absolutely nothing before Christ and may he bring us all together to life eternal.'

We keep you all in our hearts every day. We send you a message of joy to persevere in the growth of the Lord Jesus in our hearts and throughout the world.

With much love,

John Main OSB
(December 1978)

As we approached the first anniversary of our arrival, the community continued to grow in size and, because of new and gifted lay members, in variety. We were also more and more in contact with French-speaking Quebecers who heard of us and came to meditate

---

5 Ephesians 4.15.

with us or learn of what we were doing. The French-speaking Church here had undergone a traumatic reversal of fortune in the past fifteen years and the massive decline in religious practice had created a spiritual vacuum that many movements had come to fill. Many who now came to us had begun meditation as a result of an encounter with TM but were looking again at their own tradition from the new standpoint that their experience of the inner journey had won for them. Almost all were amazed to hear of a contemplative tradition in Christianity that was addressed to all and was not the privilege of a spiritual elite. 'Why have we never heard about this before?' they would ask. How, indeed, could the Gospels and St. Paul be read daily in churches and yet the experience of prayer they convey be so unknown to the bulk of Christians?

A small group of artists and craftsmen began to work on a number of projects in our basement, although we still lacked the space and facilities to develop proper opportunities for manual work for members of the community or guests. We knew this was important for giving a personal balance to our lives, both from our experience so far and from the essential Benedictine principle of the synthesis among prayer, work and study. It was another indication that the development of our work required more space.

St Benedict said a monastery will never be without guests and we were proof of it. He said also that the monks must pray with the guests and this was why our guests came. We suggested that newcomers join us in meditation for two sessions each day, morning and evening, and when it seemed natural to do so, to come to the midday session also. It was important, especially with all living at close quarters, to avoid any sense of constraint or obligation, because the journey can only be undertaken in perfect liberty and followed with a self-renewing commitment. It was clear that the witness to this was the most important teaching we had to offer and it was made as a community who had learned it from their own experience. Every member of the community shared this witness and it was underpinned by the absolute and permanent commitment of the monastic life.

In the fall we published a new set of tapes and booklet, The Christian Mysteries: Prayer and Sacrament, *which had grown out of talks I had given to a meeting of priests of the diocese. In this we tried to put meditation before the more liturgically oriented Christian by stressing the essential need for a personal journey of prayer if the outward celebrations were to be really signs and moments of growth in spiritual maturity. It had been clear more than once that our first three tapes on meditation often made deeper contact with the Christian or the non-Christian to whom 'religion' or 'worship' were secondary or unfamiliar. In Ireland these tapes had proved very popular with groups of Alcoholics Anonymous.*

We made the next important step in the community's development in October when we visited Mount Saviour. Albert Reyburn, their devoted Oblate, Father Paul, Brother Laurence and John Main drove down through New York State's beautiful fall colours and we were greeted very warmly by the Prior, Father Martin Boler. He listened with interest to our account of the Montreal foundation and of the crossroads we had reached in our monastic development. He and the community offered us their support and patronage for any step we would take to respond to the new opportunity then shaping itself before us.

6

FAITH BEYOND BELIEF

My Dearest Friends,

Peace and love in the Lord.

It seems a long time since we have written to you, but I had the joy of seeing many of you while I was in England, Ireland, and Scotland and I hope you will forgive our long silence. So much has happened since December when we sent you the last newsletter. Before Christmas Bishop Crowley came and presided at our evening liturgy. In his homily he said, 'The tremendous grace that this community can offer to an alienated, exiled world can indeed bring people back to the Spirit where they will find happiness to be like a river ... But first we must respond deeply within our hearts to the Lord our God who teaches all goodness.'

It has become even clearer to us that the service a community of prayer gives to society is an integrated response to the deepest human needs and yearnings. The monastery in the world is a sacrament of the monastic dimension in every one. The pilgrimage of prayer, followed within a community of love, the meaning of monastic communion reflects the journey everyone is called to make from the illusion of the ego to the reality of God. No society can achieve interior harmony or confidence in its own meaning without such spiritual centres of simplicity and commitment that operate, in peaceful seriousness from resources that are beyond social control. The call of God that draws us to God both transcends and affirms society because it is a call of love inviting a response of love. Although rooted in the ordinary fabric of our lives, it travels into the infinite space of God where call and response are consummated in the eternal moment of Being.

Our daily lives often seem routine and uninspiring. The vision of transcendence can be lost or become merely a memory we carry around with us from books we have read or retreats we have attended.

But reality cannot be either remembered or imagined. It can only be experienced in the liberty of the present moment, which underpins and pervades all activity and growth. If it seems that this present moment comes and goes it is indeed only a seeming. The experience is never absent. We are absent. The illusion of absence, like all illusion, happens when our consciousness becomes centred in ourselves rather than in the Other – self-referring rather than God-referring. In all our prayer here in the community we keep you in our hearts hoping that you will keep on this joyful pilgrimage always entering, more deeply and with growing courage, into yourselves in the loving Otherness of God. Many of you already know that to set out on this journey from self takes a certain recklessness. We may not be happy with our self-centredness but at least its unhappiness is predictable while the unknown that lies outside the circle of desire and sadness constantly overwhelms our capacity to anticipate it. It has to be taken on faith. Many of you also know the occasional moments of anger, grief or sense of absurdity that occur as we find that the way to knowledge is the way of unknowing. But they are only moments on the straight path to the present moment. The power by which we follow this path is not our own and so these moments of trial hold no ultimate sway over us. As we go through them the recklessness with which we started the journey is transformed into generosity, largeness of heart by the discipline of our daily meditation.

It was a joyful experience for me to see this being realized in many of the groups I met with recently. They are groups that are not complicating or saddening the journey with unnecessary self-analysis. They persevere in simple openness of heart to the Lord living in their hearts and in their midst. The members of these groups are learning to set their minds upon the kingdom as their first priority. In their own unique ways, then, they become generous communicants of the perfecting power of faith, which is human openness to the reality beyond yet containing us.

While I enjoyed the kind hospitality of the missionary sisters in Drogheda I also had the opportunity to visit and talk with some Dominican sisters. On a very cold winter's afternoon we talked together of the love of God that is first known in prayer as experience in our hearts, then marvellously communicated and shared with all we meet. As we sat and talked in the common room before a turf fire, whose beautiful soft light grew stronger as the evening lengthened,

I felt that moment to be a sign of what we were sharing at a deeper level. The power of human love is the fire of God's love centred in each person and in each community. It is realized when each person turns toward this centre and allows its light to radiate in and through them.

I found the same open-hearted seeking in many different groups in England, Scotland, and Ireland. Each of them highlighted for me the dynamic of community formation that accompanies the search for God. The journey into the God who is Love cannot be followed in isolation. We cannot pre-determine the itinerary of our pilgrimage or the conditions of our commitment. Indeed when we find ourselves planning our inner journey, steering a course so as to catch the sights on the way, it is a good sign that we have yet to take our hand off the wheel. We have yet to let the God-driven direction reveal itself. We have not yet placed our centre of consciousness outside of ourselves. Community is the context in which we learn to do this. We learn directly about the truth and power of other-centredness. Fidelity to the community is our loving openness and freedom with others. It is the complement to our fidelity to the mantra. It is all about generous, magnanimous poverty of spirit.

The way of meditation is the way of love: 'this work of love', as the *Cloud of Unknowing* calls it. So it is real not conceptual; incarnate, not abstract; practical not a matter of nice words or ideas. To act on this vision and really to begin the journey requires decisive and open-hearted commitment. There is no commitment, however, without simplicity of spirit. This is what allows us to say an unambiguous 'yes' to the call, to the invitation to journey into reality. The danger of this is that it sounds like – and can lead us into – the worst form of self-centred self-importance ... until we understand that the 'yes' we utter is Christ himself.

The Son of God, Christ Jesus, proclaimed among you by us ... was never a blend of Yes and No. With him it was and is Yes. He is the Yes pronounced upon God's promises, every one of them. That is why, when we give glory to God, it is through Christ Jesus that we say 'Amen.'[1]

This means that our commitment is already pledged in the transcendent power of Jesus, the proof of which is his Spirit dwelling in our

---

1 1 Corinthians 1.19–21.

hearts. It remains for us to realize, through our simplicity, how our incorporation in his achievement is pure gift. Our way is the way of simplicity. The simplicity of our word. The simplicity of love.

We are at a moment in history when men and women, everywhere in every tradition and culture, are coming to see that the journey within is absolutely necessary for humanity if our evolution is to continue. Everywhere people are trying to open their spiritual eyes. They are yearning for the expansion of consciousness that is the vision of God within and beyond us. The central task of the Church is to respond to that basic intuition in humanity today and to lead us to the knowledge, the opening of the eye of the heart that is seeing with the mind of Christ. It is a matter of experience, of knowledge not just preaching. It is the task of *all* serious Christians to confirm people in this search by leading them into the richness and depth of contemplative experience.

Contemplation informs action. The Medical Missionaries of Mary, for example, have a serious commitment to deep prayer that finds compassionate expression in their great work of healing around the world. Mother Mary Martin, their foundress, remains an inspiration to them because she was so evidently a woman of deep prayer, deep faith, and deep compassion. She saw clearly and knew from her own experience how the grounding reality of the Christian life is the experience of prayer. She knew that when this experience is entered with generous commitment we find, as individuals and as communities, the place assigned to us by the harmony of the love of God at work in the world: the harmony that is the Body of Christ.

The varied experiences of my recent trip were brought into unity for me by the silence of meditation I shared on each occasion with each person. Silence in the mystery of being together in his name at this time and place is also openness to the mystery of his presence within and among us. It is impossible without radical simplicity. To tread the way of meditation requires only simplicity of heart. Our talking, thinking and reading, and our theology all have value, but only to the degree that they develop our disposition to openness and deepen our childlikeness. St John of the Cross put this very clearly in Book 1 of *The Ascent of Mount Carmel*:

Only those who set aside their own knowledge and walk in God's service like unlearned children receive wisdom from God ...

If any one among you thinks he is wise let him become ignorant so as to be wise. For the wisdom of this world is foolishness with God.[2] Accordingly, a man must advance in union with God's wisdom by unknowing rather than by knowing.[3]

The cloud of this unknowing is the same cloud by which the presence of God, as well as the nature of his hiddenness, is described in the Bible. It is a cloud that both leads us through the desert[4] and draws us into itself to speak the Word[5] – the cloud in which we have only to say our 'one little word'.[6]

In prayer we enter the cloud. We set aside our own knowledge together with our expectations and our memories so as to be wholly open in purity of heart to the Word of God in the present moment. The courage to do this comes because we believe wholeheartedly, at a level beyond desire, sorrow, or imagination, that God's Word is alive, active, and in continual utterance. This is faith beyond what we normally call belief. It is a faith that is at once courage, commitment, and openness. Through it we come to know that the reality of God is the source and power of our own reality. We know it 'though it is beyond knowledge'. The daily pilgrimage of meditation takes us into the simplicity we need in order to enter the silence of selflessness. Here we awaken to hear this eternal utterance and to attend to it with our whole beings. The wonder of prayer is that we hear this Word addressed to us directly and personally. We listen to it without the distracting interference of our own cleverness. In hearing it we learn that we are continuously being called into being by Being. We share in the eternal presentness of God, who says and who is *I AM*. This kind of prayer is not *our* prayer: it is the prayer of the spirit. The mystery, ever beyond words, is that we are invited to be fully open to it with the power of his love.

Married, single people, monks, students, children, sisters, housewives, and priests – all of us have to learn that the purpose of all theology and worship and of life itself is simply to awaken us to the

---

2 1 Corinthians 3.18–19.
3 1 Corinthians 4.5.
4 Exodus 13.22.
5 Luke 9.35.
6 *The Cloud of Unknowing*, Chap. 7.

supreme reality that God is. We can awaken to this because the Spirit is awake in our hearts. The New Testament calls this journey of consciousness the way of faith – a way that begins and ends in faith. We journey away from familiar limitations and illusions into an unknown space to find ourselves in reality. There we are summoned to full wakefulness and full being. We cannot awaken to reality as if it were something external and objectifiable. Or, as if it could be remembered. We awaken to reality *in* reality – in which we already live and move and have our being.

A life of prayer is essential for everyone who wants to be awake. Prayer is an entirely natural part of our life. Contemplation is what we are created for. Modern life has encapsulated us in so many illusions that keep us at one remove from reality that today we have to take a decisive step into the freedom that bursts all bonds. This is why our dedication to the particular times of meditation, every morning and every evening, is so grounding and necessary. This is why the faithful recitation of our mantra in those times of spiritual work is so transforming.

I spent my weeks in Europe talking about the Spirit and how the power of the Spirit is working in our hearts and our communities today. What I shared with all the groups I met with was that all the talk in the world about prayer and the Spirit is of no avail unless we take the steps necessary to enter into the experience of the Spirit. Entering it is pure gift. In order to receive the gift we embrace purity of heart and poverty of spirit. This is both the purpose and the state of meditation.

We hope to be able to send you a letter soon again in the Easter season when the great symbols of the Resurrection still have their springtime power and beauty. In the meantime, we ask you all to keep us here in your hearts. The Community is at a sensitive moment of growth when we hope to expand, to receive new members, and extend our work. As the Easter liturgies will soon be teaching us, the power of all new life comes from beyond ourselves. Yet its source has been planted in our inmost being. The journey we share is to this source.

With much love,

John Main OSB
(March 1979)

Our second Christmas in Montreal helped us to realize how deeply we had already put down our roots here. A group from North Carolina drove up to see us to discuss models of community living for a number of families who had been meeting together for prayer and were now looking for a deeper commitment to the journey they were on. A leader of a London meditation group and Bishop Crowley of Montreal discussed the vision with them. It was an opportunity to air the ideas we had been putting together in the form of a 'Rule' for communities based on a common commitment to meditation – a rule that aimed not to describe structures of life as much as to clarify the principles and some of the practical considerations of a modern contemplative community. Many of the experiments we heard of in this line seemed to fail precisely because there was no inner coherence, no deeply unifying practice. This could be due to a lack of commitment, but the difficulties could also be compounded by a lack of clear language. One of the problems we discussed was how to find a precise vocabulary to replace our largely devalued religious language. How were we to communicate the meaning of 'discipline', 'obedience', or 'faith', without which there could no human community, contemplative or otherwise? At the end of January, John Main left for England to fulfil engagements and retreat, leaving Laurence Freeman with responsibility for the groups and the community. He spent the first week at Ealing, where the community was about to receive new novices and had the opportunity to talk about the way the Montreal foundation was growing. In London he also spoke to the meditation groups that had formed from our centre. He visited the Fellowship of St Ethelwold in Abingdon and spent a weekend with people from meditation groups around England at the Grail's centre in Pinner. He then went to Scotland to give the annual retreat to the Trappist monastery at Nunraw. From there to Ireland and a week's retreat to some longtime friends – the Medical Missionaries of Mary in Drogheda, an order with houses in Africa, Europe and the Americas. The travel and variety of audiences – from the lay groups and the Grail to the contemplative Trappists – deepened his sense of the university of meditation. In Dublin, an old friend, Father Tom Fehily, a parish priest, organized meetings. After a day with a group of Capuchins brought together by the Irish Capuchin who had been with us in Montreal the previous summer, he went with Father Tom to meet and meditate with a class of children in his parish school. He gave a talk at University College and another to a large meeting at Mount Sackville. His last engagement in Ireland was with the Kiltegan Fathers in County Wicklow, whose superior had spent time with us in Montreal on his return from Africa. At their house he finally met, after a long period of correspondence, with Bishop Moynagh, who had spent many years in the service of the Nigerian Church. This round of meetings encouraged him. It gave our work a wider perspective. The problems, the opportunities, the hunger were essentially the same everywhere.

7

RETURNING HOME

My Dearest Friends,

Greetings in the Lord. So much has happened since we last wrote to you on St Benedict's day in March. We must apologize for the delay in sending you this letter, but although we have been out of sight during these months, all of you have been in our prayers, in our hearts.

The first news we have to give you is that after consultation with the Abbot of Ealing, it seemed best for us to join with a monastery closer to Montreal that is also oriented to a contemplative vision of monasticism. And so we are now a dependent priory of Mount Saviour and we hope soon to establish our own novitiate here with the right to profess monks for this house.

Every Benedictine house has its own special character and direction. As each community pursues its particular vision of the monastic journey, it deepens the rediscovery of the tradition that has led it to where it is. In fact the vision itself is the result of the meeting of tradition with the unique circumstances of the present. It takes place in the open-heartedness of faith. The monastery's responsibility is to integrate its vision and experience with the tradition. It must do what it is specially called to do to pass on the experience of faith to the future. It must, therefore, be able to train its members in the light of its own vision. Our call is to follow the path of meditation, 'pure prayer.' We hope to be faithful to that call and to share our contemplative understanding of monasticism with those who join us as monks and those who live with us for short or long periods of time. Indeed, with all who 'seek God'.

Mount Saviour, founded by Father Damasus Winzen in the 1950s, is rooted in this contemplative tradition and we consider it a privilege to have been received into their family and allowed to share their heritage. Another monastery is also attached to Mount Saviour. Christ in the Desert is another dependent priory in New Mexico. Our three Houses therefore represent the spectrum of contemplative life in different settings – country, city, and desert. This points up the essential unity of the life, its freedom from constriction by outward form, its adaptability to circumstance, its fidelity to the stillness of Being, beyond complexity and division. We hope to open a novitiate here in September and we are looking for a larger site to begin the development of the monastery. We hope, too, that that Lord of the harvest will send workers into his vineyard who will generously seek his kingdom, opening their hearts to him in pure consciousness.

Our many guests and visitors in recent weeks have again shown that a community that meditates together and regularly shares the Eucharist and Office, shares itself with others at many levels. This is as natural as the bursting of a tree into leaf or the blooming of a flower – the great natural growth symbols of the parables of the Kingdom. The marvellous thing is that this happens again and again. Each time it is a new miracle, a fresh act of creation that fills us with deeper joy and wonder. I think that this happens in community when a community devoted to prayer is bringing to birth its own wholeness. This wholeness is its unique holiness. It fills us with wonder because we come to know more deeply its potential for infinite expansion. There is no limit to goodness. Prayer is the experience of Being that is, in and of itself, pure joy, pure thanksgiving. The silence of meditation opens us to this as a present reality. Theory and abstraction give way to the embodied dimension of Eucharist. In that dimension we see the presence of a light shining in and through all things, all experience. It brings life into unity. As this light grows stronger we are able to perceive and feel it more clearly. We become filled with that joy and peace which the New Testament proclaims and communicates: the joy of the Spirit, the peace that passes all understanding.

There is much misunderstanding about the 'contemplative life'. The very phrase carries with it many stereotyped images and unconscious associations. To some it brings up a picture of lifeless people sitting around all day with nothing to do except look at themselves. But real prayer, coming from the silent centre of spirit, is the source of the selflessness of love. It is not lifeless because it is the source of all energy. In that centre as the source of Being we encounter God in the power of the divine self-awareness of the Holy Spirit. It is the Spirit Jesus freely 'lavished upon us'. To find God is to find love. To find love is to find oneself in harmony with the basic energy of all creation, which is love. When a community is directed to this as its priority, ordinary limitations imposed on human relations by egoism can get flipped around. Where there was self-seeking there is a spirit of service. Where there was desire for self-perfection there is an impulse to lead others to happiness through love. The loving service of a spiritual community derives its stream of inspiration from sharing its openness to the one who became the servant of us all.

In our retreats and guests you can see something of how we have developed on the monastic journey. We have hopes for a novitiate and for future monks praying, working, studying, teaching and proclaiming the Kingdom by the simplicity of their lives and the joy of their spirit. That the monastic life can mean so much to those who are not monks shows how there is a common experience of contemplation that links the monastery to every form of life in the Spirit. Thomas Merton spoke in his later years of the monastic dimension in every person. This is the dimension of pure faith. Coming from a deep and living spring in us, it is faith that makes the monastic adventure possible but also such a rich, joyful experience for all who embrace it with open hearts.

We use the single word 'faith' to cover a vast range of human experience. For St Paul, the whole Christian life was shaped by faith: the Way of Christ begins in faith and ends in faith. This inclusiveness of faith suggests how fundamental it is to the life of our spirit. Faith is, fundamentally, the experience of our being grounded in God, rooted in him with absolute sureness and with a confidence that is always deepening because the depths of God can never be measured. This is the experience of prayer. It is falling into the depths of love with complete trust, with a complete 'letting go'. To say that 'God is the ground of our being' is not an abstract, metaphysical concept. It is saying that our reality derives from God's being, the one Reality. Our being is from Being itself. To be open to this as the great fact of all existence we need to approach prayer with confidence.

But spiritual confidence is something modern people are trained to distrust. The proper, approved, scientific attitude is scepticism. Because scientific explanations of natural phenomena change so rapidly in the light of new research, it often seems that any understanding we can have of nature or humanity has only limited, and temporary, validity. No grounds for confidence exist when everything is changing all the time. Consequently, our time has become an age of the half-hearted commitment, with the other half holding on to scepticism, self-monitoring, keeping one's options open. If this led to happiness, to richness or breadth of experience it would have something to recommend it. But, as we all discover, when we hold ourselves back on the brink of commitment we become enmeshed in a sense of isolation, of discontent, of anxious, restless desire. Whereas on those occasions when we have the courage really to let go, we have found ourselves unexpectedly more alive, miraculously borne up. The act of faith, of generous self-commitment, is the context in which we know the power of transcendence. In committing ourselves we are lifted above ourselves, out of the prison of self-consciousness and beyond our limitations. This is what St Peter means by being 'alive with the life of God'[1] and what St Paul means by attaining to 'fullness of being, the fullness of God himself'.[2] Transcending ourselves through the power of the risen, transcendent Christ, we are led into oneness with the Father, our Source.

The first step in the process of transcendence and towards union with God happens when we turn at depth to prayer. This is a moment of truth. It is a moment when we are confronted with the fact of our existence and are challenged to accept the gift of it with generous simplicity. It is a moment of silence – what is there to say or think? – and a moment of love. In this moment of decision, we turn aside from everything with faith. This is the abandonment, the letting go of prayer. It is casting out into the depth of God as the ground of being and allowing ourselves to fall back into our source. It may seem – because of the language we have to use to describe it – like a retrogressive movement. We call it a 'going back', a 'returning'. And in a sense it is. It is the returning home of the prodigal child who understood that his reality was to be found at home and not in the restless pursuit of illusion abroad. The early Christian monks used to describe it as a wandering in a land of 'unlikeness' and a return to our real likeness as images of God. This aspect of prayer as a restoration, a returning or homecoming, is profoundly important to us. It emphasizes the humanity of the journey we are all called to make. It suggests some of

---

1 1 Peter 4.6.
2 Ephesians 3.19.

the tenderest and most intimate reasons that God is known to us, and described by Jesus to us as 'Father'.

But the journey is also, and equally, a progression. We are not merely recovering a lost innocence. We are growing into innocence, becoming more like God who leads us into the universal maturity of Jesus: 'shaped to the likeness of his Son, that he might be the eldest among a large family of sisters and brothers'.[3] When we glimpse this *progression through return* as the dynamic of prayer we find the only ultimate assurance there is, the assurance of Being-in-love with God. This builds confidence in their own reality and such people of faith become confident in their acts of abandonment. Their surefootedness derives not from external forms or just from ideas but from a personal centre of gravity found not in ephemeral experience but in the experience of God. God's self-experiencing, wholly undifferentiated, is the Spirit. It is the personal love of the Father for the Son and reciprocal love of the Son for the Father. Human life reflects and shares in this. The simple and indescribable wonder of the Christian vision is that each and all of us together are called to enter this selfsame experience in the Spirit.

We find the courage to be by entering the transcendent experience in which we are delivered from our limitations and empowered with the liberty of God. Our first Pope, Peter, whom we encounter in the New Testament as such a lovable and fallible man, expresses this in daring and confident words. We have to remember that they apply to each of us:

> His divine power has bestowed on us everything that makes for life and true religion, enabling us to know the One who called us by his own splendor and might. Through his might and splendor he has given us his promises, great beyond all price, and through them you may escape the corruption with which lust has infected the world, and come to share in the very being of God.[4]

'Sharing in the very being of God' is the experience of prayer. The New Testament presents it to us partly as promise, partly as an invitation but also as a challenge. It is not enough just to 'take it or leave it', always putting off the moment of response. Our capacity to respond

---

3 Romans 8.29.
4 2 Peter 1.3–4.

to it comes through the union of our spirit with the Spirit of Jesus. It unfolds in our lives as the responsibility to attain to full human maturity. Society trains us to remain childish, dependent on external stimuli and amusement; spoon-fed on the prepackaged experiences we call entertainment. Such experiences have about as much spiritual nutrition as the fast foods or television that characterize our culture. Even when we discover the spiritual responsibility of our lives we may be tempted by our conditioning to evade it. It is easy to retreat spiritually too into childish distraction and dissipation. The responsibility of a mature response may then seem like a threat to our freedom.

This is why meditation is so important for us all. It prepares us for the real freedom that lives and rejoices at the heart of the mystery of love within us. It connects us with the movement of divine energy that is known in the stillness of meditation. To pray in the infinite depths of our spirit, which are the depths of God, is to be utterly free. Daily meditation, the deepening experience that flowers on the trellis of our discipline, teaches us the essential lesson of maturity that freedom does not consist in doing what we want. Freedom is found in being who we are. To be free is to have been liberated into being by a power of love greater than the power of our own ego. It is to have encountered and responded to the Other in humility. The liberty is the liberty to be open to God as the ground of our being and the structure of all inner and outer dimensions of reality. It is to be redeemed, by love, from the slavery of self-consciousness and self-preoccupation.

Language can be very frustrating because it has such in-built ambiguity. It is not uncommon, for example, to talk to someone about this need to be less self-preoccupied and to find that the talking is only making him or her more so. We all have a fatal capacity for spiritual ambiguity, for self-deception. The heart has to pass through many mirages before we reach the threshold of love at its centre.

What will lead us through the desert of self-deception and through all the evaporating illusions of double meaning? 'Blessed are the poor in spirit for theirs is the Kingdom of Heaven. Blessed are the pure in heart for they shall see God.' The joy of the Kingdom accepts no compromises. It is all-compassionate and all-forgiving. But it demands 'not less than everything'. In meditating with all the faith, simplicity, and childlike generosity we are capable of, we do begin to give everything. The more we give the more is demanded from us. This progression reveals itself not as a tyranny but as a wonderful grace, deepening us and liberating the spiral of being that the ego has kept repressed. The more we give the more is asked because the more we give the more we have, and 'to him who has more will be given'. Nothing shows the dynamism of love at the heart of life better than this paradox of giving and receiving, having and renouncing, possession and dispossession. It is the dynamic of the 'very being of God'.

The way into this dynamism is the way of simplicity and poverty. It is also learning to say our word, our mantra. Learning to say it is learning to turn aside from that very self-consciousness and self-preoccupation that complicate us and load us down with possessions. Those riches prevent us from becoming conscious of the Spirit within us, alive and active in our inmost centre. The 'riches' that the Gospel tells us make it so difficult to enter the Kingdom are the limited, incomplete truths that result from our self-analysis. Self-analysis is not self-knowledge nor is it even the way to self-knowledge. The little half-truths self-analysis reveal are merely refractions of a great, single, simple, and central truth. To know ourselves we have to turn wholly away from all self-preoccupation and even from the ways in which we are self-conscious. This is the great poverty of Christ centred in the Father who sent him and spoke through him.[5] It is the grand poverty, the spiritual richness and generosity of the mantra. No one could say this is easy. But nor should anyone say it is impossible. It demands only faith. To know ourselves means to discover our selves in an *other*. Our ultimate self-knowledge, which is the Spirit of Christ united to our spirit, means discovering ourselves in God. But to turn from self involves courage. At moments it can seem as if we are turning away from all we have and know toward nothing, only to find that we have lost ourselves and gained nothing in return. Yet, 'no one can be a follower of mine without leaving self behind and following me'. This is faith. Every act of faith is a step further into the infinite expanse of God.

Faced with this challenge to *be*, people can react by constructing an image of God. It is made from their own self-conscious preoccupations. They then address themselves to this image, talking to it, 'listening' to it. People are even advised to talk over their problems with God as with a therapist in an office. Hearing this sort of advice I can only recall the words of Jesus:

---

5 John 8.28.

In your prayers do not go babbling on like the heathen who imagine the more they say the more likely they are to be heard. Do not imitate them. Your Father knows what your needs are before you ask him. This is how you should pray ...[6]

Jesus then gave his followers the seven, short rhythmical phrases for their prayer that we know as the Lord's Prayer. Jesus' teaching on prayer always shows that prayer is growth, not in egotistical complexity or mental games. But in selflessness, in simplicity, in unity of consciousness with the Spirit.

There is another way we can evade this challenge to *be*. We can accept that we have to renounce multiplicity of thought and imagination. But then we just set off wandering in the labyrinths of our psyches, savouring our own experiences, selecting and rejecting what we like or dislike, setting our own courses, acting as our own guides. This is to be more turned in upon ourselves than before. More than ever, then, we turn away both from the outer guide of tradition and the inner guide that is the Spirit that we find when we take the attention off ourselves.

The pilgrimage of prayer leads us onwards between these two dead ends of illusion. Just 'talking your problems over' with God is likely to lead you into deeper ego fixation. Drifting in an undisciplined self-observation is likely to isolate you from God, from others, from yourself. This is why the simplicity and the poverty of the mantra is so vital to the pilgrimage of meditation. In saying it with fidelity we are doing all we can to turn from self. The rest we leave to the free gift of God, without desire or expectation. We begin in faith. We continue in faith. In faith we arrive. Our opportunity and our responsibility is to be self-emptying disciples of our Master. A disciple is not greater than his master. It is enough that we should become like him. Our way to imitate his wholehearted kenosis, his self-emptying, is the way of prayer. It is a real journey we are on, with real demands and a real discovery. And so we must really be faithful to our word: not just thinking of saying it but saying it with simplicity and love.

The reality of God is like the sea. Isolated from reality, we are like people standing on the shore. Some sit, like King Canute, ordering the tide to turn back. Others gaze romantically at its beauty and vastness

6 Matthew 6.7–9.

from a safe distance. But we are all called to be baptized into reality, to be plunged into it and to allow its all-powerful tides to direct our lives. To do this we have to leave the familiar shore and travel to the further shore where we have come from and where we are returning. The poverty and joy of our word leads us into the sea. Once there, it keeps us simply in the currents of the Spirit who lead us to a place unknown to us but where we know ourselves in God, in God's eternal now.

Our call is so deep and so wonderful. No fear or self-preoccupation should hinder our response. I send you our support and encouragement on the journey we share and urge you to ever more self-emptying discipleship of our Lord. May we grow into his full maturity and in his selflessness and love and so enter more fully into the power of love between him and our Father, which is the Spirit we share.

With much love,

John Main OSB
(June 24, 1979, Feast of St John the Baptist)

By June, we had transferred our monastic stability and association from Ealing Abbey to Mount Saviour Monastery. In our newsletter of that June, we expressed gratitude to everyone whose generosity had made this transition possible. We knew that not all foundations have found their canonical status as amicably and smoothly as we had done. We were now awaiting three things: the authorization from Rome for starting our own novitiate, the discovery of a suitable site in the Montreal area and new monastic candidates. The lay community provided a form of participation in our life that allowed anyone thinking of joining us as a monk to test and clarify their sense of vocation. This was not its only, or even main, purpose. We hoped to avoid too much structural rigidity in both monastic and lay areas of our life while clearly accepting the distinction between temporary and permanent commitment. There were many who questioned whether or not this could be possible just through the commitment to pray together. Yet, within that communal commitment to daily meditation together, many of the secondary issues that torment communities in endless discussions find a natural and obvious resolution. We would see. Time would tell. Our guests increased in numbers as summer approached and we encountered the familiar problem of lack of space. The variety in the ages and backgrounds of our visitors enriched our lives – from the Anglican Bishop of Ontario to workers from L'Arche and students from the USA. Benedictines and other religious were also appearing more frequently. The monks of St Peter's Abbey in Saskatchewan joined several of our Montreal acquaintances in contributing books to build up our library. The first three tapes on meditation appeared in book form to give wider expression to the vision we were living in these early days. Many groups and individuals were using the tapes as aids to their journey of meditation and they had asked us to issue the text of the tapes to deepen the quality of their listening to them. We had always felt the spoken word was the primary medium for communicating the message of meditation, but the printed word could enhance the power of the spoken word, too. In March and April, John Main gave a series of talks at the Faculty of Religious Studies at McGill University. The idea for the course originated with a group of theology students who, like their counterparts in many theological schools, felt the lack of a common living experience of the faith that they were spending so many pressured hours studying. In these meetings, the students were open and responsive, both in the talk that preceded the meditation and the discussion after it – the same receptivity that John Main had found at University College, Dublin, and with students in California. It seemed important to communicate this message in the language of the colleges and schools, but, increasingly, that showed the need for communities committed to the experience-in-itself rather than just to study. This meant places that St Benedict calls 'Schools of the Lord's service' – a monastery that, peripheral to the educational institutions, testifies to the centrality of the experience of God.

taught by one's own tradition, to be a disciple of a living tradition. And then it asks us to persevere in the ordinary, daily commitment that discipleship entails. We all tend towards a series of many 'first fervours of conversion', as St Benedict calls it in the Prologue to his Rule. We can too easily make a spiritual supermarket out of the tradition, keeping ourselves supplied with novelties and special offers. Talking to Jean Leclercq and learning from his wide experience of the Church and its forms of monastic life around the world, it became clear how immediate is the challenge today to be spiritually serious. It is a challenge the Second Vatican Council put clearly before all religious communities. We can be blinded to the urgency of the situation today by the large institutional structures that still remain around us. But these structures are dwindling. And without a living Spirit issuing from committed and open hearts they easily become preoccupied with self-survival rather than with self-transcendence. We must learn from our experience in prayer that our call is to follow Christ through death to self and then into resurrection to unlimited new forms of life in him, with him, and through him.

In July we had the great personal delight of a visit from Bishop Henry Hill, the Anglican Bishop of Ontario. We talked together daily of another great challenge facing the Church in the West: her own unity as a witness to the one Lord that all the different Christian communions serve. Many theological and ecumenical conferences have brought us a long way toward this essential unity. But they can only take us so far. What, by their dialectical nature, they cannot do is lead us beyond the multiplicity of concepts into the simplicity of God and the unity of his transcendent love found in and through Jesus. The deepest Christian unity comes from praying together.

As we spoke it seemed to us that the challenge facing the global Christian community is the same one facing each local community. We belong to a global community because locally we are each a microcosm of it. The challenge at both the macro and micro levels is to return daily, to meditate, to lay down everything we are, our very selves, before the infinite mystery of God. Even the ideas and experiences that bring us to this moment of prayer ('the sacrifice of mind and heart') are renounced, together with all self-reflection and theological speculation. The great achievements in ecumenical theological understanding over the past twenty years are only fulfilled by leading us beyond the fascination of differences to the celebration of likenesses, from the conference room to the prayer room, from words to the Word spoken to all people in silence. As with the renewal of the religious life in the Church, the challenge of Christian unity is already upon us. It demands that we respond to the moments of grace that are the opportunities for real prayer together in real communion. During Bishop Hill's stay it was a joy and a privilege for us to recognize one such moment.

Our last piece of news takes up the theme of the other meetings of the summer. On August 20 we went to Mount Saviour to meet with Dom Bede Griffiths, who was to spend a few days of quiet there after his lecture tour of American monasteries. I had last met Father Bede when he was a monk of Prinknash Abbey in England, but for the past twenty-five years he has been in India working toward the growth of a truly Indian-Christian monastic life. With the community at Mount Saviour, he spoke to us of the essential unity of the monastic order in all its manifestations in religions around the world – a unity deriving from the monk's essential task and calling, seeking God.

We agreed that the life of a monastic community truly centred in Christ has to be a life built on meditation. To the vast majority of Indians, he told us, the Church in India is seen as a wonderful worker in the social field. But it is not to the Church they go when they want to be led into deeper spiritual life. Thousands of young Westerners travel to the East every year seeking a deeper experience of the mystery of God that they could not find in the Church in the West. Some may find genuine guides and teachers of prayer with whom they can learn to meditate. But many others do not have such good fortune and are left even more confused than before. It is clear that these young people do not reject God or Christ. Why then have they rejected the Christian religious structures of the West?

Perhaps one reason is that we in the West have become too religious rather than truly spiritual. What so many today are seeking is a humble yet authoritative witness to the absolute. Our call as monks is always a call to the absolute experience of God in Christ. But this experience has to be personal if it is to be real. The young westerner will only come to our monasteries if they feel convinced that this is the primary reason for our existence – that we do truly, seek God at this level of personal experience as our very first responsibility.

The human heart longs for union – within ourselves, with others, with God. One side of us seeks to preserve our separateness, but our

Godlikeness is stronger than this egoism. It makes our hearts restless until we find the peace of union. Religion has the essential function of continually reminding us that we achieve this ideal by first entering our own mystery and travelling to the ground of our being where we come to self-knowledge. From that point of personal integration radiates the power of union with others and with God. It is simply the power of love, of God who is Love. In the depth of our being we are relentlessly summoned by a love that will not give up, to realize our union with God in whom we have being.

It is a mysterious sign of our time that this intuition of unity is accepted by so many who seek their way outside conventional religion. They have leaped back in a moment to a basic spiritual truth that centuries of organized religion have obscured. It must, then, seem as absurd to them as to St Paul to find Christians 'morbidly keen on mere verbal questions and quibbles'[1] that lead us to lose grip of the truth. Religion without spiritual experience becomes atrophied and futile, as St James realized.[2] Meditation at the centre of religious life does not devalue religion. It reinvests its value from the essential experience of religion. As St Paul also knew, experience of the spirit affirms community. Of course religion does 'yield high dividends, he tells us – but only to the individuals whose resources are within them'.[3]

Our encounter with India and the East is teaching us something we should never have forgotten. The essential Christian experience is beyond the capacity of any cultural or intellectual form to express. This is the 'glorious liberty of the children of God', that there are no boundaries. It became so clear to me talking with Father Bede that this experience has to be restored to the heart of the Church if she is to face creatively the challenges before her. These are multiple challenges: the challenge of the renewal of contemplative religious life, the challenge of finding unity in the Spirit with all Christian communions, the challenge of embracing the non-Christian religions with the universal love of Christ present in the hearts of all people and which she has a special call to release and identify. To meet these challenges we must be personally rooted in the experience of God that Jesus personally

---

1 1 Timothy 5.6.
2 James 1.26.
3 1 Timothy 6.6.

knows and that is shared through his Spirit. We do not earn this experience or create it from our own resources. It is for us to prepare for the grace of its giving. Our fidelity to meditation is our preparation, our patient and ever deepening openness to the mystery that fills and contains us. We have to be still. We have to be silent. We have to stand reverently in the cave of our hearts, the palace of God's kingdom within us.

To meditate is to 'stand still in the centre'. But it is not enough to say this is just 'centring ourselves' or even 'finding our centre'. We do this too. But not, ironically, if centring is our conscious aim. That would be too self-conscious, too focused on desire. We find our centre only by placing ourselves in the silence of God beyond any image of centre or circumference. What we think of as 'our' centre is often an illusion of the self-reflecting ego, a favourite, comfortable point where we like to take up our stand and observe God at work in us. But this can not be the way to God who is the true centre of reality.

The human fear of union, of the loss of self and of the finding of self in the otherness of God, is baseless but powerful. It keeps us centred in self rather than the other. It often blocks the Spirit in individuals, in communities, and in churches who fear to lose their personality, their distinctiveness or their exclusiveness. But the surprise of union is precisely that it does not obliterate. It is creative. Not that it absorbs, but that it re-creates. To be involved is to evolve. Teilhard de Chardin puts it beautifully and briefly: 'Union differentiates.' In union the rich variety of human mystery is known to be a luminous reflection of the unbounded creativity of God.

The many challenges that we face also point to the mystery of union we are summoned to enter. Here the challenges can be met. But we find this mystery of union, with others and with God, only when we reach in ourselves that place where Jesus experiences his oneness with the Father. That place from which he prayed, 'I in them and you in me, may they be perfectly one.'[4]

Our communities of prayer, large and small, and each of us on our unique pilgrimage of faith participate in the building up of this unified Body of Christ. Whether we can understand it or not, we are all invited to enter into the union with God himself. This communion we enter

---

4 John 17.22.

through the Spirit who breathes freely in the open spaces of our hearts.

We keep you in our heart,

With much love,

John Main OSB
(August 1979)

From June to August, we were back at the beginning of our search for a larger house. We were looking for a property with some agricultural potential, a large central house and two or three smaller cottages or barns. We felt that we would have to extend the search off the island but wanted to stay in easy reach of the city where our monastic life and prayer could continue to be of service and relevance. Our plan was to keep the Vendôme centre going for the weekly groups and as a place of continuous prayer in the heart of the city. Until the day that it might also become a monastic house of studies, it could be run by a resident lay community as an extension or sphere of the monastery. John Main gave a retreat to the community of St Peter's Abbey, Saskatchewan. In July he went to Antigonish, Nova Scotia, to a conference of sisters from the Congregation de Notre Dame to talk on 'prayer in a life of service'. The mother house of the Congregation de Notre Dame in Montreal had been kind and generous to us from our first days in Montreal, giving its furniture and equipment for our house, and continued to support us as we planned our next stage of growth. Among our visitors was Dom Jean Leclercq, the Benedictine scholar of Clairvaux in Luxembourg, who came with the committee of the Canadian Union of Contemplative Religious. We discussed together the theme of the conference they were planning to hold in 1980 – the forms of contemplative life relevant to our times and the role of the liturgy in the monastic life. Dom Leclercq's worldwide experience of contemporary monasticism confirmed our own insights gained in Montreal and London. The religious life could survive vitally only where there was a shift of the monk's centre of consciousness from external work and worship to a more deeply interior source, where the axis of his life would be the journey into the mystery of God, the inner journey of prayer. It was not easy to describe this. To many religious, it sounded unbalanced – an undervaluation of monastic service to the world in education or in the missionary field. It was refreshing and encouraging for us to talk to Dom Leclercq, so deeply rooted in the monastic tradition, and find that we shared a vision for the future. Far from restricting its development, restoring the priority of contemplation to monasticism would set it free to expand. As it had perhaps never been free to do so before, monasticism could serve the modern world at the level of its deepest need. We had a second and longer visit from Bishop Henry Hill, who spent a two-week retreat with us – working, praying and sharing his wide experience of different Christian communions. In August, Laurence Freeman travelled south to visit the Monastery of Christ in the Desert in New Mexico. On his way home, he visited the charismatic Benedictine Abbey at Pecos and brought back a vivid account of the range of Benedictine life that these two communities witnessed to within 100 miles of each other. A further dimension to the breadth of the Rule of Benedict struck us at the end of August when we met with Father Bede Griffiths at the end of his US lecture tour. During the few days we spent at Mount Saviour with him and Brother Amaldas of his community, he spoke of the courageous and troubled founding of his Benedictine ashram in southern India by Father Jules Monchanin and Dom Henri le Saux (Abhishiktananda). Of particular interest to us were the discussions we shared on the state of Western monasticism and Father Bede's own belief that the contemplative life in the West would be revived through networks of small ashram-type monasteries located in the main population centres as a living witness to the journey from self to God.

9

THE AUTHORITY OF EXPERIENCE

Dear Friends,

Peace and love in the Lord.

Father John was about to prepare this newsletter when we learned that he required urgent surgery. The substance of this letter will be taken from notes he prepared for a talk he gave to a group of Anglican Bishops and their advisors in Quebec City in September and from notes for his proposed talks to the Lakeshore School.

In Quebec City Father John spoke of the vision of the Church that has begun to emerge from the contemplative experience of our time. It is difficult, he said, to generalize about the state of the Church today, covering as it does such a spectrum of belief and devotion. But what the rich variety of the Christian communions reveal today more clearly than in the past is the mystery of the Church as the mystery of person-hood.

From every part of Christian thought and life today comes the same intuition that abstract or legalistic answers to the riddles of our lives are inadequate. Rulebook regulations applied without human com-passion for the uniqueness of each individual are inadequate. They are as futile as the neat intellectual formulas that have no integral power to change the way we live. But, he went on, the risk we run in giving due importance to the personal criterion of truth is that it can lead us into mere subjectivism or self-indulgence. We also need the discipline, the teaching, of tradition. One of the most damaging divisions in our fractured society is the split made between personal experience and tradition. What the Church is empowered to proclaim out of the vitality and freshness of her knowledge of the Person of Christ – which is her collective contemplative experience – is that in the moment of pure love experience and tradition are one.

The mystery of God is available to humanity in the mystery of the

Person of Jesus. It is a living mystery, overflowing the normal limits of thought and feeling just as it transcends any human organization that tries to contain or control it. It is a mystery greater than each of us and greater than all of us. Yet it is one to which we are closer than we are to ourselves, because it contains us. The immanence and transcendence of the mystery, like the realities of tradition and experience, are seen as one in the moment of contemplative vision. Loving so generously that we rise above ourselves, we see no longer with our own eyes but with the eyes of God, the mind of Christ.

We can know all this conceptually inasmuch as we can put it into words. But how satisfied are we at the end of all our word-making? Don't we feel only more deeply impelled to enter into a direct, undifferentiated experience – the experience itself? It is this response that leads to full personhood because although the mystery lies beyond our power to understand, it does not lie beyond our experience. Indeed, we are each of us summoned by the very fact of our creation to experience it. What this demands simply is the courage of love. What it means simply is being fully human, fully alive.

Simone Weil has said that goodness can only be known in the act of goodness, never in anticipation or in retrospect. What she was saying is what every human being (and in particular every child) knows from his or her own experience. The difference is between thinking of someone and being with them; between looking forward to an experience and being inside the experience; between image and object, illusion and reality. It is so astounding that, once we have left the relative simplicity of childhood behind us, we so easily forget this. We become idea-centred rather than experience-centred. The difficulty facing all Christian teachers today is to convince people that this is not esoteric knowledge but plain simplicity. A group of children who come to our monastery in Montreal to meditate each week could really communicate this silence and fidelity to the older meditators much better than all the rest of us!

What I am suggesting is this: our society has become personalistic after a long history of dominant legalism and intellectualism. But at the same time it has lost a vital contact with its tradition and so it is pursuing an experience-centred course. This is not bad in itself as I have said, but presently it is lacking the stability and centrality the tradition needs to give it. What the Church must proclaim is that this tradition is the central human experience of the mystery writ large. To be in contact with the tradition is not to forego the validity of our own experience. It is the grace of the opportunity to make our experience complete by making it other-centred, purifying it of all egoism, all self-preoccupation. The tradition is also one with the community of the faithful as the Person of Christ. It is the universal hinge upon which we swing away from ourselves to God. At no time in history has the richness of this tradition been more universally available to us. Why, then, do we remain so trapped in the prison of our ego and why does our experience, deep as it is, fail to reach its full potential in the vision of God?

We all know of people who have had visions. I do not at all doubt their sincerity. But my own conviction, based on the teaching of the tradition, is that the greatest enemy of *oratio pura* – simple prayer as our participation in Christ's experience of God – is our imagination. I have tried to find ways of putting this more palatably to people who are shocked or offended by what seems to them an insult to their humanity or intelligence. But I do believe, and I believe it is the belief of the tradition that the more we 'think' about God, picture 'him', or stir up our imagination for autonomous visions of him, the less we can experience him. This is not to denigrate theology, philosophy, or art. But these three fruits of our minds and hearts relate to truth only so far as they clarify, encourage, or purify our journey to the frontiers of the limited human consciousness. On this frontier we are met by a guide, who is unlimited consciousness, the person of Jesus Christ. We reach this frontier only if we travel light, if we have left all behind us and if we embrace the one who meets us with absolute trust. At that moment we know from our own experience that he is the Way, the Truth, and the Life.

The deep spiritual search of our contemporaries is for this personal experience that authenticates them in relation to the Absolute. In St Paul's words, they are seeking 'justification'. The danger we face in this search is that it has lost its stabilizing contact with the common tradition. As a result it so often leads straight back to self-obsession and self-indulgence, sometimes even by way of the easy options of religious nostalgia or legalism. The Church must provide the centrality of insight and teaching that will prevent this. In our global crisis, we can ill afford further delays in an effective proclamation of the Kingdom. She must proclaim, from the rich depth and variety of her tradition, that this search of modern people for authentic experience of God is her own foremost concern and indeed the reason for her existence.

It is not enough to talk about the mystery of God in Jesus. We have to talk from within the heart of the mystery where we are led by the Spirit. Any talking secondhand will fail to communicate the life-giving word and instead merely provide definitions and dogma. But if we have allowed ourselves to be led into the secret of Christ within us, then we will speak with power. It will not be us speaking but the Spirit speaking through us. This is experience in service of tradition. We all know that the last ten or fifteen years have shown that the search for experience out of context only leads back deeper into the labyrinth of egoism. The desire to possess one's experience, to hoard or cultivate it, that has characterized much of modern spirituality, is ultimately self-defeating. We can only be joyful if, in Blake's phrase, we 'kiss the joy as it flies'. If we bind it to ourselves we kill it.

The context for all authentic personal experience that leads to the redemptive moment of transcendence is tradition. This is why St Paul says we are authenticated, 'justified', by faith. We have come to think of faith merely in terms of knowledge. We say people have a 'good grasp of faith', if they are well read in scripture or theology. And, in a way, faith is knowledge. But not our knowledge. It is the knowledge Jesus enjoys of his Father and yet becomes ours too. It is the communion of love that is God's knowledge of himself, so personal that it is the Holy Spirit. We are redeemed from the limitations of our narrow selves into the glorious liberty of those born of God by our personal contact with this self-knowledge of God. It is not a contact we can have from the outside, touching God as an object, but only from within God himself. This is possible for human beings because Jesus is the innerness of God, the divine self-revelation. To know him is to know the Father. To be open to him is to expand far beyond the frontiers of our self-regarding consciousness into communion with his consciousness, unlimited and fully human. This is the knowledge beyond knowing that St Paul urged the early Christians to accept. It is the secret of faith and the living power of the tradition that has been passed on in the loving community of the faithful from the first century to our own. It is a knowledge that is forever present, always unchanging, and ever expanding. It is within the infinite mystery of the God who is. To possess this knowledge is to allow oneself to be possessed by the infinite love of God and to re-find oneself transformed into servants of that love. We love one another because 'we possess the mind of Christ'.

I hope this serves, as Father John's other letters have, to encourage all of us to deepen our poverty and fidelity on the pilgrimage we follow together, in obedience to the Lord's will for each of us.

Please keep Father John in your hearts.

We send our love,

Laurence Freeman OSB
(October 1979)

At the end of August, John Main gave a retreat at the Cloister in Maryknoll and spoke on meditation to the Knights of Malta at St Benoît du Lac, the large Benedictine abbey about 100 miles from Montreal. For some time he had been experiencing pain and, when he was examined, colon cancer was discovered. Surgery soon followed. It happened as Laurence Freeman was about to make his solemn monastic profession at Mount Saviour. He had been ordained to minor orders, the first step towards ordination to the priesthood, in early September. Bishop Crowley had come to us at Vendôme for compline and meditation and bestowed the orders at a ceremony in which several of our friends participated. It also fell to Brother Laurence to greet our former abbot, Francis Rossiter, from Ealing, who came from England to attend the profession and meet our new brethren at Mount Saviour. Bishop Crowley also participated in the ceremony and led a group of our friends from Montreal down to Elmira, New York. John Main's illness placed extra responsibilities on Laurence Freeman's shoulders, not the least of which was the continued leadership of the community and the meditation groups. Among our guests were students from the seminary in Toronto, a missionary doctor on leave from Uganda, an English monk studying monastic liturgy in North America and a Philippino Sister preparing to return home.

10

GIFTS OF OBEDIENCE

My Dearest Friends,

How good it is to be able to write to you again. After a major operation, when we sail close to the perimeters of life and death, we have a finer perception of life as a sheer gift. We feel more deeply and clearly that presence of beauty and goodness that gives meaning to our life. So I am full of thanks that I am able to write once more and so full of gratitude to all of you who have kept me in your hearts during these days of my recovery.

I am pleased to tell you that as a result of the wonderful care I have received from all the community, I have made an excellent recovery and now feel stronger and better than I have for months past. This is especially good as we are moving into a period of much development in our foundation, as we seek to expand and make firm the growth of the community.

Dom Laurence made his Solemn Profession at Mount Saviour Monastery in New York State on October 18. Prior Martin Boler received his vows and presided at the Mass of his Profession. Bishop Crowley of Montreal concelebrated at the Mass along with our former abbot, Dom Francis Rossiter who came over from Ealing to be present at this first Solemn Profession for our community. Several members of the community and friends from Montreal also travelled to Mount Saviour to share in the occasion.

In December I participated in a conference of the Principals of Anglican Theological Colleges from across Canada. I shared with this influential group my convictions about formation in prayer. I tried to say to them that I considered the essential foundation of the professional formation of theology students to be pure prayer. This depth of spiritual practice is the essential discipline of all Christian discipleship because it is the essential learning process of becoming Christlike. This approach to Christian and ministerial formation obviously demands a re-evaluation of what we mean by discipleship. It asks for a reaffirmation of our whole understanding of discipline. First there is the discipline of studying the tradition, being grasped by it and rooted in it. There is also the discipline of personal daily practice, inner renewal, the pilgrimage that the real appropriation of the tradition involves. My very strong conviction is that it is not enough for us to study the Christian faith or to profess it. We must also come to experience the Christian truth ourselves, in ourselves. This is the real, foundational 'knowledge' of the Christian way.

We have also started a group of oblates of the monastery. An oblate is a person who shares the ideals of the community and seeks to follow them in the circumstances of his or her life. We hope to establish groups of oblates in any place where there are interested people who have come to this through their practice of meditation. An oblate seeks God by living by the spirit of the Rule of St Benedict. It is a spirit characterized by stability, ongoing conversion and obediential listening to the Word of God. Its priority is love, generosity, liberty and the wise virtue of discretion that serves the kingdom of peace. The oblate joins the community in this spirit each day by saying the Morning Prayer and Vespers of our Office and, after each of these, spends half an hour in meditation.

Taking the step to become an oblate of St Benedict is a movement toward the 'new' life which is the good news of the gospel. In this Christmastide letter we think of the new life of Christ and our own rebirth in grace as the result of his birth in the flesh. I would like to put before you some thoughts on the spirit of St Benedict in this letter because it is a spirit that flows so directly from a knowledge of the Word made flesh in ordinary life, in community and in individual lives – the Word that is also born of us through the love of God.

For Benedict the first quality we require to respond to Christ and be open to his life in our hearts is the capacity to listen. The first word of the Rule is 'Listen!' As you know, this capacity is one of the great fruits of meditation through which we learn that the condition of true listening is silence. We can only listen to the Word spoken to us by another if we ourselves are silent of all words. The wonder of Benedict's spirit as it speaks to us in the Rule is his understanding of how the prayerful heart is so naturally and humanly integrated into the whole of life. He does not see silence in the monastery, for example, just as a regulation to be obeyed. He wisely knows that there are times when charity will demand words even when the rule of silence is in force, such as when guests arrive unexpectedly. He understands silence as the fundamental condition of the heart, an attentiveness to a reality larger than our immediate activities or concerns. A heart wrapped in silence is wholly attentive to the word of the Master. We are not attentive to this only at set times. Attentiveness is the way we live. Silence is the state of being in which we respond to the gift of life. It is one of the creative paradoxes of the Spirit that only in this attentive listening, this silent openness, can we respond to the deepest mystery of our life appropriately. Our busyness, our noisiness, our distracted attempts to cover all bases are ways we reduce the mystery of life to a solvable problem. In these ways we miss the creative moment. We fail to see the gift as it opens before us. We lack the necessary spontaneity of spirit on which readiness for the kingdom depends. We become dreamers of possibilities rather than tasters of real life

Everyone who is conscious is seeking a way. The problem is that we so often accept the way only on our own terms. We see ourselves as choosing God. We invite ourselves to the Master's banquet. We make an immature response to the gift of being, a childish underestimate of the infinite potential of the life that has called us into being to share its own plenitude of joy. This is where our spiritual tradition is of such importance and why we need to be formed and rooted in this tradition. The way of our tradition is a heart that is opened to the infinite mystery of God by awakening to itself. And we awaken in silence.

I have often urged you to be faithful to the recitation of your 'one little word' in the time of your meditation, because it is the way to silence and the means of leaving behind the self-centred noisiness of your words and thoughts. At this time of Christmas, the time of the Incarnate Word, let me urge you again to utter faithfulness during your morning and evening meditation: the word and only the word. Part of the difficulty in understanding this simple teaching today is that we lack a confident vocabulary in which to describe our experience. We hesitate to be simple because we confuse simplicity with naivety. To be vulnerable seems wrong because the catchwords are 'strength' and 'self-sufficiency' and so we think vulnerability is weakness. Our traditional religious vocabulary, which should help us towards silence has been made largely redundant. No word in this vocabulary is so misunderstood by our contemporaries as 'obedience'.

Generations of pious people have been brought up to believe that it means merely 'doing what you are told to do'. Conformity, submission to authority, surrender of responsibility. Yet in its first verses the Rule of St Benedict links obedience to silence through the mature condition of listening. It describes obedience as the glorious armour of the true child of God or, in other words, as the way of standing in the knowledge of our true relationship to God.

Obedience is the capacity to listen to the other. In awaking to the other, we hear the word within which we ourselves come to be. We know life as the mystery that is simultaneously the mystery of shared identity and of uniqueness. We become disobedient, we stray from God when we lose this attentiveness. No amount of talking or thinking about God can substitute for this silent listening. We stray off course by drowning out the Word with our own egocentric noisiness and the complexities of our imagination. We stifle God's life by our self-fixation and by all kinds of selfish behaviour. The wise teaching of the Rule is that we are continuously invited to return to God by obediential attentiveness. We are meant to learn how to be listeners. The Latin root of 'obedience' is *ob-audire*, to listen. The follower of Benedict follows this teaching in all aspects of life, committing himself or herself to a sustained attitude, a continuous practice of listening and attentiveness.

As you know from your own experience in prayer, attentiveness is itself a journey. It takes us into a wonderful and undreamed-of conscious silence. Here, for the first time perhaps, we can taste fullness of being. We learn this depth of attentiveness only with faithful, daily practice. The early monks saw this faithful regularity of returning to prayer as the way of bringing out the spark of God from stony hearts. St Benedict, inheriting their teaching and re-transmitting it, calls on his monks to 'open their eyes to the Divine light'. The responsibility of faithful practice falls on anyone who is trying to respond to life as gift and to become the person we are called to be. Through Jesus we know that this responsibility is a light yoke, not a heavy burden but a gift and calling that fills us with joy.

Regularity and faithfulness to meditation brings us closer to this mystery. At first we hear it as something remote, alien, or meant for others. Then we may see it as relevant to ourselves personally but like a distant mountain range, beautiful but unattainable. Meditation takes us away from this distancing and objectification of God.

Through the daily practice our faithfulness brings image and object ever closer together, into an undifferentiated union because the journey brings us closer to our selves. The light to which St Benedict urges us to open our eyes is in our hearts and the light is Christ. Our pilgrimage of prayer is the wonderful discovery that our journey is into an ever fuller realization of a mystery that can never be fathomed or forgotten because it is the mystery of the God who is. The wonder, too, is that if we will only undertake the journey seriously, then once we find this light in our own hearts we have found it in the hearts of all. This is why St Benedict makes this inner and outer transformation of the journey of prayer the foundation of community. A great mystery of prayer is that it is the true foundation of a vital Christian community that is being built up by people who, by awakening to this light in their heart, also awaken to others.

Our journey into deeper attentiveness is the work of the silence of meditation. It also brings us closer to the personal mystery of the Church – another religious word that has lost its power today. A word full of meaning, it has been bankrupted. Only a return to the experience it signifies can restore its meaning. It means the communion and community of the faithful. But only those who know what it is to be faithful listeners can discover their communion and mediate this meaning. Community does not just happen. It is built, step by step, by the courage of individuals leaving self behind to love those with whom they live. It is created through perseverance in giving of themselves even when they fear being exploited or unappreciated and the ego urges them to put their own interests first. This is the risk of community. It is an ideal that is unattainable and could break us if we relied only on our own strength. Early on the pilgrimage of attentive, obediential silence we find that if we can even begin to turn from self then a power far greater than our own is opened up in us. In this power we make commitments. In and with this power we make our journey.

This power reveals the vital connection between Christian community and personal fidelity to the pilgrimage of prayer. Christian community is characterized by its quality of being embodied in the ordinary and yet rooted in the experience of transcendence, not otherworldly but truly spiritual. The medium of transcendence is silence because we have to accept the inadequacy of words to bring us into the full light of reality. A community that knows the mystery of being silent together, hold their hearts in readiness and attentiveness, become an embodiment of the light of reality that fills all hearts. This is what church means.

The pilgrimage is not a part-time activity. It is the only activity that sheds the light of reality on any of our activities. The same faithful perseverance that makes the individual pilgrimage real also makes for community. The faith of a community comes from the same faith of discovering the light in our hearts. Once we discover this light of Christ and begin to communicate it (because its dynamic is self-communicating), then we begin to manifest the life of Christ in our midst. His life *is* his presence. We know his presence through his Body, which means the community of faith.

A Benedictine community in the understanding of St Benedict's Rule is simply a gathering together in faith by those who journey together with the light of Christ as their guide. It knows that this light is love. So, by their love for one another they let the light of their guide burn more brightly. They know the light as an emanation of their Master's Word constantly spoken in their midst, one to another daily. They try to listen to it all the time and to respond with ever deeper attentiveness. The wonder of such a community is that, despite its faults, it shares in its Master's transcendence of all that blocks or refracts his Light. It is because the light passes freely through an obediential community that it can share itself and its journey with others. Even those whose outward circumstances of life are very different from life in the monastery can share directly in its experience. This is what makes the oblate community possible.

The Benedictine community spirit is one of largesse, growth, and visionary generosity. Benedict speaks to us of a monastic experience that leads to expansion of heart and consciousness. He describes such a community as making rapid progress on the pilgrimage with a love whose tenderness, he says, is beyond words. Benedict's wisdom is the teaching of the Master. What he is saying is that the love whose full-ness is indescribable can only be experienced in itself. It cannot be remembered or anticipated because it is the supreme reality of the God who is. In face of this understanding of community the best words that express what monks, oblates and all meditators are doing are these: Be still and know that I am God.

Christmas is a feast that can deepen this stillness. It can open the hearts of all to the presence of Christ, because it puts before us the universal qualities of innocence and hope. We need these if we are to awaken to his light. Christmas also fills us with confidence because it tells us that the old age has ended. The new age, a new creation, has begun and our point of departure for finding it everywhere is finding it as a reality in our heart. Our journey then is to our heart. All of us are invited to enter this temple and to receive this new life. We have to see this time as a moment to put off everything in us that is dead, everything that prevents us from embracing the mystery of our own creation and entering into the fullness of life that we receive as pure gift through the eternal act of creation.

The meaning of the Christian teaching of the Incarnation is that the mystery of God in its eternal creativity is not only brought closer to us but really united to us. We no longer need to distance and objectify the mystery if it has taken up its dwelling in our hearts of flesh. Awakening to this reality is a possibility for each of us because it is an incarnate encounter. The human happiness which Christmas reminds us of is real because this awakening is not something of our own creation. We are no longer isolated or dependent on our own inadequate resources. It is not our own power or wisdom but his love present as the light of supreme reality in our hearts. The humility of the child Jesus is our guide and teacher. In his light we are conscious. In his love we have love. In his truth we are made truthful.

Christmas is a feast and time of wonder and full of hope for us all. It is a new dawn for humanity that begins with a faint glow but whose strengthening light transforms the world until perfect day. Here in Montreal, as we celebrate the Mass of the Aurora of Christ, the Mass of Dawn, we shall remember all of you. May the New Year to which it gives birth be for each of you a year of renewed hope and light.

With every blessing and very much love,

John Main OSB
(December 1979)

John Main convalesced well after his surgery for colon cancer and was declared by his doctor a 'textbook recovery'. By mid December he was able to relieve Brother Laurence of some of the responsibilities he had been carrying since Father John's cancer had been diagnosed. In December, Laurence Freeman was ordained to the diaconate by

Bishop Crowley at a ceremony where about 200 friends of the community helped make it a prayerful and symbolic moment in the history of our community. Guests continued to enrich our life in both the perspective they opened up on our work and sharing of their own insights and traditions. A Unitarian minister and chaplain at Cornell University visited and discussed the problems of communicating our tradition of meditation to young people so alienated from the disciplines of any tradition. We welcomed Father Placid, a monk from Mount Saviour who had been a co-founder of the monastery and, like ourselves, originally a monk in the English congregation. The weekly diocesan priests' group continued to meet faithfully with a core of six to seven members. In December, they spent a day with us in prayer and discussed the question of how to communicate their conviction about meditation to their fellow priests. A new venture was the formation of a Benedictine oblate group. The relationship of an oblate to a monastery – being dedicated to the religious life, but not taking full monastic vows – offered a traditional way of developing our contemporary monastic witness to the world. The ceremony of receiving oblate novices for a year before their oblation underlined the spiritual participation in the monastic journey, while the presentation of a copy of the Rule and the Medal of St Benedict symbolized their entrance into the Benedictine tradition. Rooted in this by their twice-daily meditation, they would come to share in their own experience of St Benedict's vision of the harmony of prayer and work. Our first oblate was Rosie Lovat – received on the last day of her month's stay with us. It seemed right that she should be the first oblate as she had given so much of herself to the community from the beginning. Two days later, Bishop Hill became our first ecumenical oblate, followed soon after by Louis Chavez, a young married man, a new immigrant to Canada working in the civil service in Toronto.

CONTINUOUS CONVERSION

My Dearest Friends,

In his chapter on the Observance of Lent, St Benedict describes it as a season of joy. He tells us to prepare for the great feast of Easter, the centre and climax of the Christian year, with the 'joy of the Holy Spirit'. And, as everywhere else in the Rule, he sees the basis of the Christian response to life's gift as purity of heart, rootedness in prayer.

As we read this chapter of the Rule at Compline last night, at the beginning of Lent in the year we celebrate the 1500th anniversary of St Benedict's birth, it struck me how unnecessary it is to think of any part of life in a sombre or depressed way. Lent, no less than Christmas or Easter, is full of the Risen Life.

Even the hardest parts of life point us into freedom. They are times, of which Lent is the great symbol, when we live through the preparatory stage of the Paschal mystery. We need to be prepared for the gift of life, to be ready for it as infinite gift. Lent is a time of preparation when we get ready to enter, once again but more deeply, into the great awakening of Jesus, his Resurrection. Our preparation itself is joyful because this awakening has already taken place, in time and into eternity. In Jesus the cycle of death and rebirth is definitively completed and perfected because he has broken the cycle that kept humanity within the circle of the finite. Jesus has transcended all the limitations of human experience that we recognize and confront in ourselves during Lent. He has led humanity into the infinite circle of God, whose 'centre is everywhere and whose circumference is nowhere'. This is the realm of liberty and joy we enter daily in our prayer.

Because we can observe Lent in the dawn light of Easter it is a time of joy. The Paschal mystery is completed and we enter it through the Spirit, preparing ourselves with the silence and stillness of our meditation. There is nothing punitive about Lent. We are not punishing ourselves or being punished. Christians are free of such old religious compulsions because they are freed by the forgiveness that gives them fullness of life and affirms that life. Christians enter into the person who frees them. In their turn, they forgive those who bear hostility toward them. Perhaps the gift that our violent and fear-filled world needs most is forgiveness. And during Lent we deepen our experience of ourselves as forgiven and set free from fear. Through the Risen Life we are summoned to communicate this to all.

Since writing to you last, I have given talks to Benedictines in St Louis and Cleveland. My aim was to share the conviction that monasticism today enjoys a great opportunity. In an age so dissatisfied with its own shallowness – a dissatisfaction that is the cause of much of our violence – the witness of a monastery is to the satisfying depth and absolute value of life centred in Christ. Not merely by ideas, but in the incarnation of this faith in life, the monk's message to the world is that everything falls into chaos when the centre is lost. His knowledge is that Christ is the universal centre, the centre of each person and of the world.

When we read chapter 16 of St John's Gospel or St Paul's letter to the Ephesians we can be enthused by seeing how the universal and the personal are united in the centre of Christ. But the big difficulty is to believe that this vision is really possible, for us, now. It has to be made *our* vision, not someone else's that we as outsiders admire. This is where the monastic life can be so important. In the monk we should see someone to whom this vision has spoken with absolute power and has evoked an absolute personal response. But in the monk we also see an ordinary, weak human being. His or her ordinariness is an essential part of the monastic witness. In the monk's ordinary life we see humanity redeemed from shallowness and inserted deeply into the great order, the essential structure of the universe. We see the monk's life witnessing to the fact that God alone is to be worshipped because God alone is good and this goodness endures eternally. In more contemporary language, the monk's life proves the possibility of founding life on the reality of absolute value, no longer condemned to the shifting sands of passing fashion.

To illustrate the challenge to us as men and women of today, I tried recently to put before the monastic communities I spoke with in St Louis and Cleveland, an understanding of the Christian life as a call to transcendence. Here the monastic life has an essential witness to make.

For St Benedict, the monastic life was a continuous conversion, not a mere change of social status. The ground on which this conversion is realized is the heart of the monk, his most simple and most absolute level of being. And so, his ongoing conversion should lead him into an ever deeper authenticity. More and more he should not merely believe what he says but be what he believes. The essential conversion is not concerned with externals because it is not a change from one form to another but from form to essence. The monk's conversion of heart is a conversion from idea to reality. When he encounters the vision of St John or St Paul or his own monastic tradition, he opens himself to the personal reality of what they communicate. And, in the monk's radical openness, that is to say in his prayer, this vision *is* realized, made real, converted from theory into a living truth.

The dynamic of this conversion is transcendence. And, because a total transcendence is involved, a 'loss of self,' we must understand transcendence as an expansion of our whole being, a pushing back of the frontiers of our limitations. It is a dynamic motion, a re-centring beyond ourselves and a shedding of the limitations of self-centredness and egoism. The principle of transcendence is a creative development of the whole person, not merely a specialized part of it, not mere imitation, but a deepening of the integral harmony of mind and heart. It can only be realized when we are turned away from ourselves. This is the movement of prayer. In it we begin to find ourselves as persons created for an eternal destiny. Our self-conscious frame of reference cannot comprehend this destiny. But experience teaches us as we find our true significance, no longer in terms of our limitations, but in our potential for infinite expansion, in Christ. The monk, even in his fragility and ordinariness, is uncovering the sublimity of this essential, human meaning.

Conversion leads through transcendence to union. But how can we say that we find our true meaning if we are truly in union, which means wholly absorbed in God? Our modern consciousness holds back from union, and so from transcendence, precisely because it demands always to know what is happening to it. It fears to take the risk of a union that seems to spell the death of self-awareness. The truth involved here is a paradox and the only way through a paradox is to enter it in person. Paradoxes do not have answers. And it is the integral Christian paradox that whoever wants to find his or her life must first lose it. A phrase of Teilhard de Chardin's illuminates this paradox for us when he says that 'Union differentiates.' The more we are absorbed into another, the more we become the person we are called to be. This is the nature of our union with God in Christ. There is no other way to find our selves, the meaning of our life, except through this union. Just as we can only know God by the power of God's own self-knowing, so we can only know ourselves by that same power because God is the ground of all consciousness. It is the supreme joy as well as the destiny of each person, to discover that this power is the power of love. Our origin is in love and our culmination is in love because only love truly *knows*.

It is this vision of transcendence in love – through the ordinary – that authenticates the Benedictine place in the Church and its value for the world. We hope that this year of interiority will deepen our understanding of both of these. A monastery exists precisely to provide the incarnate and participatory context within which the love of Christ can be fully known. St Benedict's vision in writing the Rule was not just to provide monastic 'ideals' but to lay down the practical guidelines, the living of which would bring everyone involved into the ever deepening experience of the reality of God.

Ideals are dangerous. There are many who want to talk about prayer, read books about it or do courses on spirituality. But St Benedict advised to say as little about prayer as possible. The monk who wants to pray has simply to enter the room and pray. Because of this priority of experience monasteries have much to offer the world just by being places of practice, where the turning to Christ, the ongoing conversion, is the clear basis of their whole life. It is not that the monks are supermen or superwomen but that they have organized their lives with an utterly clear priority. In their conversion they first turn from themselves to their brethren in the community, then to Christ in prayer, to God in Christ and to the world in love. This is the clear Benedictine tradition. When it is fully alive in the hearts of enough men and women it has the power to help convert, to turn to Christ, all who come under its influence.

The love we experience in our monastic life is not in the first place our love for God, but God's love for us. This is the source of our monastic peace which is the great treasure we have to share with the world. The harmony of a monastery flows from the knowledge that our beginning and our end, our point of departure and our destination, are both found in the same centre, the only centre, who is Christ.

Now, monks as people of prayer know this not as a sublime theory but as practical knowledge given to them by the gift of God's light and their own brothers and sisters in the community.

I feel a great sense of urgency to share this with all of you. It is a constant wonder and happiness to me that you all take the time and trouble to read these letters and to pass them on to friends. What I want to say to each of you is to be open to this prayer of Christ yourselves – in the most practical way. Meditate every morning and every evening. And in the time of your meditation be poor, be simple: recite your word and only your word.

The marvel of prayer is that it is transcendence realized. As we pass over from self the love of Christ is set free in our hearts. All the illusions and images that restrict or distort our vision are transcended. Prayer is the work of finding and realizing our fully human liberty of spirit. This is also freedom from desire (even the desire for God), our freedom from sin and from illusion. Desire, sin, and illusion are all transcended because in prayer we are made real by being in harmonious contact with the ground of our being: God's own free-flowing and all-embracing love.

What the monk discovers as, in all humility, he tries to lead his conversion of life is that prayer is not the isolated moment of ecstasy. It is the movement of our whole being, through all of life, from self to God. This movement is the structure of the monk's life. And, after a lifetime in the monastery, it becomes the structure of his or her being. The monk's witness is not to an ideal but to a real presence –the reality of the transcendent Presence that summons human being to an infinite expansion of spirit.

Thank you again for all your messages of goodwill. I am glad to tell you that after my week of talks and lectures I feel very well. Perhaps my illness has given me a sharpened awareness that life is for living and that we must live fully in the *now*, the moment that is eternal only if we enter it fully.

With much love,

John Main OSB
(February 1980)

The community of St Augustine's Monastery in Nassau extended, in both senses, warm hospitality during John Main's convalescence there after Christmas. From within the framework of their monastic life, he was able to regain strength and write. On his return to Montreal, our search for a larger home felt more urgent as our first monastic candidates were applying to join us. As soon as he and Laurence Freeman returned, the weekly groups at the monastery resumed with new energy.

12

SUMMONED TO SANITY

My Dearest Friends,

When we last wrote it was to say that the deepest Christian understanding of Lent makes it a time of joy. Now, in the middle of the Easter season we can understand why. The great ceremonies of Holy Week mirror the stirring of life and beauty in the world around us. They remind us that our Lord, who has risen, has awakened to all that is, to the All. And because he summons all now to awaken to him everything we do communicates his joy. We send you this letter with great joy!

Every year the Easter celebration reveals a little more clearly the depth to which the love of Jesus, his own fullness of life, has penetrated our human heart. The Easter Vigil repeats the same ceremonies annually but we are never the same people who celebrate them. Each year we have grown in our capacity to understand and enter the mystery of Life they point us toward. We have been made more capable of receiving the revelation of his love – both through our deepening commitment to meditation and through all the many new challenges of our life. And so each year we take another step into full consciousness – toward the full knowledge of the personal mystery that underpins everything we are and do and without which we would lack meaning and purpose. Each year the radical change that the death and resurrection of Jesus has worked in our ability to see God rises a little further in our experience. The risen life that wells up in our heart at prayer and whose tidal flow is felt in every part of our life takes us more confidently into the mystery of Oneness. This is the mystery that is the Resurrection.

This has been our third Easter in the monastery in Montreal, and I have to feel a sense of wonder at the growth we have been blessed with. We look forward to our first candidates for the novitiate later this year and on June 8 Dom Laurence will be ordained to the priest-hood. We have seen our work reach out in many unpredictable ways both in North America and Africa and our own commitment has been encouraged by the serious way many individuals and communities have responded to the pilgrimage of meditation.

The journey is a simple one. It requires a certain vision of its importance, a certain humility to begin, and a certain fidelity and courage to persevere. It needs above all, perhaps, the willingness to be led into fullness. These are all essentially human qualities that are needed for any fruitful contact with life. And the journey is an ordinary one. We don't follow it in order to sensationalize life but to see every aspect of life as the mystery it is. The greatest danger and temptation is to complicate. As far as I can see, if we are actually on the journey, if the poverty of the mantra is the rich core of our lives, then we grow more and more simple. Increasingly, we see the utter simplicity of the call Jesus addresses uniquely to each one of us, to leave all things and self behind and to follow him into the infinite freedom of his union with the Father.

If this is the centre of our vision of life the rest gradually falls into place in the particular pattern that we are called to bring into ever more resonant harmony. That harmony we may discover in different ways. Each moment of discovery is an eternal moment in which we open our eyes to the divinizing light of Christ. Our life is a growth in simplicity because all things are bathed in the light and held together in the new creation of the Resurrection. To see this is to see ourselves also as an integral part of the universal harmony that is Christ. All that is needed is to look away from ourselves.

This sounds so wonderful we can hardly believe it is real or, if it is real, then possible for us. Yet it only requires that we are on the way, that we have the humility to begin and the openness to the power of Christ to persevere. Then we know that this is not only real and possible but essential for us. The complications seem to arise on the side roads and dead ends, not on the straight way we are called to follow. Any of us can wander off on these diversions, into distractions, triviality, self-importance. The great power of liberty and confidence that permeates our life, however, is that we do have a way back to the straight way, to simplicity and other-centredness. Our way back is simply the love of Jesus that is always present to us, in our own heart, not as something we have to earn or conjure up but as something that simply is. It *is* so simply that it underpins and surrounds us in the roots of our being. It loves us into being and cannot leave us until we have freely accepted the gift of being it bestows.

We live in an age that has lost the experience of simplicity and so is losing the experience of transcendence. We are trained to recognize value only in the illusions of complexity and we are absorbed in transience. This would be bearable, although miserable, if we could make ourselves in the image of the machines we create. But we cannot. Our humanity demands that we travel to a deeper level of awareness where we see and experience the reality of God. Our hearts are restless until we have learned to be still and silent at this deep level. There are many spiritual 'techniques' that operate at the superficial level of our being, where we are carried along on a stream of distraction, and that promise more or less instant results – spiritual experience by demand. No one can say that, in the ways of providence, people might not be led from this superficiality to a more serious and mature commitment. 'Sin is behovely,' as Dame Julian said. Nonetheless, we need to remind ourselves that the stream of distraction is not the ocean of God. It is only too easy to anaesthetize ourselves, to be so soaked in our own self-images and self-reflection, to drift along, floating in a realm of self-conscious piety. But it is also possible to take the journey to reality, to be led by Christ the risen and enlightened One into the great awakening to his Father and to realize our vocation to sanctity. By ourselves we could not make the journey. But we are not by ourselves because we are 'in the Spirit'. Nor can this experience even be understood just as our own experience. Our vision is the vision of Jesus and our knowledge of God is a oneness with his knowledge.

The call to the deeper level of our being where this union is found cannot ultimately be repressed by any amount of distraction or evasion. It is the Word spoken eternally by the Father. Our own being derives from its utterance. If we could finally shut it down we would ourselves immediately cease to be. Listening to the Word and awakening in the full consciousness of God to the point of our creation is the task and very meaning of our lives. It is the way of our meditation. The challenge of life and the deep responsibility of the Church as the community of those who are faithful to the pilgrimage of life, is to show that this is the way for all people. To show that we become simple only if we turn from self-centredness, from trying to find our centre in ourselves. Because our centre is in God we have to turn beyond ourselves to him.

Our growth into this experience of God, of the liberty of spirit that comes from other-centredness, is entirely natural. We have simply to clear the ground and to be open to the energy of God's love that makes it possible for us to enter God's mystery of communion. The task is to be simple and open and to remain open while the process of growth unfolds itself in our heart and throughout our lives. Like every process of growth, the condition for it is patience. We are conditioned to distrust patience as a waste of time. In a world-view tied to the finite dimension time seems the most precious of all values. It *is* precious, of course, but only because it is through and in time that we awaken to the eternal. The right use of time is patience. Time is given to teach us patience, to teach us to be still.

Any technique of prayer is by definition impatient. It sets out to make things happen according to the desire we have for God, to possess God. This is a desire that operates only within the limits of our sense of time. Such spiritual techniques, designed to speed up the journey into God, will be disposable methods used until they produce a desired effect or dropped if they fail our expectations. Meditation is not a technique of prayer but a discipline of life.

When we were in Victoria, a college student who had come to the cathedral to find out what Christian meditation was all about attended the nightly meeting of the meditation group. In the discussion period after meditation he said that he was familiar with many techniques of prayer, mostly from the East, but that he was not very familiar with the Christian tradition. Why, he asked, did we seem to be making such an absolute claim for the Christian tradition of meditation? Was the Benedictine tradition derived from John Cassian really so different from the others? I think we have to understand why this question could be asked to understand in what type of world the Gospels have to be preached today. If we are to communicate the gospel as a living tradition today we have to be sure from our own experience how an integrated Christ-centred life provides the full answer to that young man's question.

I responded to him with what I have just written here about the nature of techniques. A technique is goal-oriented, necessary if we are learning how to drive or to grow roses but misguided if we are learning the way of unlearning, the way of prayer. A technique in the realm of spirit intensifies our self-centredness. Why, then, is meditation in the Christian tradition different from a technique? First, because it is best understood as a discipline. It is a way we follow regardless of our immediate experience because it takes us, beyond egocentric attachment to our passing moods and desires, into the liberty of the children of God. It is a discipline in the richest and most positive sense of the word: a learning, a discipleship, a yoke (meaning 'union') that Jesus tells us is necessary but, when freely chosen, light to bear. Techniques are limited to a functional area of experience, whereas creative discipline integrates and harmonizes life as a whole.

Contrary to prevalent belief, commitment sets us free, seriousness brings us joy, and discipline leads us to transcendence. This is the understanding with which we can communicate the gospel and our Christian tradition of meditation. To underestimate the absolute demand the gospel presents to each of us is to also underestimate the absolute joy and fullness of life it offers. We have to be clear that we are not communicating a short excursion but a way that spans our lives, a way that St Paul tells us begins and ends in faith. The best answer to the student in Victoria, then, is 'faith'. Faith makes the difference. Meditation in the Christian way is the way of faith. Christ is our way to the Father. Christ is our faith: relationship, trust, spiritual knowledge. Christ's risen life supports us in the journey of our life.

When we begin to meditate it is natural to ask, 'How long will this take?' We need to be told – and our living tradition tells us – that it takes no time at all. This is the same as saying that it takes only as long as it takes us to realize that it takes no time. This is why the real use of time is patience. In the moment of pure patience, simple openness, the little ego that keeps us self-centred fades away into the nothing it came from. Our spirit, centred in Christ, flows into the plenitude of God as its beginning and its end, its alpha and omega. Our faith is our patience, our openness to what already is. We are not so much waiting for God to arrive as for ourselves to realize that God is with us in Christ. Emmanuel, God-with-us. We have to learn, not to 'make God happen', but to become sufficiently still, sufficiently silent, to allow the consciousness of Jesus to expand and push back the frontiers of our being, and reveal that we are in God.

To pray deeply is to be faithful. To be filled with faith is no less than to be filled with the power of the love of Jesus – which is the selfsame love with which he is loved by the Father. His openness to the Father opens our heart to the Spirit. Our greatest challenge then is also our greatest opportunity: to become faith-filled, to root and found ourselves in Christ as the source and being of our faith.

This is just what we do by following the way of meditation. Every day is built into the faith with which we leave self behind and journey into the mystery of God. It is the faith we open ourselves to each morning and each evening because our mantra is the way of faith and the sacrament of love. To say our word continuously throughout the time of our meditation is our simple task. What could be simpler? But as we know, simplicity is not simplistic. It is not easy to be simple. Commitment to simplicity is the essential spiritual discipline and it makes all compromise a false option. The way to simplicity must be itself simple. We have cause to rejoice that in the mantra we have found this way.

The way of the mantra is a way of generosity, of expansion and deepening. It is a 'narrow way' but not in the sense of exclusion or narrow mindedness. A mystery of this journey is that it makes us grow in sensitivity to the presence and goodness of God in many unexpected areas of our lives. Often it is not easy to explain how this is so and it cannot really be understood outside of the experience. To turn from our thoughts and imagination at the time of prayer and to be wholly faithful to our simple task of saying the 'one little word' – how can you explain by image or concept that this is a way into the silence in which God reveals himself in Jesus as the source and foundation of all creation? Yet we know, when we have followed this way even for a brief while, that the poverty of the mantra enriches us in a movement of love. It fills every part of life and awakens us to the mystery in which we are inserted. We see more clearly each day that this mystery is closed to us as long as we remain centred in ourselves rather than in him.

To understand what it means to be simple and to discover it in our own experience shows us that we become simple by becoming other-centred. Although we are trained to put our trust in complexity, we know at a deep level that real peace depends on our going beyond complexity and becoming simple. The wonder of the Christian revelation is that, while outside of Christ all is uncentred and complex, we find simplicity by discovering ourselves centred in union with him because 'he himself is our peace'. In and through our meditation we see that this peace is not a passive stillness, not any kind of negation. It is pure affirmation, as is the faith and poverty of our mantra itself.

Also, this peace reveals itself progressively as nearness, our nearness to the source of all creation. We know, as St Paul tells us, that in Christ we, who were once far off, have been brought near, and that a world which was without hope has now been filled, made radiant with the knowledge of our nearness to the Father.

The Christian who awakens to this mystery has, by the nature of the experience of love itself to communicate it. There are many, shaped by our materialistic values today, who would say that this Christian vision is illusory – a myth of an old world. There are some who say that it may be true but only for the few. No one can, of course, quantify God's self-revelation and self-giving. This is the deepest and most personal movement of love. It is absolute. But if our faith is in harmony with that of the New Testament we must believe that the words of Jesus were addressed to all. And the letters of St Paul, containing the highest claims about human relationship with God, were written to ordinary men and women in the first Christian communities. The call is universal. Our greatest fault as Christians has been that we have so tragically underestimated both the universality and the wonder of this revelation. There is nothing worse than a shallow Christianity. We are not invited to hover in the shallow netherworld of our ideas and images. We are summoned to go beyond all limitation, all the restrictions of self-consciousness, and to expand in depth to infinity in the heart of the Trinity. We are called to realize that the primal power and energy of creation flows in our hearts and that this power is the energy of love. Upon it, upon its wellspring in Christ, our peace depends. To find this peace, we need to know ourselves but to go beyond even self-knowing.

Our destiny is to know that we are known. Our roots are in God. In meditation we discover the resonant harmony between the being of God and our being. Language fails us but we have to try to use it to direct our attention to the depths of the mystery. Into these depths the mantra leads us. Like God's harmonic it roots itself in our heart until every part of us is opened to God's love and its power pours freely into us.

Sanctity and wisdom are simply names for the knowledge of reality. God alone is real. We discover in meditation and in our daily fidelity that the godliness we are summoned to is full sanity, flowing from the full power of God's love. Each of us, by the very fact that we have been given being, that we have begun to share in the reality of God himself, is invited to discover that goodness and godliness flow freely in the depths of our heart.

The wonder of the Christian revelation is that this is not theological poetry. Each of us has infinite importance. Our creation is designed in a mysterious way by God to fulfil the design of God's own holiness. When we have turned to God we reflect the divine glory we have received back to God. This is our meaning, our vocation. It is in Christ that we turn. We could neither know nor realize our destiny without Jesus who awoke to it in his human consciousness and who has realized it in the Spirit he sends into our heart. 'In Christ the complete being of the Godhead dwells embodied and in him you have been brought to completion.'[1]

Each Easter the experience of the risen Jesus calls for a deeper response from us and we grow a little further into the completion he brings us. To commit ourselves to this growth is the greatest opportunity any of us could ever have. In the fellowship that we share in him, let me urge you to deepen your commitment to the simplicity that we need for this growth. We keep you all in our hearts on this pilgrimage.

Wishing you every blessing and with much love,

John Main OSB
(May 1980)

John Main went to Victoria, British Columbia, with Laurence Freeman at the invitation of the Bishop and cathedral clergy there. They gave a week's 'mission', talking and meditating twice a day in the cathedral. They saw again how widely and diversely meditation can be taught and understood by people. After Easter, John Main gave a midweek retreat for priests organized by the core members of our Tuesday morning priests' group. He visited a group that meets regularly in Plattsburgh, New York, and Laurence Freeman visited Toronto to help start two groups – an ecumenical group meeting at an Anglican religious house and another run by two of our oblates downtown. On his return, he stayed with Bishop Hill in Kingston and spoke and

---

1 Colossians 2.9.

meditated with a group of young Anglican clergy and their wives. Our oblate community had its first meeting in March. From our more distant oblates in Vancouver and Louisiana we heard how supportive their membership of our spiritual community was to them by encouraging their discipline of prayer as the grounding reality of each day.

Two · The Present Christ – First Harvest

13

THE SILENCE OF REAL
KNOWLEDGE

My Dearest Friends,

One of the challenges the human person faces is to be continually sensitive to the unfolding of God's plan in our lives: to give free and open assent to the destiny God's love is shaping for us. It is so easy to lose that sensitivity. Much of life is dominated by the mechanical, by programmed responses or reactions that are scripted for us, by impatient attempts to predict or anticipate growth. The danger is we lose contact with life as mystery and so, eventually, with life itself. When we lose wonder we begin to see existence merely as a problem, a series of complex, interlocking processes. But life is whole. The wholeness is both in its mystery and its simplicity.

The wholeness of life is the harmony of our experience. It is both an inner harmony, the sense of consistency that life persuades us it possesses, and the harmony with which it resonates with everything around us. Reality stretches far beyond the frontiers of our limited experience and in time we come humbly to realize that a greater whole actually contains our experience. Experience, however, does not become significant and life is not charged with meaning until it begins to repeat itself. The outer harmony and inner consistency of life reveals itself in patterns of experience. Every pattern is the projection of creative repetition. But no pattern is ever completed. It can only be finally complete within the boundlessness of God's inner expansion where all is both new and familiar. This ever-freshness is eternity. Any fixed pattern we try to impose on reality, as if it were complete and final, falsifies the truth of the mystery that is both eternally present and ever unpredictable. Dogmatism, fundamentalism, rigidity, the closed mind or heart, are signs of an attempt to avoid the challenge to be continually sensitive to the unfolding of our destiny and to cooperate with it. Fear of the expanding interiority of truth tempts us to protect the ground gained rather than pushing the frontiers further. Self-cultivation rather than selfless exploration then becomes our default response to all situations. A growing insensitivity to life's mystery then wraps around us like a strangling vine, stifling the circulation of our spirit and making us ever more closed in upon our own pain and fear. Increasingly, this creeping spiritual death manifests in the diminishing returns of all our attempts at self-distraction, a cold anxiety and a deepening fear of boredom. This closed kingdom of the ego is a joyless world of laughter at what ceases to amuse and a monotonous seeking for something new.

To live from day to day merely within the perspective of fixed patterns is to waste our deepest response to life on what is passing away. We have not engaged with life on that level where things endure. To remain unaware of the eternal unfolding itself from within our inmost being is the saddest of fates, the betrayal of human destiny. The great Christian insight is that this fate need have no power over us. ('Fear not for I have overcome the world.') Whatever befalls us, the divine perspective is a redeeming reality because all possible human experience, every kind of reality, has been shot through with Christ's redeeming love. He has already visited everywhere we can go. Each person is called to respond to life from within this pervading consciousness and indeed to be wholly penetrated with his consciousness. Human destiny *is* this call, made simply because we are human and our meaning is to be fully human.

The gift that facilitates this is spiritual knowledge, Holy Spirit. The capacity to know by participation is the great gift of life. Whatever our patterns of experience may be, the Spirit continuously recalls us to the grounding realization, the consciousness of simple and pure being which is joy and fills us with joy. Knowing that being is joy constantly transforms the patterns of experience. ('Though our outward humanity is in decay, day by day we are inwardly renewed.') Each time we meditate we return into this joy-full, grounding consciousness of Being. After each meditation we return to the changing patterns more firmly rooted in joy and better able to see life as mystery and to communicate this joy to others. The very ability to see this is itself part of the gift of our creation, the gift of coming into being that is given with ever-increasing generosity moment by moment. Creation is not an historical past event but a present reality. Our personal creation is ever expanding in harmony with the spring of overflowing love in the secret depths of the Father's timeless mystery. As God's being fills our being, our heart is purified and we are led deeper into the vision of God that is God's own infinitely generous self-knowledge.

The gift of vision is the wonder of creation. We are empowered to see the reality within which we live and move and have our being. It is not a gift we can ever possess because it is one we are continuously receiving. In returning it, in letting go, we receive it again even more fully. That is why, the longer we have been meditating, the more we do so without demands or expectations. Knowing that God has created us to share in being takes possession of us without our knowing it. Yet the light of consciousness we expand into is complete in ways that the ego's dim self-consciousness never can be.

We live no longer but Christ lives fully in us. Christ is light. He is the light that fills and gives range and depth to our vision. He is also, in his fully realized human consciousness, the eyes with which we can see the Father. Without his light our vision would be tied to the dimension of limitation and finitude. Our spirit could not soar above itself into the unrestricted liberty and pure clarity of the unified being that is God. Consciousness would remain forever an observer on the imagined periphery of God's boundless space. We would remain hellishly unfulfilled by union with Christ's consciousness and uncoordinated with his Body. Without the Holy Spirit 'dwelling in our mortal bodies' and opening up the dimension of Being within our spirit, we would be prevented by our limitations from moving into the liberty that is our destiny. The light that empowers our weakness and makes of our limitations a crucible in which God's power is brought to perfection, has been freely given. It has been poured into our heart as the pure effulgence of the Father. For Christ is the radiance of the Father. The light of our vision is not less than this radiance, the glory of God itself. 'For the same God who said, "Out of darkness let light shine", has caused his light to shine within us, to give us the light of revelation – the revelation of the glory of God in the face of Jesus Christ' (2 Corinthians 4.6).

For those humbly treading the pilgrimage of prayer into light, this is the essential knowledge we need. Knowledge is experience. It is also the Word that once uttered makes conscious whoever hears it. It summons us out of the old fixed pattern and inspires us to breathe more deeply into the expanding reality and to place our centre of consciousness beyond self-preoccupation. It is to discover that our centre is in God. How we may come to this journey is less important than that we do begin it. To begin, it is necessary to enter somehow into real commitment. That moment of self-giving, of surrendering the ego, is the hole in the wall of the ego that, however fleetingly at first, allows in the light. Light will flow in more and more powerfully until it overcomes whatever blocks translucence. This moment of commitment is always available to us. It is not an absent ideal, a theoretical possibility, but always a present reality accessible through faith. The question is, are we sufficiently present to ourselves to see it, to hear the invitation and respond? Every moment is *the* moment because all time has been charged with divine meaning. 'Now is the acceptable time.' All time is the 'moment of Christ'. Like a lover, like a gardener, God patiently awaits our response, our growth.

Day-to-day life is the field of the mystery of transformation as our destiny is worked out in the power of Christ. Once it is seen in his light no detail of experience is insignificant because the 'recapitulation' of creation in Christ is all-inclusive. Nothing is left out. But our daily times of prayer are of supreme value within the expansion of consciousness if our spirit is to expand in harmony with the greater whole. Nothing should interrupt the rhythm of prayer in daily life because that would retard the process of expansion and obscure the light. Nothing can block us except our own heedlessness, our preference for postponing or for remaining unconscious.

The besetting social fault of every period of history is that people become so busy about so many things that they forget that only 'one thing is necessary': to be one as God is one. The plan being worked out in the life of each individual is the same as that being worked out in the whole of creation, the bringing of all that is into unity with Christ. Unity is indescribable. It cannot be objectified because nothing stands outside it to observe it. No part is left outside the mystery of oneness. It is at once the primal simplicity of being, the unrefracted consciousness of innocence, and the highest end-point of evolutionary creation, the omega point that is also the starting point, genesis of infinite growth. We do not have to be able to describe or even to understand this mystery in which our deepest meaning is rooted. But we do need, and in this life, to have begun to experience it as a personal reality in our own heart, to know our coming – into – being as an act of creation in love and to have felt the joy of the knowledge of oneness with the One.

Then we will have begun to know. Daily meditation will confirm that the first phase of this movement into unity is achieving wholeness within ourselves. As the mantra roots itself in our being, it gently but surely draws all the distracted and scattered parts of our being together. It calms and disciplines the unruliness of the mind, the tree filled with the chattering monkeys. It takes us beyond a self-centred attachment to our moods and thoughts and it transforms all desire including spiritual desire. It takes us through those turbulent, difficult periods of meditation in which our unconscious fears and anxieties are run off, often disappearing for ever without our necessarily knowing what they were. Through all this the mantra is the discipline that allows us to be silent. In silence our spirit naturally expands. From day to day an inner confidence in the true nature and reality of being deepens. The fear of slipping into nonbeing or that we do not exist at all – these fears are the demons of our time – are exorcised. The unfolding experience of our own harmony becomes a sense of wonder and beauty allowing us to recognize the wonder and beauty of all creation. The real wonder is that we are becoming fully conscious of our own creation, knowing that we are being brought to completion. Yet we are not coldly detached observers of this. We are one with our creator The uncovering of our inner harmony sets up a resonance with the source of all harmony. To find our own centre is thus the opposite of being self-centred. It is to awaken to a centre beyond ourselves from which we are created and to which we return with Christ.

I spend much of my time talking with good people who agree with all this at the level of theory. Yet they are often reluctant to set out on the pilgrimage that puts it into practice. The ideas and the language we use to express it can be so intoxicating that they make the pilgrimage, in its wonderfully earthy ordinariness, seem by contrast very mundane. The need for novelty is satisfied by the wares of a spiritual supermarket rather than by the simple labour of daily meditation. We need often to be reminded of the practical and simple ways in which the mystery of life is manifested and how we are made real in its emerging. It is hard to understand how the tradition that teaches us this can be read, preached and lectured on and yet so rarely followed. The teachers of Christian wisdom all point to the same simple truth. They say that the way into the mystery of life is love and love is becoming centred in God, the way of pure prayer. For John Cassian in the fourth century the way into this simplicity was taught as the way of poverty of spirit in prayer. By becoming 'grandly poor' in the utter simplicity of the mantra (the 'formula' or single verse) inner and outer harmony were realized. For the *Cloud of Unknowing*, too, it is about prayer as a journey of progressive simplification, the true humility of self-knowledge, a going beyond words and thoughts in the honesty of the 'one little word'. More and more it seems to me that talk about prayer without taking account of this silent, contemplative, interior dimension cannot lead to the deeper experience of the mystery. With its injunction to 'become as little children', the Word of the Gospel lies at every turn across all our theorizing paths. The mantra may not be the only way but it is certainly a means that is at one with the end: a way both simple and absolute. Our daily fidelity to meditation and our fidelity to the mantra throughout the meditation are signs that we have really heard the radical call of the Word. Each day that rests on the twin pillars of the morning and evening meditation is a step on the pilgrimage from theory into reality, from idea into experience. As we shed complexity trivial concerns are re-evaluated against the ultimate standard of truth, reprioritized in the experience of being one with the One who is One

The silence of meditation releases the power of the glory of God in our heart. Silence is a power within us, the life of consciousness, the power of the Spirit who 'in silence is loving to all'. In the poverty of our mantra meditation is what the Upanishads call the 'work of silence'. As we approach the creative silence that is the Spirit in our heart we know that it is also the light that enlightens everyone who comes into this world, the glory of God's self-giving that attracts us ever onwards and inwards. In the transforming energy of this silence the greater becomes our wonder, the deeper our joy that we are on this pilgrimage of being.

There are days in our lives, days of epiphany, when the unfolding revelation takes on a wholly incarnate form and the plan of the mystery is made visible. On such days what seems the toil and labour of the pilgrimage gives way to enfleshed grace. The centre of the pattern dilates and touches us with a sureness beyond the power of any pattern of words or experience to contain. Such a day for our Community was June 8th, 1980, the Feast of Corpus Christi, the Body of Christ, when Laurence Freeman was ordained to the sacred priesthood.

Understanding can only emerge from within if we accept that there are many things we cannot understand or can at least only apprehend very dimly. The deepest Christian experience is entered into when the wisdom of this humility has dawned on us. Only then can we allow the mind of Christ full realization in our consciousness. Only then can we understand that we know the Father only by means of union with Christ. Only thus can we 'know it though it is beyond knowledge'. The power of the sacraments is to awaken this knowledge. In sacramental participation with reality we know 'in him, with him and through him' by allowing him to know us. We can talk of the Body of Christ. We can talk of the Priesthood of Christ. But words cannot sound the depth of the mystery. Only silence takes us into the vision of God.

The intimacy of human participation in God's self-revelation creates an awe that makes silence the most natural response. It is such a deep involvement because the mystery is closer to us than our own words and ideas about it. It is not simply that God is drawing us closer by the revelation of the divine plan but rather that in Christ we are participating in the eternal communion of love that *is* God. Human beings are not meant to be mere onlookers at this mystery. When God the Creator passes his life into Adam on the ceiling of the Sistine Chapel, God looks into humanity's inmost depths, creating the potency of consciousness from which our awakened recognition of God arises. God knows God in our humanity, not as we hear the echo of a voice in a hollow chamber but in the liberty of human love. The full flow of the divine current is earthed in humanity. It fills us and creation with the beauty of the Spirit.

The sacraments are dynamic manifestations of the 'joy of Being' earthed in the human realm of signs. Through the ordinary fabric of experience, water, wine, bread, oil, touch, they remind us that our meaning is to be transfigured by the power of God flowing through us and bringing us into the fullness of creation. The greatest moments in which mind and heart advance into this fullness are moments of pure silence. The deepest silence during the ordination ceremony is the actual sacramental moment of power when we allow all that words and rituals have prepared us for to dilate in the sacred space in which we have gathered and fill us. It is a still moment, full of energy, the loving energy of God delighting in the realization of the plan in each human life. In stillness we are filled with a reverential fear: not fear of punishment but an awe that flows into supreme confidence in the presence of the one who is self-disclosed by love. Everyone present is turned in the same direction, drawn and at the same time liberated by the power that unveils a reality encompassing the bishop, the priests, the one being ordained and the whole community present. But it goes beyond all into the mystery of God in whom space and time subsist. It is one of those moments of transcendence when we are taken beyond ourselves and yet are never more truly the person we are called to be.

The sacrament of Holy Orders, like all sacraments, is an outward sign, a sign of an inner reality that is pure openness to God and the power of love. In the generosity of that openness the barriers preventing the free flow of that power are swept away. By knowing the reality of the great communion of this love we know that all things are held together by love. Because this is the inner dynamic of the sacrament we celebrated with Bishop Crowley in the Chapel of the mother house of the Congregation de Notre Dame in Montreal it is no idle thing to say that all our friends around the world were there with us, as Laurence was led deeper into the mystery of his creation.

Every individual life is charged with meaning from within. Patterns we impose from a merely abstract level of consciousness, from outside, falsify the truth. This is always the danger of language because whatever we say about the mystery of God expanding in our life, or about meditation, misses the wholeness and the simplicity of the reality. One aspect or other must get ignored or distorted while we talk or think about another. In talking of meditation, for example, as the way to lose our life and go beyond self-consciousness we can neglect how it is equally the way to find ourselves and become more alive. Similarly, we talk of silence as the medium of this discovery. But talking of silence may suggest that it is only the absence of sound or image. Silence has to be experienced to be understood. Only in the mystery of silence can we see that it is the union of love, total and unconditional acceptance. Silence is the overcoming of time and space. All limiting patterns of mind dissolve in communion.

To understand this in our own experience it is only necessary to begin to commit ourselves to it as *truth*. Confirmation follows commitment. Then externally we begin to see reality as only true interiority can reveal it. Vision and understanding expand from the centre where the mind rests in silence in meditation. Let your mind rest in the heart, say the Upanishads. Set your mind on the kingdom before everything else and all else will be given to you as well, says the gospel. We are most truly ourselves when we are rooted in the silence of this centre. The problem is only our distracted possessiveness. But the Spirit waits patiently for us in its own eternal stillness. Our daily pilgrimage of meditation gradually teaches that we are there *already*, with 'my Father and your Father', the One who creates and calls us to be here and who loves us to be with him.

Awakening to this is expansion of spirit. With expansion comes liberty of spirit that extends the range of consciousness through union with the human consciousness of Jesus that dwells in the infinite space of his love in the human heart. He dwells there with the most perfect respect for our freedom. Destiny is not fate. Our destiny requires our freedom. Liberty is our capacity to enter with undivided consciousness into this destiny as the perfection of love. Experience, the spiritual knowledge that flows from this knowledge is not theoretical. It is touching the most immediate and personal heart of our being. We are not meditating long before our spiritual eyes begin to open upon epiphanies of love in life that before we were too short-sighted to perceive or not generous enough to receive.

Liberty is the fruit of rootedness. Our materialistic, egocentric instincts dispute this. The ego sees freedom as the avoidance of commitment, freedom from ties, keeping options open. This negative self-protection temporarily offered by the ego demands the fruit before the seed. But while the ego is being melted away and desire dissolved in the faith of meditation, the kingdom dawns. The mantra leads into the rootedness that bears fruit beyond imagining. Through all the meanderings of the mind the simple faith of the mantra word keeps us homed on our true destination, the reality of God's love. Then we enter the breathtakingly boundless expansion of heart that liberates us once and for all from narrowness, insensitivity, fear, fantasy, all the shadows of the ego.

Language frustrates unless it leads back into the refining silence. Spiritual language is a language of opposites, the paradoxes in which we see our spirit expand beyond all fixed patterns. Mind cannot know this as a separate reality, to analyse, remember or quantify it. Mind is itself transformed by this knowledge. It is the knowledge proceeding from the heart's silence that only the heart can know at its source. The knowledge of love is only knowable in love's alchemy. The mind finds peace in stillness of heart. In the union of mind and heart we awaken to a still greater union of which our being is a sacrament: the union of all in Christ who unifies all by the grace and power of his union with the One who is all in all.

With much love,

John Main OSB
(July 1980)

Among those coming to visit and enter our life during the summer of 1980 were a number who came exploring a monastic vocation with the community. John Main spoke at a wide variety of gatherings in Montreal and the USA. The ordination of Brother Laurence Freeman by Bishop Crowley was a milestone in the development of the young community. The spacious chapel at the mother house of the Congregation of Notre Dame on Sherbrooke Street was needed to receive the large numbers who attended.

14

ABSOLUTE GIFT

My Dearest Friends,

There is a deep and urgent need in the world today to recover true experience of spirit. By 'true' experience I mean experience that is fully personal and made authentic by the engagement of our whole person. It is not enough to be moved by accounts of the spiritual experience of other people. Nor is it not enough to approach the dimension of spirit with merely part of our being, intellectual or emotional. The fullness of the spiritual experience to which we are each summoned requires not less than everything we are.

I would like to suggest an aspect of this conviction which was emphasized for our community this summer as we meditated with our missionary guests – men and women who meditate daily through lives of active and often very courageous service. The same insight was highlighted for us with the Dalai Lama, spiritual leader of one of the world's oldest contemplative monastic orders.

Meditation is a way of life centred faithfully in daily practice and with the discipline of prayer is our way into this true experience of the Spirit. As anyone who follows this way soon comes to know in their personal experience, the demand of meditation upon us expands with each step we take along the pilgrimage. As our capacity to receive the revelation increases so too does our natural response to make greater openness, deeper generosity and more unpossessiveness. Strangely and wonderfully this demand is unlike any other demand made upon us. Most of the demands upon us seem to limit freedom, but this one is nothing less than an invitation to enter into full liberty of spirit – the liberty we enjoy when we are turned away from self. What seems scarily to be the demand for absolute surrender is in fact an opportunity for the infinite realization of our potential. But to understand this, we cannot flinch from the fact that the demand *is* absolute and so, consequently, must our response be.

We are so used to what is relative rather than absolute, so used to making compromises, that it may often seem that any absolute response is only an ideal, not a practical possibility. 'It would be nice if we could but it just isn't realistic,' we say about many things we believe in. The urgency facing the Church today is to awaken to the fact that not only *is* it realistic; but it is the *only* way to come into contact with reality. The Church, no less need than the rest of society, needs to recover the true experience of spirit as the central priority in its life if it is to be true to itself, its Lord and its vocation. Only if it has personally recovered this knowledge in lived experience can it point the way forward to the fundamental truth of the human mystery. which is the mystery of Christ. The absolute commitment required was described by the early Church as faith – faith in the utter reality of God's revelation in Jesus.

This challenge to the Church is, in fact, the same one facing all men and women – to understand that the absolute is the only realism. Perhaps for those who are awake to the mystery of Christ it is easier to understand how practical is the absolute because what they are awake to is the incarnation of the one who says 'I am'. The Spirit dwells in us as absolute gift, unconditionally. It dwells in our ordinary humanity, that is weak, vain or silly, that knows failure, mistakes and false starts. Yet it persists within us with the complete commitment of love. It dwells within us through the humanity of Christ and it is through the mutual openness, the union of our consciousness with his that we are empowered to make that absolute response which is the secret meaning of our creation.

Any life which fails to place this mutual openness, which is prayer, at its centre loses its balance as it moves away from its centre of gravity. Then it can only fall into one or other extreme of solemnity or triviality. Between these two extremes is the discipline of seriousness, the truly serious approach to life that both prepares and sustains us for the response to the absolute. In that response we enter into the experience of pure joy, the joy of being, the joy that underlies everything we are and everything we do. Beginning the journey of meditation is to begin to understand that it is for this joy that we have to learn to prepare ourselves. Our capacity to receive it with open, generous hearts depends upon the generosity of our discipline.

Our response to the absolute nature of reality is something

absolutely ordinary. We live in a world where it is the extraordinary, the phenomenal, that fascinates and attracts attention and we often see this manifested most of all among religious people judging spiritual authenticity on the basis of 'special' experiences. Underlying this kind of sensationalism is the pursuit and worship of novelty, which is a loss of faith in the mystery of life as it is actually given us – the absolute gift of living to the full in the present moment. What we lose in the cult of novelty is the sense of wholeness that is essential to the survival of the contemplative experience at the heart of human life and society. The mystery of life is woven into its wholeness. And the wholeness of life is the mystery that, from deep within the ordinary, continually deepens the perspective of consciousness. If meditation seems to many people to be an unrealistic, impractical, non-incarnational fringe activity of spiritual life it is because the experience of wholeness has been lost or become an abstract notion. The truth of the Incarnation is that the absolute reality of God has touched and indeed united with the variable, contingent reality of human existence. God became human so that human beings might become God. The early Fathers of the Church expressed it just like this. Staggering as such an idea is and feeble as our capacity to grasp it may be, it is realized through the reality of the person we are within the ordinariness of daily human life. For this reason we meditate as an ordinary fact of daily life, every morning and every evening. It is part of the routine of our daily life. But unlike all the other, largely unconscious parts of our routine these times of meditation are moments of an ever deepening wakefulness, an ever fuller consciousness.

The creeping sense of unreality that is overtaking our culture often leads people to intense self-consciousness about the mundane things of life, like diet, body shape and exercise. Once begun such self-consciousness tends to spread to the whole of life and so intense self-consciousness about food is not infrequently linked with intense self-analysis about 'methods of spiritual realization' and the quest for new experiences. The tragedy of this type of self-consciousness is that it originates in the loss or corruption of that pure consciousness which is the basis of true spiritual experience. Even though it is an attempt to recover that pure experience it is doomed by its very nature to be counter-productive. The simple truth is that to enter into undivided consciousness, into purity of heart, we have to leave self-consciousness behind. Whoever loves their life will lose it.

After we have been meditating for a while the self-conscious novelty of it begins to wear thin and the ordinariness of it begins to appear. Ironically it is at this moment, when self-consciousness is beginning to fade and the experience of wholeness begins to emerge, that many people give up. The quality we need to persevere and which allows the mystery to dilate at the centre of our being is what we call *faith*. The Church has always known that faith is pure gift. It is not earned. It is not bought. The personal quality that empowers us to travel ever deeper into the ordinariness of meditation also calls forth from us a mature acceptance of the gift of our being. Yet it is never, in any possessive or self-dependent sense, 'mine'. The Christian knows it as the faith that Jesus himself communicates to us through his pure consciousness dwelling unitively within and among us. From a source deep in the centre of our spirit where Jesus' Spirit dwells, this gift is breathed into us. We also experience it from the *word* of faith spoken to us in innumerable ways by others, both saints and sinners, in the faithful community of humanity.

Hearing the word of faith is to meet a challenge, addressed to our deepest sense, of self to realize our wholeness. We find many ways of postponing or evading this challenge. Our lives are busy and distracted. Social pressures and indeed our own fear of stillness can make us prefer to be busy and distracted even while we complain about it. How many people, seeing a little free time in their day or a spare evening in their week, react automatically by immediately looking for something new to fill it? Our social programming makes it almost second nature to fear that if we are not doing something we will cease to be. Our very being, we are encouraged to believe, depends upon our being busy.

This delusion makes us spin out of our spiritual centre, both personally and collectively. It is a fundamental inversion of reality. It is not necessary to do in order to be. In fact, it is only if we can first learn to be that we become fit for all doing.

The danger today for us is that this truth seems bizarre and abstract and so, by current values, impractical. Then it remains, what for so many Christians the gospel can remain, just a beautiful theory. Spiritual life is life committed to reality. All theories are dangerous because they can so easily become ways of keeping our minds busy while in daily life we live at one remove from reality. If theories are applied idealistically to ordinary life they can produce extremism, an inflexible lack of humanity. If they are insulated from ordinary life in an ideal realm (the Sunday Christian, the weekend or binge meditator), they lead self-destructively to alienation and inauthenticity. The fundamental truths are discovered through practice and grounded in the ordinary.

For many people, of all traditions, who have lost touch with the ordinariness of the spiritual, a truth like meditation can seem great theory but impractically idealistic. So it becomes something at best to be practised in one's rare spare moments. A great danger for religious people is that they can feel so at home in their verbal formulas and rituals that they fail to recognize such an absolute and fundamental value of the spiritual life as silence. Recently I saw a great number of religious people in a place of worship enter into and taste this value for themselves. It was the most refreshing and inspiring aspect of the inter-faith service held in the Marie Reine du Monde Cathedral in Montreal to greet the Dalai Lama. Several thousand people of different traditions meditated together in deep silence for about twenty minutes. This gave depth and significance to the readings and the speeches that nothing else could. The Dalai Lama remarked on this to me afterwards adding that it was the first time that he had meditated in a Christian church. Yet at the same time it was the meditation that made this special large gathering a realization of unity in spirit that was so intimate and wonderfully ordinary.

Our lives are not only busy; they are usually also very noisy. If life is to be charged with meaning from its depth dimension and lead to true growth in consciousness we have to be rooted in silence. This means to be rooted in the spirit, whose depth can never be plumbed or analysed and whose full meaning is found in the consummation of union. Each of us is called to enter with wonder into this mystery with our whole being, in the total immediacy of the present moment which is the eternal moment of God. To be touched with this wonder is to know reverence. It is to know, in the absolute certainty that belongs to our own experience, that the energy of creation, the power of love, dwells in the human heart in silence and in the stillness of pure consciousness. The meaning of awakening to this power of our first creation is the true meaning of our being that we thirst for. It dawns as we simply open our consciousness to its source. To receive a gift is to return to union with the giver. Our goal is awakening to the source. Every aspect of life, leisure or work, relates directly to this meaning. Nothing lacks the significance of being related to this spiritual dimension. That is why the greatest sacrilege in any human life is triviality. Rejecting the ordinary, pursuing the sensation of the new for its own sake is to trivialize, to reject, the gift life. When we have committed ourselves to understanding this more deeply an entirely new perception of the harmonious relation between being and action, stillness and movement, silence and speech, begins to dawn on us.

These dimensions of reality seem contradictory. You can't know both at the same time, it seems. But the opposition between these dualities is only conceptual or verbal. Thinking classifies. Experience unifies. To be open to reality through the ordinary practice of meditation reveals the mystery of God to be pure activity. Pure stillness and silence, are not inactive. They are harmonized energy, energy that has reached its highest formless form. In this harmony the creativity and the meaning of all movement is contained. The stillness of divine being that we enter through stillness is love. It is the focal point, the centre and source of all goodness. Our stillness in meditation *is* the divine stillness precisely because our centre is in God. The ordinariness of meditation reveals to us – as lived knowledge – what thought alone could never convince us of. That being is pure action.

Daily meditation, then, is in no way isolated from the meaning of our ordinary activity. The set times of meditation, like our fidelity to the saying of the mantra from the beginning to the end of each meditation, are the essence of all our activities because meditation is the realization of Being, of pure action. Meditation is pure activity. It purifies all our activity from the distractedness, business and egocentricity that cloud and confuse its clarity. Indeed meditation *is* action, in the sense that it is the positive, purposeful deployment of energy, an ordering and focusing of all the energies that make up the mystery of our whole personhood. Properly practised, it can never be a merely passive state, because what is both energetic and still is at the highest point of action, energy incandescent – consciousness. We know this in very immediate experience, the experience of persevering in our journey up the mountainside of daily life. The faith demanded of us by the pilgrimage requires the quite un-passive qualities of courage, perseverance and commitment.

Meditation is pure action. It purifies all other activities. It is pure because it is selfless, wholly other-centred. Most of our activities, our hopes and plans are carried out with a predominant concern for verifiable, material results. At its worst this obsession is just self-interest, egoism at its most intense. But, in fact, any fixation on results, any attachment to the fruit of action that interferes with the selfless-ness of the work itself, betrays a possessiveness which disturbs the integrity of the activity. In meditating day by day, however, humbly and ordinarily, beginning our pilgrimage at the point we have received the gift of faith to begin it, wherever that may be, we set out again and again into the mystery of selfless, other-centred activity. We may well begin meditating with a superficial concern for results, trying to esti-mate if our investment of time and energy is justified by dividends in knowledge or unusual experiences. Perhaps anyone formed by our society is conditioned to begin in this way. But the ordinary practice of meditation purifies us of this spiritual materialism. Practice purifies motivation. As we enter into the direct experience of being, of pure action, we find all our other activities progressively and radically purified of egoism. To put all this more simply – because meditation leads into the experience of love at the centre of our being, it makes us more loving persons in all our ordinary lives and relationships. Meditation teaches us what reading theology alone could not convince us of, that being is Love.

The redemption of our society from the constricting, complex self-consciousness into which it has fallen calls for this fully personal knowledge of being. The experience of Being – as purity of motive and as love – is recoverable. This is our hope. But human society can only be redeemed and restored to whole and other-centred consciousness if enough people enter into the practical pilgrimage that it demands. Society can return to sanity, to wholeness, wisdom and true religion only if enough individuals and communities within it undertake the journey into reality, into the renunciation of self-consciousness, into love. Only in this way can human life be healed and transformed by the power of love that is Spirit. Our life is a holistic growth, a move-ment into wholeness infinitely greater than ourselves. It both contains and fulfils us. Such growth must have a centre. If we can find that centre we would find both our point of departure and our home-coming, the convergent point of all humanity. Where then is this focal point of the whole life, where we find both the spiritual reality from which we come into consciousness and the faith that empowers us to embrace it? Where is the reality in which human consciousness infinitely expands because it awakens to the mind of Christ with which it enjoys a union of love?

In terms of the mystery of our own being this convergent point of wholeness is the heart where we are one in body, mind and spirit. In terms of ordinary life it is the centrality of meditation in our day, the two periods of meditation on which every day is balanced. The boundless centre of ordinary life is pure prayer. The great wonder and joy of knowing this is that the purity of our meditation, purity of heart, clarifies and unifies all our activity by bringing it all into true harmony, into the dynamic state of other-centredness which is loving service of others. The selflessness of the mantra progressively liberates us from all self-centredness. It frees the spring of compassion and profoundly summons us into the mystery of the wholeness of life.

To enter into wholeness is to enter into self-identity and this is to enter into God. In this movement of love our life finds true spiritual focus and direction. Thus it becomes love of God, love of neighbour and love of self.

So let me encourage you with what St Benedict calls 'the support of many brethren' in your daily commitment to this daily journey. In understanding its ordinariness you will awaken to its absoluteness. Then you will know the infinite enrichment of your whole life that is the liberating power of love. Liberated from self-centredness in order to become ourselves, we are led into the experience of communion in which being and action are one, that communion of love that is Spirit, the selfsame Spirit dwelling in all of us.

How? We have only to begin the journey and to remain faithful to our beginning.

With much love,

John Main OSB
(October 1980)

Shortly before we moved from our first home on Avenue de Vendôme, John Main was invited by the Archbishop of Montreal to welcome the Dalai Lama, as a fellow monk, at an interfaith service at the cathedral. After the event, the Dalai Lama accepted John Main's invitation to visit the community for meditation, lunch and discussion. He joined us one Sunday for the midday Office and meditation and, after lunch, he and John Main withdrew and spent an hour or two together in conversation. A friendship began that was to bear fruit many years later in the 1994 John Main seminar, 'The Good Heart', led by the Dalai Lama, and in 'The Way of Peace', co-led by the Dalai Lama and Father Laurence Freeman who, as a junior monk had served them lunch on that auspicious day. In the summer of 1980, the McConnells, a prominent family in Montreal, offered us a large house and estate that miraculously answered our need for growth. It stood in three acres of wooded garden on the slopes of Mount Royal, yet was only a few minutes from central Montreal. Around the same time, four young men came, seeking to begin the monastic life within the community, and this gave a special sense of providential design to the move. Among our increasing number of guests were several missionaries who were between assignments. Meditating with them reinforced our conviction that the way of meditation is relevant and necessary to all walks of life and kinds of vocations, even (indeed, especially) for the more active. The Benedictine oblate community continued to expand in a monastery without walls, with new members from Canada, the United States and Europe. In Toronto, interest in the work of the community led to an invitation to John Main, from the Christian meditation groups associated with the priory, for him to speak there in November. During the summer, John Main went to Ireland to lead meditation retreats for Benedictine nuns at Kylemore Abbey and for Dominicans in Drogheda. Later, he gave a retreat to the Benedictine monks at St Louis Priory, Missouri.

15

PREPARING FOR BIRTH

My Dearest Friends,

With all the pressures of consumerism attached to Christmas today it is easy think of it just as a period of hectic preparation and a quick day of celebration followed by a time of recovery. We can easily forget that it is more than a feast. It is a season. Like all seasons its essence is a cycle of preparation, achievement and then the incorporation of what has been achieved into the larger season of which it is a part, the season of our life.

As Advent, the four-week period of preparation for Christmas, draws to a close and as we approach the feast itself, I would like you to know that we all here wish you much joy and deeper peace as we are led more deeply into the mystery of the Lord's birth. The period of preparing to celebrate the mystery is itself a joyful time, because there is a quietly deepening understanding of whose birth it is we celebrate and just how eternal an event it is. Each year of celebration, the mystery of the birth of Jesus becomes greater. And yet the greater it grows the closer it comes to us. In a society that has lost so much of its capacity for peace and so much of the patience needed to prepare for anything, we risk being left only with the worship of the instantly visible, the immediately possessed. We are then left only with the aridity of the instantly forgotten. A liturgical season of preparation, which tunes the deeper rhythms of our spirit, would then become not just a religious but a psychological anachronism. Why celebrate such a thing at all?

So much depends upon being prepared, upon having firsthand experience of being ready. If we want to know the truly spiritual meaning of Christmas, the celebrations and rituals at home and in worshipping communities, we have to know with well-prepared and peaceful hearts what it means to enter the space where celebration becomes joyful. This is what the daily pilgrimage of meditation teaches us from within. In that simple and humble journey we discover what it means to make space in our heart. We feel what it means to prepare the heart for the great celebration of life. As we prepare, and as our spiritual materialism and egocentric expectations drop away, it dawns on us that the event we are preparing for precedes us. The great liturgy has already begun in spirit and in truth.

So often we have the experience and miss the meaning. Afterwards we know the hollowness and disappointment at what was merely said or done in external signs that did not connect us with their underlying realities. This is the sad result of being unprepared, of being lost in the superficial. But once we have found true relationship at depth, everything that happens to us is drawn into a meaningful pattern. It is only necessary for us to prepare our hearts and we are prepared for everything.

One reason that Christmas can still mean so much to us spiritually, despite all the materialism and busyness which accompanies it, is that it continues to remind us of our innocence. Often, however, our sense of innocence is romantic rather than Christian. We think of a period of 'lost innocence' and are filled with that great enemy of all maturity, sentimentality, and that great enemy of prayer, nostalgia. In any season the spiritual balance and clarity of life can be disturbed by emotional self-indulgence, by the cultivation or indulgence of an image of self. These are the common ways we stifle our sensitivity to truth and our capacity for empathy with others. Instead of playing the game of lost innocence we are meant to realize our present innocence. This is the potential we have, right here and now, for a direct response to reality. First, we must cease limiting the mystery within the forms, habits and ready-made formulas of interpretation by which we say we 'make sense out of things' but which too often mean committing the non-sense of trying to control life and thus devitalizing it. The true character of innocence, by contrast with this, is pure energy, free adaptability and a joyful wonder that derives its power from an expanding experience of mystery. If we could begin to know ourselves as naturally innocent in this, actual, present moment, we would be preparing to enter not just into the full experience of the Christmas season but of our whole life.

What does it mean to know ourselves to be innocent? To answer this we have really only to look clearly into our experience. In a moment of pure sensitivity to beauty, or when we are suddenly over-whelmed with wonder at the sheer power of love to create a new world, or when we are led, beyond all our own self-expectations, to set another's interests before our own – in such ways we have precious insights into the real nature of things and into our own real nature. Elaborate theories and formulaic systems simply crumble before the power of this actual experience of the present moment which is so self-evident, so simple, that it transcends all expression except self-expression. It can only be communicated by sharing the experience-in-itself. Any description of it, as when we try to treat it as something observable, distances it from the authenticity of the present. Whatever can be observed or objectified in this way is static. The nature of inno-cence is to be wholly dynamic.

In the dimension of innocence, the state of a pure consciousness and an undivided heart, we know the joy called 'liberty of spirit', in which we realize our potential for self-transcendence. The exhilaration is to know the goodness of life unfolding itself in an infinite generosity of self-giving throughout our whole self. We sense the extraordinary inter-relatedness of the mystery, the way *my* life is connected inti-mately with the lives of others and how all together weave the great mystery that extends far beyond imagination or intellect to that plane of reality where all things are being brought into unity in Christ. These are ineffable glimpses of the supreme reality, of supreme love. At the same time they are absolutely ordinary. We know that no amount of contrivance or experimentation, no kind of fascination with the out-of-the ordinary could have led us into so natural, so real, so simple and so whole a way of being. It is not so much that we see or understand something new as that we *are* someone new. Or, rather, the old person we were is graciously led to completion. Reality is not made, certainly not made by us. To be real is to know in ordinary experience what philosophers or theologians can make sound complex and pompous, that to be is to be joyous, because Being is bliss. To be is to be simple because Being is ONE.

We know only because we are known. We understand only because we are understood. This is the great Christian insight into the human mystery. As St John says, 'this is the love I speak of, not our love for God but his love for us in sending his Son ...'. To be innocent is to live in accord with this truth of our being known and loved. It is to receive a gift, even the gift of being itself, with delight, and generosity, without possessiveness. A child's wonder and happiness at Christmas is a sacrament of its true meaning. It is with the same simplicity that we should receive the supreme gift we receive in the love of Jesus.

The problem is of our own making, when we turn gift into possession. Then the outward sign cannot signify the inward reality. Celebration becomes hollow. At Christmas, and at many other times too in our society, we are tempted to remain on the surface level. Without meeting the challenge to sink our roots deeper into reality we drift discontentedly between desire and disappointment. Our society's infatuation with novelty keeps us endlessly supplied with objects of desire and with counter-distractions to cope with disappointment. We need depth-living to reverse this. We need a spiritual response to life to be able to escape from *samsara*, this round of death and rebirth. We need to make use of the innocence we already possess. Even though we have known such moments of truth, though we may have golden veins of clarity and joy running through our life in the form of relationships, creativity or meaningful work, often these are not integrated into higher unity. They are not linked to the living centre. If we are not *deeply* inserted into the reality of this centre that sustains us in being, we feel fragmented. We lack essential unity and so we lack peace. We are parts waiting to be made whole. Just to dare to go beyond the superficial, is to encounter a realm of faith, not just a beautiful idea, not a fascinating image, not a reflection of our own self-consciousness but wholeness itself. Our essential unity is touched awake. We discover that all is one and we are one with the all within the great, simple heartbreaking truthfulness of Christ – the one who is one with the Father.

It is easy to get stuck in the conviction of our 'lost innocence'. For many kinds of reasons and wounds we slip into the divided consciousness and self-rejection that characterize our time. One major reason for this state of sadness, and half-life is that we are so habituated to live in the past. We look for emotional or spiritual resources in past experiences instead of taking the risk of leaving the past behind and becoming poor, empty, once more in the present. We carry so many memories of the tarnished riches of the past with us that we do not have hands free to receive the real, living gifts being offered to us now. In this state the past exerts a terrible fascination upon us, consciously and unconsciously. It lures us with the narcissistic gratification of endless self-reflection. One of the ego's most enervating pleasures is regret.

Another and similar reason for our belief in 'lost innocence' is our obsession with the future. We invest ourselves so exclusively in future plans and dreams, imagining what might happen, trying to control what we think should happen, that we are dis-membered from reality. In either case, living in the past or in the future, the present, where the real is, where the essence of life and the simple secret of joy await us, goes unnoticed. We become closed to the God who says, 'I am.'

Absurd and tragic, the consciousness that misses the present moment drifts rootlessly in the shadows of past or through the fabrications of the future. It is lost in the state of self-alienation and the longer it remains separated from itself, the more tired it becomes. It exhausts itself by its imprisonment in the self-consciousness of the ego. I have often thought that what many people identify in themselves (with the terrible inaccuracy of egoism) as guilt, their intrinsic loss of innocence, is usually not so much the weight of sin as the oppression of boredom. Boredom – with self, with others, with the hope that the presence of God makes present to us – proceeds from an implosion of spiritual energy that prayer reverses. The greatest task the Church faces today is to extend that invitation to deep prayer as convincingly and as universally as her nature demands. This is to teach prayer as a way open to every man and woman in the ordinary circumstances of their life. To pray is to be prepared for the celebration of life. Meditation teaches us to see that Christmas is the feast of the divine explosion – the love of God revealed in the poverty of Christ.

Loneliness and self-rejection, the boredom that the desert monks called 'acedia', these are perhaps the most virulent diseases of the modern world. They are as much a social threat and psychological epidemic as a spiritual crisis. The crisis of our spiritual life is, however, the fundamental crisis of our time. If Christian communities are vital, if they experience the transcendent dimension of faith, if they are praying communities rooted in the prayer of the living Christ, then they will address this crisis. But, if they lack these essential Christlike qualities, they will be infected by the rampant egoism of a culture suffering so intensely in its addiction to the superficial. They will become preoccupied with their image, their success rate, their numbers, their own psychologies. These are not the concerns of a Christian community. A spiritual community has one concern: to set its mind upon the Kingdom before all else. All the rest will be given in the measure needed and the way best suited. To set our mind upon the

Kingdom, not just as individuals but as integral parts of a community is the simple, single-mindedness of innocence.

The authentic Christian response addresses itself less to the symptoms and more to the causes of sin. This avoids a merely theoretical charity. Compassion and concern become all the more practical because they are inspired by insight into the underlying causes of suffering. In the alienation and spiritual and mental suffering of so many today we see not just economic or sociological causes but spiritual blindness. We see not just cases or problems but human beings of infinite value and lovableness capable of healing and restoration to their true relation with themselves, with others, with God. It is this belief in the curability of the disease that makes compassion faithful and faith compassionate. We know this because we ourselves are being cured. Healing often begins with small steps. If the slightest aperture can be made in the wall of a closed spirit the love of God can enter and work wonders beyond all imagining.

The experience of love working the wonder of God in the heart does not just offer temporary relief. Nor is it a false panacea or a distraction. This faith-filled Christian vision of social and individual healing today communicates a diagnosis of life's suffering that carries within it the power to cure. It is a life-giving word. It is a powerful, awe-inspiring message and also a heavy responsibility. We cannot pretend that the cure does not entail a certain rigour. The way to freedom passes through commitment and mature discipline. Absolute freedom is absolute commitment. The power of this saving process comes from beyond us. But it has taken up its dwelling in the human heart and for every surrender of self we make in that sacred space we win a thousand victories.

If our communities are to show the way into this space of the heart they must themselves be on the way, travelling from afar by the power of their own innocence to become epiphanies of the Kingdom. The journey is from materialism to a renewed sense of the spiritual quality of life discovered in its ordinariness. It is also the journey from the boredom of consumerism to the vitality of loving service of others. The frame of the journey is the commitment to prayer which brings community to birth in the first place. Until that commitment is made, the community is little more than a group waiting to begin a journey, reading timetables and travel-guides, discussing routes. It is a journey to be prepared for but not one that can be predicted. It is made wholly in the present. Every day we travel a little deeper into the fullness of God's presence. It is a journey we may postpone but ultimately not one that we can decide not to make. It is a simple journey, not an easy one, or a difficult one. Once begun, so many strengths are given to us. The greatest strength is that it attracts fellow-travellers. Whoever begins alone will be joined by others and in that mystery of communion the Church is reborn, rekindled in many quiet corners of the earth. However small the corner, it is born in fullness because Christ is born there, humble, vulnerable, and fully human. In those very qualities of the Incarnation Jesus brings the fullness of the Father's love. This is why authentic Christian community, like Jesus himself, has an influence out of all proportion to its size and numbers. The Kingdom, realized in the innocence of a community persevering in prayer, may not conquer the world. But it can love the world and redeem it by its love.

Of course, abstractions can be the great enemies of true religion. Blake spoke of the 'holiness of minute particulars'. Restoring the world to its own innocence, to the capacity to delight in the gift of life without attempting to possess it, is the work of a free-flowing spirit in touch with the flesh of this world. All is made real, not in the media, in programmes or courses, but in the minute particular of the heart. To begin to realize this we are meant to undertake the daily labour of preparing the heart, of clearing space within it. This is the simple, humble and entirely practical work of daily meditation. Each morning and evening we make space for the kingdom to expand a little further, firstly *within* us and then *through* us. Our mantra is our work, our faithful and continuous recitation of the little tool of the mantra that clears the space and opens the heart to infinity.

One of the fears I most often encounter in people beginning a daily pilgrimage of meditation is that the journey to their own heart, to this infinite space, will be lonely. They fear it will take them into isolation away from the comfort of the known into the strangeness of the unknown. This is an understandable fear, initially. To let go of the superficial means leaving behind the familiar and this can cause a feeling of emptiness as we become increasingly exposed to depth and more substantial reality. It takes time to adjust to a new sense of belonging, a new relatedness that sets all our relationships in a new pattern. Our coming home can seem like homelessness. Reflect a little this Christmas on the homelessness of the stable at Bethlehem.

In time we realize that the new experience of innocence, of delight in the gift of life, is only leaving childishness behind and entering into the full maturity that Jesus enjoys in the Father. The fullness of his love enters and expands our hearts in the Spirit. It is not only now, at the beginning of the pilgrimage, that we need the human love and inspiration of others. But it *is* now, when we see an unfamiliarly vast horizon, that we specially need the strength of community. Our openness to others on the same journey in turn expands our sensitivity to their needs. As the mantra leads us ever further from self-centredness we find ourselves turning more generously to others and we receive their support at deeper levels of trust. In fact, our love for others is the truly Christian way of measuring progress on the pilgrimage of prayer.

To those of you who have only recently begun to meditate I would like to send you especially much love and encouragement. The commitment this journey calls from us at first is unfamiliar. It requires faith, perhaps even a certain recklessness to begin. But once we have begun, it is the nature of God, the nature of love to sweep us along. It teaches us by experience that the commitment we are making is to reality and that our discipline is the springboard to freedom. The fear that the journey is 'away from', rather than 'towards' is eroded by experience. This is the journey where ultimately only experience counts. The words or writings of others can add only a little light to the wholly actual, wholly present and wholly personal reality that lives in your heart and in my heart. Miraculously we can enter this experience together and discover communion just where communication seems about to break down.

The journey to our own heart is a journey into every heart. In the first light of the real we see that this communion is the Kingdom that Jesus was born to reveal. He is born again in every human heart to realize it. We have left behind loneliness, confusion, isolation. We have found communion, sureness, love. Our way is simplicity and fidelity. The simplicity of the mantra. Fidelity to our daily meditation. And, as we travel this way, we are drawn ever closer together by the power of love that unites us.

With much love,

John Main OSB
(December 1980)

As we prepared for the first Christmas in our new home, the community was very aware of its own growth – indeed, of a second birth. There was little time for self-reflection, however, in all the work of settling in and, not least, of keeping warm in a house that was large and beautiful but not well insulated. Even amid the bustle of the moving day itself, we had all stopped at noon for the usual meditation. Through the busy weeks and months ahead, the stillness of these times would underpin our life ever more securely. The new house soon began to fill with guests and community members. On 13 December, three of our novices received the monastic habit. The evening groups – of beginners on Mondays and regular practitioners on Tuesdays – almost immediately grew to fill the larger room. Several new oblates were received, including one from Germany who was to introduce our work there and translate some of the key teaching texts into German. While sharing with us our last days at Avenue de Vendôme and our first, very active, weeks on Pine Avenue, our first oblate and John Main's close friend, Rosie Lovat, made her final oblation.

16

FAITH AND BELIEF

My Dearest Friends,

As our society becomes increasingly less religious its need for the authentically spiritual intensifies. As the religious and social support systems fail, we are faced with the urgency of the ultimate, the challenge to experience the meaning and value of life.

This is best expressed in Christian terms as the essential difference between belief and faith. A great deal of ink – and blood – have been spilled through the Christian centuries over beliefs. Even today, in an age – not of faith but of scepticism and anxiety – what we believe, or think we believe, can often be a source of division, conflict and religious hypocrisy. We should ask how often the violence with which people can assert or defend their beliefs betrays an instinct to defend their certainties, to convince themselves that their beliefs are authentic? The spectre of realizing that we actually are not so certain about our belief may be so frightening that we can be plunged into fanaticism, extreme and self-contradictory ways of imposing our beliefs on others rather than co-existing and simply live as sincerely as possible according to what we believe. There is another extreme reaction to the disturbing, repressed suspicion that our beliefs are not absolute which is just indifference. Sensing our inauthenticity we evade it by collapsing into the emotions it creates, fatalism or pessimism. But whatever the extreme, bigotry or lukewarmness, the cause is the fear and self-doubt arising from the gap between what we believe and what we experience. If this gap makes us inauthentic our message – even if it is the gospel message – will convince no one until it has convinced us that we are transformed by it.

Whenever this fear of secret unbelief grips the Church what should be a joyful, tolerant and compassionate community united in celebrating the wonder of a common transcendent experience becomes instead either a lifeless observer of formal routines or an intolerant and pompous agent of repression. From a historical perspective we can look back on a Church that has often been both of these. In fact, because of the complex and volatile society we inhabit, we can probably find both extremes of Christian unbelief in different arenas of the same Church today.

It is an ever-present danger, because the life-force of the Christian tradition is so precarious, so personal and so delicate. It cannot be compromised or diluted without ceasing to be what it is and becoming instead mere pious wordiness or arrogant religiosity. Yet this life-force that St Paul calls the Spirit – the Spirit we must neither sadden nor stifle – is a power of irresistible joy and peace. Its power is released if only we allow ourselves to be who we really are, to believe what we really believe and to say what we really mean. If only we can find a way simply to be ourselves, then this Spirit of truth and authenticity dilates within us and absorbs us. Then we find ourselves being in practice what we often just talk of being, apostles of the reality that is Christ, Christlike communicators of the life of his gospel.

One of the great ironies of history is that although many attempts have been made no one has ever been able to institutionalize this energy. No experience of reality can be known except through direct and spontaneous participation. It is only too easy to codify, formalize and institutionalize the memory or the written record of the experience. But this easily becomes inauthentic experience, the image of a brief glimpse of reality's true light. It is this memory, many times removed from direct experience, that then passes into codified beliefs passed on to successive generations.

This gap between the authentic experience and the received memory can become the chasm between honesty and hypocrisy. This is a possibility that threatens the religious practice of every tradition. It is the gap, simply, between credal statements and experience. Seen positively (because such a gap there will always be) this gap is an opportunity for spiritual growth and human development but only if we acknowledge and accept it in a spirit of humility. Religious believers find it hard to be humble about what and how they believe.

It is true, of course, that we know more than we can prove. This *gap* within the very act of believing exists also because we are born into a long, rich and complex tradition. To accept a belief or, more accurately, a belief-system (because beliefs come in clusters) is not as the agonizers of doubt think the final step. The tradition we are formed by convey many beliefs to us almost automatically, through social conditioning. It is difficult to say how we could ever choose what to believe. But if this tradition is alive, evolving and spiritual it will insist that all beliefs be realized and grounded in personal experience. The supreme test of a tradition's authenticity is the degree to which it teaches the way to this realization to all its followers, not merely to an esoteric few. The distinction of the Christian tradition in human history is that it teaches this personal authentication as a possibility for all in this life. This suggests why the gospel is minimally creedal. It is not obsessed with right and wrong beliefs or with a religious law. Instead it uncompromisingly presents the directly personal truth of its message. The message is the *person* of Jesus and all that his person contains. Jesus does not firstly call us to *believe* or to *do* but to *be*. That is faith, the courageous commitment to be ourselves. Then we become fit for all doing, and for believing in the right way.

Without faith and being, however, the gap between belief and experience becomes a limbo of unreality that is only too easily institutionalized. It will then attract us in the way unreality attracts because it provides an escape from reality. Such zones of human consciousness are well populated by institutions and by individuals who are agreed not to tell the truth to each other. It makes for a world of self-complacency, false piety and intolerance. A place of slow dying and protracted suffering, it defends the half-life that masquerades as truth. But there is no reason why anyone should settle for half-life. We are irresistibly called to fullness of life from the deepest core of our being. And fullness does not have to be earned or even to be achieved, only realized, only accepted. We accept it through a journey of faith across the gap between belief and experience. On that narrow, direct path we are purified in the darkness of faith, beyond belief. We make a transition to the deeper levels of reality by letting go of the words, concepts and images that tie us to memory, to abstraction or to the ego's systems of fear and desire. Then we enter the extraordinary purity of the present moment. Entering humbly, realistically, into the fact of our own incompleteness teaches us how wonderful is our capacity for infinite growth. But to be taught this we have first to learn to be dispossessed, to let go our grip on belief. Blessed are the poor in spirit.

Over the centuries great numbers of men and women and whole societies have affirmed their belief in Jesus and the gospel. All Western culture is permeated by this belief even now when believers are a small minority. This has changed the world. But why has it not *transformed* the world? This is a vital question for Christianity today. We must face up to it, not just by blaming the institution of the Church but by accepting personal responsibility for Christian authenticity at large. A good part of the answer, I think, is that we have too glibly confused belief and faith. We have thought that we could convince others of the truth of the gospel by beliefs alone. Those others we labelled 'non-believers' and saw them as inferior or underprivileged just because they did not believe what we believed.

Beliefs tend to be stronger than faith until we understand that faith – unconditional, open-hearted commitment – operates at the fundamental level of our being through participation in the life of the Spirit. Belief is the tip of the iceberg most of whose substance is invisible. Faith makes up the greater and more essential part of our commitment to truth and to the person of Christ. His person is universally present in the energy of his love for all peoples, all faiths and all creation. He is the invisible reality we enflesh in our lives. Faith is the invisible but realistic way of being ourselves that allows us to share in the mystery of Christ's life, work and self-communication. As *a way of life*, faith is a power to heal, forgive and enlighten. It is a power, a grace and gift within us, that silently communicates itself to others even as it is being set free and growing within ourselves.

The Letter to the Hebrews describes how faith helps us to perceive that the visible comes forth from the invisible. Beliefs are the visible expressions of faith, forms of our personal commitment to the person of Jesus. Because they are expressions they find form mutably in words, concepts and images. Beliefs change, dogma develops, language evolves. The sense of inauthenticity that overtakes the religious mind is often caused because we treat the transient as if it were enduring. We overtax the resources of what is finite and changeable. All the forms in which beliefs exist and are expressed are constantly in the process of passing away. In belief the mind has 'here no abiding city'. Only in the heart can we experience the enduring reign of God. Whatever has form, like our beliefs and bodies, is always in transition to a new form. Beliefs always seek new definitions, new words in which to re-form and dress themselves.

When I studied theology Catholic belief in the Eucharist was summed up in the word 'transubstantiation'. Since then many new

words, like 'transfinalization' and 'transignification', have been proposed as more apt expressions of the mystery of the sacrament. The
Eucharist is most obviously the mystery we can experience in faith but
never solve in words or belief. Yet our beliefs about the Eucharist have
often led to its becoming a symbol of division and scandal rather than
a sacrament of unity. As words and their meaning change so do our
beliefs. The fact that we ourselves are changing, being changed by life,
means that our beliefs must similarly grow, mature and become more
attuned to the mystery that is greater than they are. Faith endures. It
changes only by growing to be more perfectly what it always is, our
personal commitment to truth. Faith grows pre-eminently in pace with
our commitment to meditation which is the quintessential journey of
faith. In the faithful commitment to meditation, each morning and
evening, we accept and gradually come to see the priority of faith over
belief. By repeatedly emptying ourselves of all that is passing away –
all words, ideas and images – faith grows and goes deeper. The
creative matrix of faith is silence. From human relationships we can
see how much faith we need to have in a person to be silent with them.
Our faith in a person is deepened by such silence. It is the same
dynamic as the silence in meditation. In contemplative work faith
becomes active in love. Silence realizes God's love for us as it is
expressed in the love of Jesus. In the silence of faith we are invited to
enter into the enduring reality where Becoming is embraced by Being.
What is visible passes away, what is invisible endures.

Because of Jesus and the communication of his Being to us, this
reality is no abstract, platonic idea. It is fully personal and wholly
incarnate. The person of Jesus is the revelation of the person of God.
And the gospel, which is the continuous extension of his teaching and
presence, reveals the priority of the personal over all secondary, institutional forms. An extraordinary discovery is waiting to be made. It is
that the goal of each person's pilgrimage is the transcendent completion of each person realized in Jesus. We are made one with him
who is one with God. To call this a 'relationship' with Jesus attempts
inadequately to express the mystery of a union that is realized both in
the power of our faith in him and his love for us. It *is* a relationship
with Jesus but it is also an undifferentiated participation in his life.
The deeper our journey of faith takes us the more it appears that this
life is the life of God. We call it the Trinity, the explosion of love that
is the Being of God, who is the ground of all Being. Because God is the

infinitely uncontainable energy of love, because God simply *is* love, God seeks himself beyond himself. In obedience to the dynamic of the divine being, God seeks another to whom he can give himself, into whom God can empty and lose divinity. For Jesus *we* are that Other. He has sent the Spirit of his self to dwell in our hearts.

The wonder of all this is too much. It is so overwhelming that it must make us humble. It also fills us with confidence. The personal vocation of each person is to experience it in the immediacy of faith and so to share, as St Peter tells us, in the 'very Being of God'. To experience it we need to let go of all secondary forms and expressions. We need to pass over beyond belief to faith. In the new state of faith we are drawn into the ever-expanding self-knowledge of God. We know God only with God's own self-knowledge. We know ourselves and others only in God. This is only very inadequately expressed as a 'relationship'. The mutual presence and self-giving that is the love-force of the Trinity transcends difference but does not obliterate distinction. In the same way, our relationship with God in Jesus is infinitely greater than the dialogue of two self-contained individuals. There is achieved between us a common consciousness, a single ground of being we can only call love.

Any of the many mysteries of love that make up and point to this reality is the fruit of faith rather than belief. With those we love we have a mysterious bond, something so close it is indefinable. It is a mutual commitment to each other's uniqueness and an unconditional acceptance of inalienable communion. This is just how we are loved by God and how we are empowered to return that love. The wonder of love is that it always creates its own universe, transforming the mundane and finite into a world of meaning and mystery radiant everywhere with a primal clear light that originates deep within our own spirit. This new creation generated by love builds up into an expanding universe through the power of faith – unconditional commitment to what is real but unseen.

The world desperately needs men and women filled with this faith. It is faith that is both the precondition and the medium for the communication of any personal reality. As the ultimate revelation of the personal the gospel is, as St Paul says, a way that begins and ends in faith. Perhaps never more than today has the world needed a Church filled with men and women of faith – their 'eyes fixed on Jesus', the Invisible One among us, as the Letter to the Hebrews puts it. If it is to respond to this need the Church must sink its consciousness deeper than its beliefs and into the roots of faith, in fact into the mind of Christ. We do this only at the bedrock of our being where the pure consciousness of Jesus fills and sustains us. In a sense Jesus himself *is* our faith, just as the person we love is really our love.

As a Church we are not travel agents handing out brochures to places we have never visited. We are explorers of a country without frontiers. We discover little by little it is not a place or a state but a person. We are not communicating a script, because we are neither actors nor audience. In harmony with this person and in the light of Jesus all roles have been burned away. Only persons are left, open to each other in love. This is the Church.

To meditate is to accept that the exploration of the universe of God is the meaning and authenticity of our life. It is to become rooted in faith, like Abraham obeying the call to go out to a land destined for himself and his heirs and leaving home without knowing where he was going. After meditating even for a short while you understand that commitment in faith to this reality is always deepening. There is always the home, the familiar ground of our ideas and plans and dreams, to leave behind us as we move more surely towards the heart of reality.

The price of a gospel of absolute power is absolute commitment. As we sit to meditate each day we encounter and are made one with this power at a level of reality deeper than belief and more enduring than the images and concepts of belief. And as we get up from each meditation to re-commit ourselves to the responsibilities of life we bring the power of this purer reality into every part of our ordinary life. It is through meditation that we put faith into practice.

We *are* invited to believe in Jesus. But belief soon leads on to something greater, to faith in him. Our faith then becomes the potential to resonate with him, to be in harmony with him who is in harmony with God. It is a wonder beyond explanation that we have found the way to place ourselves within this harmony. The way of the mantra is the harmonic of faith. Saying the mantra *includes* belief but also sets us free from the inherent limitations of the ideas, images and words of belief. The mantra bridges the gap between belief and experience because it bridges them as the sacrament of faith. Travelling across that gap is going beyond ourselves just as Jesus has gone beyond himself before us and from that further shore (within us) calls us to follow.

We must cross over too if we are to awaken in the heart of reality, in Jesus, who is awake within the heart of God.

As we prepare to enter another Lent, to strengthen the disciplines of this passing-over let us keep one another in our hearts. This is a time of conversion – a time to turn from what is passing away in order to be at one with the one who is eternal.

With much love,

John Main OSB
(February 1981)

After Christmas, the coach house on the monastery grounds was converted into a guest house, which enabled us to receive more women and married couples. We continued to receive many guests, particularly in this period from Europe, where, we kept hearing, weekly meditation groups were forming. Bishop Henry Hill, one of our first oblates, resigned from the Anglican diocese of Ontario and came to live in the community as a resident ecumenical oblate while continuing his work of dialogue between the Orthodox and Anglican churches.

17

THE PRESENT CHRIST

My Dearest Friends,

We celebrated the Easter liturgies of Holy Saturday night here in the monastery with our resident guests and many others. During the Vigil it became very clear to me in a fresh way how much the mystery of Christ consists in his *nearness*.

If something is distant it is strange or foreign, rather than truly mysterious. For example, when we objectify something (or someone) we may admire it but its essential identity remains alien because we have set it at a distance, or on a pedestal, far from ourselves. We and the objectified remain mutually isolated. And so even if we contemplate it from this distance we are unchanged by what we 'contemplate'. But if, as when we are truly present to the mystery of God, instead of objectifying it we are humble enough to be one with it in its nearness; if we can resonate finely with the mystery, then we *are* changed. We enter another and more creative way of being. The agent of all objectification, all distancing and alienation is the ego. It is the subliminal voice in our consciousness that urges us to be separate, even from what we worship or love. The fading of this voice of the tempter is also the dawning of the reality we enter as the Kingdom of Heaven. It is a reality we discover in and through union.

We know something or someone fully when we experience and simultaneously understand the experience. This happens when subject and object are transcended in the consciousness of the state of union. We can only fully understand how close Christ is to us from within this egoless state of union. We only know him with his own self-knowledge. This knowledge of union is love and it is more than what we generally mean by 'relationship'. It is more consummated than what we usually call dialogue. And it is more incarnate and tangible than an 'idea'. The deeply moving symbols of the Easter Vigil brought all this home to me because they point beyond themselves and beyond ourselves towards a fuller dimension of meaning. Not even the most sacred symbol, word or gesture can express the fullness of the reality of Christ; that is a reality known in an intimacy that transcends sign and ego and is felt as both personal and universal. When we bless the fire at the beginning of the Vigil we become part of a pre-historic dimension of humanity. Appropriately, we begin the night's re-enactment of human redemption with a ritual that dates from the dawn of human consciousness. The fire we light burns right into our deepest atavistic memory. A few moments later, in the lighting of the paschal candle from this same fire we are reminded of the nearness and presentness of Christ throughout history.

Later in the evening when we bless the baptismal water we re-enact a primary symbol of the source of life and consciousness which is also full of meaning as a force of purification and clarification. By immersing the candle in the water we enact the unique synthesis that has occurred in Christ. We are transferred from a distant way of being to encounter what is immediate and present. The symbols remind us that the flame of the Christ consciousness has come to dwell in our hearts and that 'we possess the mind of Christ' (1 Corinthians 2.16).

Christ's personal presentness to us is an aspect of his universal presentness in all time. As Christian thinkers understood from the beginning, the redemptive love of Jesus universalized for mankind on the Cross is situated in the centre of all consciousness by the Resurrection. It travels both backwards and forwards through space and time, uniting every human consciousness in him. From this historical moment, both 'in and out of time', humanity has been plunged into a radically new way of being present to the mystery of God. We have been touched by a pure ray of reality that has opened our eyes to the ambiance within which we live and move and have our being. We are now empowered *to be with* God in an unprecedented way by participating directly in the plenitude of God's Being. We no longer have to regard this Being as an external reality, an object of devotional or intellectual projection. And so we no longer have to imagine our creating source as an external object. This objectification alienates us from God and is the root of what we call 'sin'. Christ's redemptive forgiveness of sin is not the reprieve of a judge but the embrace of a lover. Because redemption *is* our being brought near to God in Christ we need no longer focus on God as an external object. Instead we are lifted beyond all images to be in the presence of the truth revealed in silence of perfect communion. The eye with which we see is the eye that sees us. Our vision itself is Christ.

In the Resurrection we are absolved from the need to objectify God. No longer do we have to talk to God, to appease or petition him. 'Your Father knows what your needs are before you ask him,' Jesus assures us. From that eternal moment in time when Jesus awoke to his union with the Father humanity passed beyond the stage of its spiritual infancy. In that moment it matured into the 'full stature of Christ'. This moment of Christ is found in the centre of our being, in our own heart, where his spirit lives and grows like a seed buried in the ground. Finding that moment is the work of meditation. It is a joyful and vitalizing work because we move into the heart in a faith that knows that the moment has already dawned and is born imperishably. Once we know this union in our own experience our whole existence is reborn. It is known to be united in a wholeness that is holiness. And this is all the work of a moment, the moment of Christ.

We are not only freed from the need to see ourselves and God dualistically. We are actually summoned *not* to. 'The time has come, indeed it is already here' when we are called to worship God in spirit and in truth. By saying this to the Samaritan woman Jesus calls us all into a new dimension of spiritual consciousness. We can no longer persist in the dualism of spiritual infancy and be in the truth of the moment of Christ. The indwelling of the Spirit of Christ is not just a gift, a special offer, a grace we can accept or decline. It is a reality, the door into the sheepfold of boundless union. It is the force in our destiny that brings us to completion. The wonder is that this summons is made by love and that it educates us with infinite gentleness.

The gentleness, however, is purposeful and determined. It is linked to the movement of all creative energy back to its source. The energy of the Spirit of Christ is unquenchable and so ultimately it is unavoidable. Even in the ordinariness of daily life it is steadily, wonderfully present. There is more than just symbolic meaning in that the power of the Resurrection reaches us in the springtime of the year when we rediscover all nature's energies of growth, cosmic and yet creative of the delicate marvels of earth's beauty.

The human condition is growth in all its aspects. In those aspects of our life we can measure, growth happens within the cycle of birth and decline. We bud, blossom and fade. The more subtle dimensions of life are not measurable. They are not conditioned by time or space and so their growth has infinite potential. Growth can occur only in union, through the interconnectedness of being. Like all growing realities we lean into our destiny, fullness of being and we need roots to connect us unitively with the nourishing source of life. In our true nature the root is Christ and the source is the Father. Union with Christ is the fruit of the mingling of his consciousness with ours at the most truly human level. It is the heart of the human mystery and within it all growth, finite and infinite is a conscious awakening to it. Perhaps the greatest mystery is that even the most finite growth experienced in the cycle of birth and decline is radically transformed by the power of this union. The Resurrection is the saving of the whole person, heart, mind, spirit and mortal body. This affirmation of the divine potential of the whole human condition happens because the life-source of the Father flows into us through our rootedness in Christ. The channel of com-munication is the human consciousness of Jesus open to the reality of God and to us also, dwelling with the Father and in us. The openness of his human consciousness to the Father allows us to realize union with the Father also, through him, in *our* human consciousness. With him, in him, we travel beyond ourselves, through him into the heart of God. This is transcendence realized.

Jesus told his disciples, 'all that the Father has is mine'. He has revealed to us everything he has heard from the Father (John 15.16; 16.15). As a result of this oneness of Father and Son and of the Son's oneness with us we are able to grow into fullness. Human beings are innately restless in their condition of growth because we have such an expanding capacity to be in the truth. We are impelled by the inner expansiveness of our own being to align ourselves to our destiny and to enter the hard-won simplicity of the egoless state that growth demands. We need to let go of the past in order to venture upon what is to come without the resistance imposed on growth by desire. We are insatiable for truth. Above all we thirst for the truth of our own being because only there can we be sure that we are not engaging only with an image or theory of truth but with truth incarnate. This experience born in self-knowledge is what we intuitively recognize as reality.

The self-revelation of the Father that occurs in our union with the consciousness of Jesus is the authenticity of human life. Without contact with this source of being we remain rootless, meaningless, theoretical and static. Without the touch of truth we stay as imaginary creatures, struggling to make fantasy or intellect substitute for the real. Attraction to the truth is the deepest characteristic of the human spirit. By growing towards the real, the true, we are far more deeply in touch with ourselves than in fantasy. Until we abandon illusion and touch the centre of our being we think this centre is a hidden place where we are most alone, closed in on ourselves. This is why so few complete the journey. But once there, an opening of self occurs, towards an unbounded wholeness that is God's manifesting in us. Here we find an utter simplicity in our contact with truth. The revelation of the Father becomes actual. The Greek word for truth is *aletheia*. It means a revealing, an uncovering. To find the self-revealing truth we need not images but an open heart.

Christ reveals humanity's new involvement in the truth and it makes us wonderfully, terribly present to God. Even rituals and symbols cannot distance or objectify the one who has drawn so near to us: God with us, Emmanuel. If we learn to reciprocate, to be with God, we grow in union and the divine presence (closer to us than we are to ourselves) becomes not a source of fear but of peace. 'He himself is our peace', a harmony of being that is both the union and fulfilment of all creative energy. Harmony is achieved when we take a step of faith into the silence where truth resides, the contemplative step from image to reality. In the marvellous dispensation of God we have only to take the first step for us to be swept along by the Spirit's power for the rest of the way. The truth we yearn for is not a cold platonic wisdom but a movement of love. The indwelling of the Spirit of Christ is itself this movement of life resolved into a person and it lingers within us with the ache of love until it evokes a fully personal response.

The presentness of Christ to us is what drives our transition from image to reality, from fantasy to person. We are the 'heirs of the prophets' as the New Testament declares. In the new modality of being in which the risen Christ is the universal centre all signs and symbols explode with meaning. Even the most sacred and potent symbol is now only a stage in the revelation of a reality with which we are already one. So, we are called to 'worship the Father in spirit and in truth', because in the immediacy of Christ's presence this oneness is palpably manifest. In communion 'to be with' is 'to be in love'. An early Christian writer put it graphically: 'Who bows to the statue of the King when the King himself is present?'

This is what makes the Christian revelation so contemporary in every period of history that it can be said to define the term 'modern'. Perhaps even what we call modern consciousness is in fact the Christ-consciousness of union. This is the awareness we hear in the New Testament when, for example, Peter, in the portico of Solomon, declares with the authority of transcendent experience, 'and so said all the prophets from Samuel onwards; with one voice they all predicted this present time' (Acts 3.24).

The faith generated by Christ-centred consciousness contains this extraordinary sense of having reached the fullness of time. Of course, repeated just as a theological formula it sounds astonishingly arrogant. But spoken out of the experience of the Spirit who inspired the prophets to imagine such a time it becomes mysteriously persuasive and inclusive. 'All these things that happened to them were symbolic and were recorded for our benefit as a warning. For, upon us the fulfilment of the ages has come' (1 Corinthians 10.11).

To hear this proclaimed with authority helps us to awaken to an unprecedented experience – to the presentness of Christ in all the dimensions of time and also to the unity of humanity that this presence creates. We can recognize human unity today because we meet in the same place and time and before the same mystery. The universal presence of Christ creates unity and it is why 'he himself is our peace'.

It is intoxicating to think that we are in the convergence point of human evolution when the destined growth of consciousness in all creation returns to its source. But it also carries with it a huge responsibility. If we are no longer in the infancy of humanity then we are summoned, personally not anonymously, communally not institutionally, to a new level of maturity of spirit. Because of the seductive power of illusion we prefer to postpone rather than engage with the work of this maturing. And yet because the end of one period of preparation soon becomes the beginning of another phase of perfecting we are summoned to reach out towards this perfection. Our human vocation is no less than to be holy. Not as the word might suggest to modern ears, 'holier than thou', but holy as God is, in whose fullness of being we already share (2 Peter 1.4).

The truth of human destiny that Jesus has uncovered for us is the new age of presence. It calls for a correspondingly new understanding of how we share in the Trinitarian mystery. Because of the new Christo-centric consciousness we understand, in ways that are disturbingly personal *and* universal, that we do not so much exist in relation to God as subsist within God as the ground of being. We are called to know, and know fully not just notionally, that no one can be outside the ground of being that God is. This is why in the light of the new Christo-centric consciousness prayer is not talking-to but being-with.

In the past humanity thought of itself as a creature summoned to *surrender* to the Creator. Human beings were dominated by a sense of the infinite transcendence and superiority of the divine mystery. This extreme sense of the otherness of God, however, did not lead to true transcendence. We were not swept out of and beyond ourselves, into the mystery of our being but rather locked into a fear of what exerts so powerful a force over us. Human prayer in this paralysed condition of fear and non-growth became no more than a psychological technique of coping with what is perhaps our most fundamental terror – the fear of extinction. However great our suffering or disappointment, we are more deeply terrified by the idea of non-being. If knowledge of God stops short at this fear of divine transcendence God becomes little more than a threat to our survival. Then prayer becomes no more than a way of pleasing or placating, petitioning or manipulating God in the hope of turning his anger away from us. All the time fear grips us in the vice of paralysis.

This is God merely as *Creator*. Jesus uncovers God to us as *Abba*, Father. In this most personal and yet universal of the many divine self-revelations human dependence on God shifts from being a source of terror into a source of infinite joy and wonder. We are because God is. God is our being and therefore our being is good, as God is good. We have nothing to fear from such goodness because the nature of his goodness is pure love. The Trinity's explosive and loving creativity burns away fear. The ground of our most haunting fear – the fear of isolation and extinction – is exposed as illusory. The dream-world created by the ego which is the source of our sense of isolation, fear and loneliness, the feeling that the world itself is only a terrible mistake or a meaningless accident, is dissolved by that experience of love.

In the Christian vision of reality prayer is the way we see and feel that the human condition is not separateness but communion, being-with. This is the effect of the Christo-centric consciousness. It both commands and empowers us to *be-with* everyone in the harmony of our experience of communion. 'Love one another as I have loved you.' In giving us his whole self Jesus authenticates this teaching of human and divine unity with absolute authority. In the light of his teaching we no longer think of ourselves summoned just to 'surrender' to God. In any act of surrender we remain within the limits of human failure to dissolve the illusion of dualism. There always remains an *I* to surrender, and a *You* to be surrendered to. It matters little whether such dualism is retained due to fear or false piety. In either case it is a kind of spiritual schizophrenia. How can we 'surrender' to the one with whom we are already united?

But we can *awaken to* and realize our *empathy with* the Christo-centric consciousness. For modern people the most urgent task is to come to terms with this new way of being with God. Our relationship with the divine has to be understood primarily in terms of union rather than surrender. Nevertheless in order to realize this empathy with the divine a kind of surrender *is* involved. In fact this is the dynamic process of all experience of love where self is lost in the other. But rather than seeing it as surrender *to*, better see it as the surrender *of* – of isolation, fear, possessiveness, self-centredness and all the other demons lurking in the breeding-ground of the ego. It is the surrender, the *letting-go* of this reflective, divided self and of the false image of self projected in self-consciousness that we most fear. If we can, even for a moment (the first step of faith), move aside from the distorted field of egocentric vision we glimpse reality from the Christo-centric perspective. We gaze upon the selfless state of love with unimaginable wonder and excitement. But the knot that seems to bind us is a self-contradiction, a strange compulsion, because we are frightened to lose our fear.

This becomes evident quite quickly to anyone who has begun to meditate. We become aware, almost simultaneously, of the wonderful new perspective on reality *and* of the strange reluctance to leave the old, narrow world of the ego. The meditator comes to learn that the way through this double-bind is the way of poverty. We learn this by embracing the freedom of the poverty of the mantra. The results are at the same time the loss of fear and the winning of freedom. It is difficult to communicate this to people who are not meditating. Yet it has to be communicated. There is an apostolic dynamic in the deep interior poverty of the Christo-centric consciousness, the need to tell others about it as Jesus saw and instructed his disciples to do. How? Somehow, provided the poverty is generously embraced it communicates itself. This is why the mantra is rather caught than taught.

The most frequent objection I hear is that this is not what Jesus meant by loss of self or that this is not about Christianity but a form of Platonism or impersonal Eastern mysticism. In response to this, I can only say that if Jesus meant a partial loss of self he would have said so and that the mystery of Jesus is precisely his oneness with God and his oneness with us. How can we understand what he meant when he said 'the Father and I are one' unless we enter into the personal experience of our oneness with him? To enter that experience is prayer and so it is also an entry into the prayer of Jesus. The koan of the saying, 'the Father and I are one' is mysterious, irresolvable. But it dilates beyond logic in the experience of the Spirit, which is the bond of oneness between Father and the Son, the prayer of Jesus that becomes our prayer.

'We do not even know how to pray but the Spirit prays within us.' The Spirit guarantees the hopefulness of laying down our life, of leaving self behind. There are other forms of selflessness which are not so positive: self-rejection, self-hatred, merging ourselves with mass-hysteria or materialism or wilfully anonymous ways of denying life. These are those forms of surrendering-*to* that intensify the anguish of isolation. In meditation, on the other hand, we embrace the healthy surrender *of* isolation and we do it in the power of the Spirit of oneness, the Spirit of love. The mistake we often made in the past was to believe that we had to be *thinking* about this Spirit for it to be there to help us. The Spirit, however, is unceasingly present and active within and among us. By its silent abiding presence it calls us into its own unified consciousness. The irony is that while we are trying to conjure it up by thinking about it or by imagining what it would be like to experience it, we are not present to the Spirit. The first step in contemplation and the beginning of a deeper life of faith is to stop thinking about God at the time of prayer. We have to *believe* that he is with us and we in him, not just mentally but with the whole of our being. This turns belief into faith and helps us to experience the meaning of the words of Jesus, 'Dwell in me as I in you.'

The path of meditation is the path of faith. The sacrament of faith is silence. The door to silence is the mantra. Once we begin this path it is not long before we understand that loss of self is not abnegation but empathy, not an extinction of individuality but a communion of persons. As we become more rooted in the deep ground of our being we experience clarification and affirmation in the purifying silence of the mystery that manifests its presence in our heart.

The power of the Resurrection of Jesus collects all time and space into a single, universal focus. Within the microcosm of the human heart the cosmos has also been radically transformed by this power condensed into the single point of pure and limitless love. We are freed from the illusion that we are outside creation or outside God. Through the power that dwells in the open space in the centre of our being we pass beyond ourselves into divine fullness of being, the *pleroma* of Christ. We need only to be simple, to be rooted in reality, faithful to our pilgrimage of meditating each morning and evening. Then we realize union with our point of origin. Our destination and the teacher, our source and companion are one. Jesus assures us that 'I call you servants no longer; a servant does not know what his master is about. I have called you friends because I have disclosed to you everything I have heard from my Father.' It is this sharing of himself that makes the pilgrimage possible.

With much love,

John Main OSB
(April 1981)

Through the spring of 1981, a great enrichment of our community life and a source of theological stimulus came, as usual, from the Benedictine charism of hospitality. Guests came to deepen their meditation with us, but they also shared in the daily manual work and shared in other spiritual practices, such as the Office, the Eucharist and periods of lectio divina *(spiritual reading). Bishop Crowley paid us one of his regular, encouraging visits. It was unusual for a bishop to understand so well what a monastery is about. His farseeing vision of the Church made him open to development within the tradition and an agent of change. Laurence Freeman visited meditation groups in England, France and Germany and spent time in Trosly-Breuil, the headquarters of L'Arche – Jean Vanier's communities for the mentally handicapped. In Germany, he visited our young oblates in Wurzburg who were teaching meditation at the university. Returning to Montreal, he took over the editorship of* Monastic Studies, *a journal of monastic theology and scholarship formerly edited from Mount Saviour Monastery. The work of the community extended further through the publication of John Main's* Word into Silence *in England and the USA. With the* Communitas *series of his taped talks on meditation, made at the weekly groups meeting at the monastery, a new outreach for his teaching was launched. This series of cassettes began as a monthly subscription and continued in five new issues. (Now also on CD, they still inspire new and ongoing meditation groups around the world.)*

18

SACRAMENTAL VISION

My Dearest Friends,

Greetings in the Lord. Today we have been celebrating the Feast of St Benedict. It seems an appropriate day to send this letter as I know many of you share with us his vision and are inspired in your daily life by what he taught.

Benedict understood the Christian life as a commitment to ordinary reality rooted in the contemplative experience. For 1500 years this has inspired people in diverse walks of life to follow their different vocations to the one God. I remember hearing some years ago an old monk quoting a description of monastic generosity of spirit: 'on things of no account an unaccountable zeal bestowing'. It is the particular and the way we do small things that reveals the universal. A commitment to perfection in all we do for its own sake enables us to leave ourselves behind. The genius of Benedict's vision is that, whereas this approach could easily become fanatical, he renders it humane, compassionate and tolerant – truly Christian. The power of his vision is its humanity. Often a religious vision of life loses its human focus but for Benedict it was through the humanity of Jesus – and our own humanity – that we enter the divine mystery.

In June I returned from Ireland in time to celebrate Corpus Christi (the Body and Blood of Christ) with the Community. Annual feasts like this have an important part in clarifying the Christian rhythms of daily life. They do not become merely routines as they are never celebrated in exactly the same way if we have ourselves grown in the interval between the celebrations. Like the Mass itself the great feasts express a mystery we are continually growing into. Although the outward rites are the same, each time they can convey a deeper, clearer aspect of the mystery. If we are committed to the continuous penetration of the mystery our rituals never become routines and the mystery expands. Each year the feast of Corpus Christi gives us an opportunity to focus, within the liturgical mystery itself, on how we have developed. Like all liturgy it does this by bringing thought and experience into greater harmony. This convergence is necessary, especially in regard to the Eucharist, which focuses our whole religious and sacramental life and provides us with a vital means of strength to remain on the pilgrimage.

The general experience is that for a Christian who has been meditating for some time the Mass becomes a more meaningful mystery. This is especially clear when, as in this community, meditation is integrated with the Mass immediately after the communion. Meditating at that point brings home very powerfully the true significance of all the words and rituals used in worship. They are then seen not communicating something to God but as preparing ourselves to enter communion with God. In the light of meditation we see that all religious words point and lead to silence of spirit in reverent attention to the presence of God.

The Mass is the supreme symbol of the Christian mystery of Incarnation. In a concrete and tangible form it teaches us that reality is incarnate not conceptual. It reminds us to commit to this reality just as we are, fallible and fickle but redeemed by a power that is totally committed to us. The extraordinary revelation of the gospel is the value of the ordinary and its potential to be transfigured by this divine, universal energy of love. A life built on the discipline of morning and evening meditation is rooted in an ordinary way in this power and so our ordinary lives are constantly being touched and transformed by it. What at first we might seem to lose by sacrificing the time for meditation in a busy life is not worth comparing with what we gain. Indeed we regain even what we think we lose in the heightened clarity and calmness of mind which meditation brings to even ordinary decision-making and also because of the better sense of the value of time and priorities along with a growing reluctance to waste it. Above and beyond this a light is shed on life and radiates everything to reveal its true meaning and sacredness. Meditation deepens our appreciation of the Mass because it awakens a sacramental perception of our whole life as a ritual of the love of God.

As meditation highlights even the most ordinary, routine aspects of life it draws out their latent sacramental value and hidden meaning. There is so much discontent and frustration in our world because so many have lost touch with this value and meaning. Looking at life and work for meaning people find only a series of self referring egocentric values turned in upon themselves. The search for meaning is also a search for the sacramental nature of the ordinary and immediate. The mysterious nature of the world and the value given to it by its divine origin is there waiting to be found. It is not our invention. It is not even our own meaning reflected back to us by the world. The things and processes of the world have an innate meaning and value. This is why we are transported in wonder at the beauty of creation and feel ourselves to be more meaningful by being part of it.

Our own human meaning and purpose, however, point us towards the originating centre of all meaning, to the Creator. Divine reality is absolute because in God the meaning of all is focused and realized. In God we live and move and have our being. So we cannot awaken to God without awakening in wonder and compassion to the reality of our humanity, in general *and* in the particular persons who are for us the sacraments of God's mystery and with whom we turn towards God's presence. The sacramental value of people, processes and things all lead us to this presence. Modern people are so often sad because they think this value has been lost or exposed as an illusion. The truth is that neither we nor creation have lost the divine radiance. But we *have* lost the faculty of seeing it. To be saved is to regain it and redemption is achieved when we see creation through the eyes of Christ. Extraordinary though it may seem we can see even more: with the vision of Christ we see into the divine mystery itself.

St Benedict reminds us in chapter 19 of the Rule that 'the divine presence is everywhere'. As our spirit matures in the course of life we grow in our capacity to see this presence in every dimension of our being and in all our experience. Yet we cannot see it unless we are prepared to become one with what we see (just as we are one with the very power of seeing). Union with Christ is the way into union with the Father. This progressive process of unification is the deepest mystery of life and the greatest power in creation. We can only be aware of it imperfectly and through experience. No one can stand back on a spectator's bench and watch the process at work because *we* are not the centre of the process. Even our own centre, our objectifying consciousness, is being unified through the experience of seeing. All this, the process of 'oneing', is the work of the Spirit. The Spirit itself is one with her own work as she is with the Father and the Son, from whom she proceeds. The form and manner of the process varies according to the material which it is happening through, but it is 'the same Spirit working in all and through all'. The Spirit crying 'Abba' in our heart leads us into union with the Father through the Son. The Spirit unites the bread and wine with the body and blood of Christ and unites those who stand around the altar with each other and with herself.

The Spirit is the power of God who is love. One of the discoveries we make through the experience of love is to find our own *innerness* in the *other*. Our self becomes the temple of their interiority. This is the loss, the transcendence, of self-centredness as well as the restoration to real selfhood in the beloved. Another way of saying this is that the division we assume to be so definite between the inner and outer worlds is simply dissolved (gradually, perhaps, but no less surely for being gradual) by the power of love. All the energy we had used to maintain the illusion of dividedness is transformed into liberty of spirit and is expressed in the joyfulness of the person who is 'in love'.

We see reality divided into inner and outer worlds because our mind is divided. The accumulative force of meditation heals this wound in consciousness: the effect of healing is to make whole. Increasingly we see reality as a seamless whole. As we become one with ourselves we are no longer spectators watching the world (and ourselves) through cracked spectacles. What power restores us to the sense and knowledge of wholeness in ourselves of the harmony between self and creation? It is the power of the wholeness itself, the uninterrupted presence of God in all persons and all things. To experience God as Creator is to experience the liberation that every encounter with truth – with things as they really are – provokes. We know God as Creator, always creating, by encountering reality in ordinary experience as having a transcendent centre and meaning: *all* reality because reality cannot be divided. There is not a 'sacred' area where this vision is seen and other 'profane' areas where it is not. To see it is to see it everywhere. The religious response to life springs from wonder and a sense of the yet to be completed potential of life. As the etymology of the word implies, religion 'relinks' us to the power that brings life to its destined fullness, which is its wholeness. The different parts of ordinary experience are then no longer alienated from each other. We are empowered to see one area of experience in relation to all the other areas. We see with the vision of God. We see the same presence of God shining with supreme, benevolent simplicity in both the mental and material dimensions.

The presence of God is never a partial revelation of love. Wherever God is God is wholly present. This is the human ability to be only 'half-there' because of our divided, distracted nature. Do we not know this only too well from the sad experience of being with someone who is evidently not as present to us as we are to them; or of being unable to concentrate on what we are doing? To meditate is to know the value of paying complete attention to whatever we are doing or to whomever we are with. Learning to do this is the work of simple fidelity to the mantra. It opens the way to 'sharing in the very being of God' which, St Peter says, is human destiny. God turns with complete and undivided attention to humanity in Christ. Wholly turned toward us means wholly loving. That is why we do not say just that God is loving but that God is love. To be wholly loving is to be love, to be one with what we see.

If God were in any degree self-centred – not wholly attentive and concentrated in the movement of love – then we would be able to analyse, to objectify God. We know God as an object, a manifestation of reality rather than the ground of being. Then we could 'see God and live'. As it is, the divine wholeness means we know God only by participation in God's own self-knowledge which is the ever-flowing stream of self-transcendence, creative other-centredness. To enter the life of the Trinity through union with the Son is not at all settling down to contemplate a finished picture. It means to be swept off the side roads of self-centredness onto the highway, the living stream of God's eternal creative love.

The presence of God would be imperceptible to us in daily reality if we did not already 'possess' that presence through God already knowing himself in us. 'The love I speak of is not our love for God but his love for us,' St John said. We are touched into consciousness and self-knowledge by God's attentive, loving presence. The Holy Spirit is 'breathed into us'. We awaken to this inner and outer presence with an ever growing wonder and joyful confidence in our own reality. We cannot see reality until we ourselves are seen, realized, made present by God's presence. To know ourselves is to know God in us, to know with the knowledge that God has of us. This dynamic of growth in consciousness that is so profoundly *reciprocal* underlies the paradox of Jesus: that we find our life in the losing of it. Expanding the frontiers of being by growth in the mind of Christ is a centrifugal process. It happens from the centre of our being outwards. We make this journey 'outwards' by the 'inner' journey of meditation.

In the Eucharist we have a real, living symbol of the unity of the inner and outer faces of reality. What is the 'real presence' of Christ in the Eucharist? It is not that the presence of God-in-Christ is *less* real in other dimensions of life. God cannot be more or less present because God is indivisible. But we can be more or less open to God's presence because we are divided. In the Eucharist we engage a fully human particular sign that realizes Christ's universal presence. We call this presence real because *our* grasp of reality is stronger at that level of human encounter through which Jesus gave the gift of himself. Human love is the necessary first stage for the realization of the full nature of divine love. 'The glory of God is man fully alive,' exclaimed St Irenaeus. In the Eucharist, we encounter the human love of Jesus. Because it is fully humanized it is integral with the reality of God who is love. Having loved wholly he becomes love. In the Eucharist we meet, not an effect or reflection of Christ, but his own person, given to us and universally present in its unique and particular human nature. We enter into communion with the one who is the human sacrament and incarnation of God.

The universal presence of God in the universe manifests the divine reality underlying both matter, mind and spirit. It reminds us that our experience of reality is always incarnate but has an unlimited potential. This may seem an abstract way of talking. How can we imagine 'creation'? Yet, out of a primary experience of love, we can see and believe in this presence. We can then continue to commit ourselves to the vision of reality that love initiates. To believe without imagining is faith. It is faith that is the condition for the knowledge of God in every degree. The meaning of the Eucharist is an experience open only to someone who is in this condition of faith.

The nature of God is to be universal. Ordinary human nature is particular. We feel this most often when we make ordinary choices (our fundamental choice is assenting to the gift of our own being). God, however, does not have to choose, as all options coexist in the divine present. We, in our as still unrealized finitude, express the divine universality through the particular. The particular is the condition of choice. The Eucharist is the human mystery of Jesus choosing the particular meal of the Passover, with its particular (but universally meaningful) symbols of bread and wine, to express the universality, the divinity, of his love for all his human brothers and sisters.

We are moved to our deepest core by this universal love. In a profoundly moving way the Eucharist utters the weakness and limitations of the human. Some particular thing had to be *chosen* to express the universal. This in itself suggests the tragic nature of our finitude but it is also wonderfully appropriate when we see it as part of the larger mystery of which the Last Supper was an effective symbol. This larger mystery is the Cross; or rather, the acceptance of the Cross as the particular point where the love of Christ and the vulnerability love entails would culminate. The silence of the Cross stirs an essential question in every human heart. How did the finitude and weakness of the man Jesus break through to universal presence and power?

Limited and vulnerable, Jesus was like us. But he made what we alone cannot make – a total gift of self. His love for humanity was in his fidelity to truth and this expressed his commitment of self to all. It is what makes him still the 'man for others'. The totality of this commitment was the love of God at work in Jesus. It was not that he merely co-operated with this love, but that he was one with it and, in his essential identity, was so from the beginning. 'True man and true God.'

The folly of the Cross is the wisdom of God. Entire and unlimited as was the spirit of Jesus in accepting the Cross, it was still necessary that the Cross was his experience of failure, defeat and death. In the radiance of his integrity, however, the finality of the Cross becomes the beginning of something of eternal meaning. To those who see it with faith it shows that the spirit not only survives death but is glorified, made fully alive through death. The Cross is the extreme point of the development of human finitude, of man's being limited by the particular. But by the completeness, the wholeness of Jesus' commitment to this particular, it becomes the universal means of liberation into the reality of God.

In the Eucharist we encounter the frailty of the human, the immediacy and the ordinariness of the bread and wine as well as the fallible persons in the community which is itself a real part of the sacramental presence. As St Augustine said, we ourselves are upon the paten that the priest raises to the Father. We encounter the Cross. We die with Christ. We do so in the power of his Resurrection which sheds its light both backwards upon the Cross and forwards upon the gathering together of all creation in Christ. The Cross remains a particular moment of complete human weakness. The Resurrection does not negate the tragedy of the Cross. But it is charged with the Presence of God that made the Resurrection happen.

The Mass transforms the ordinary into the mysterious without betraying its particularity or frailty. Similarly, meditation leads from the particular to the universal without betraying our wholeness or the strange gift of our mortality. No part of life is left untransformed by meditation because we meditate from the centre outwards. And as we travel deeper into this centre the outward is transformed and unified with the inwardness of God's presence. The mantra consecrates our whole life and, like the sacramental mystery of the Eucharist, it becomes an outward sign of an ever deeper inner reality that is fully known only in faith.

Around the eucharistic table there are no observers, only partici- pants. If anyone is there to observe themselves or others, then *their* presence is not real. The Lord, however, is still present to them – for 'if we are faithless he remains faithful for he cannot deny himself'. The complete and unconditional fidelity of his being present to us exposes us to a power of love that will eventually impel us to turn our self- centred attention outwards to him who dwells in silence and love within us.

This is the dynamic power of our stillness in meditation. The aspect of consciousness that is looking for results, searching for experience or calculating spiritual progress is simply not part of this movement towards God. On the pilgrimage we find that this is of no significance. God's presence to us is stronger than our absence from God. All we need to do is to be open to the condition of faith that is our integral openness to God's presence. By faithfulness to the mantra, which is an incarnate movement of faith, we allow the power of this indwelling presence to radiate outwards. By being fully and personally open to it, it is *realized*. So we are made real by reality. Just as the eucharistic community is made one by faith in the Body and Blood of Christ, so our personal inner unity is realized by the faith we bring to each time of meditation. From that inner unity we move outwards to realize our unity with others in the mystery of God.

We see the presence of God in Creation because God is present within us. We see reality because we are made real and we are made real by that presence. It is only necessary to be in the presence of the divine wholeness of God in order to be transformed. What is vital is that we learn how to be present. To learn it we have to accept the ascesis of unlearning a great deal about God and about ourselves. Thus unlearning and relearning is work because we have so complicated the simple truth encountered in meditation. It is the simple truth that the natural movement of our spirit is to rise above self-centredness by the opening of our consciousness to God *in the mind of Christ.*

Great harm to our understanding of this truth, which is integral to our ability to pray, is wrought by the impersonality and materialism that our society develops in all our attitudes. The value of *presence* has been replaced by the idea of function. What counts is not what a person is but what he or she does. The truth is rather that the value of action consists in the quality of being. Our experience of love contradicts these false assumptions, but they remain deep-rooted in modern consciousness. Meditation challenges it at root because when we meditate we are not trying to do anything. We are simply attending to the divine presence and learning to be present to it.

Each step we take, each time we meditate morning and evening this presence strengthens. We discover that to *be* does not mean to be isolated but to be realized in communion. Christ is eternally present to us and we grow in the capacity to be present to him. In realizing this reciprocal presence in communion the divine self-transcendence sweeps us out of the netherworld of self-centredness into the reality who is love.

We send you encouragement and support in the commitment you are making to this journey into the reality of God. We keep you present in our heart and ask you to hold us in yours.

With much love,

John Main OSB
(July 1981)

We heard about the development of the weekly meditation groups in Toronto and Ottawa. In May, John Main visited them and other Canadian centres to encourage them on their journey. In Montreal, we continued to grow in the richness and unpredictability of community life. The stroke suffered by one of our elderly resident oblates deepened for us St Benedict's words on the care of the sick, in whom, he said, we see Christ with special clarity. Another oblate, who had come with us from the lay community in England, married and moved to an apartment near the monastery. After conducting visitations and presiding over an abbatial election in the Irish Benedictine monastery of Glenstal, John Main went to Dublin to visit his old friend, Monsignor Tom Fehily, who had started the first Irish Christian meditation groups. Returning to Canada, he addressed a large assembly of religious sisters in eastern Canada.

19

THE CHRISTIAN CRISIS

My Dearest Friends,

The great challenge facing Christianity today is also a most vitalizing opportunity. This is the chance to put the essential Christian experience before the world. This may seem obvious enough until we distinguish between the *essential* and the *superficial* experience.

The redemptive and liberating power of Christ is *preached* at the superficial level but it is communicated, shared and *known* on the essential level of being. The superficial levels of life are not unimportant, however, because daily life and work are also integral to the spiritual journey. But the superficial easily becomes trivial, just an empty sign, unless it continually springs from the depths of spirit where our whole being is centred, renewed and daily refreshed. It is only too easy for very religious people to live very superficially because they become alienated from the depth of the reality which they proclaim and pretend to experience. The need to be in touch with the personal experience of that depth is essential to the teaching of Jesus and the whole Christian tradition. To be a disciple of this master means to be constantly mindful of the depth of spiritual power that lies beyond religiosity. The whole, living person always resides behind theology and philosophy.

This sense of personal, experiential depth is central to Christian teaching. We hear it in the Letter to the Hebrews and how modern it sounds:

> Let us then stop discussing the rudiments of Christianity. We ought not to be laying over again the foundations of faith in God ... Let us advance towards maturity, and so we shall, if God permits. (6.13)

One can be sincere enough living on the level of the ideas and images of religious faith but, as ordinary experience constantly reminds us, sincerity alone is not enough. Our call as Christians is to go to a level deeper than thought and image and sincerity. We are called to the depth encounter with reality itself which makes us authentic. We are not only called but *empowered* to respond by the transformation of consciousness that has occurred through the life of Jesus. The consciousness of a fully human being has opened in love to the infinite mystery of God. It has been swept out of itself into God without ceasing to be itself. The mystery of the Incarnation means that Jesus was and remains fully human, fully alive to us and also to the Father in his glorified state. So it is through his *human* consciousness that we make the journey he made into authenticity. Our call is to be realized by being bathed in the light of that reality, the reality that has glorified him. This is not only possible. It is in a unique way for each of us, unavoidable – or avoided at the cost of a wasted life. The Letter to the Hebrews calls it 'maturity', St John 'fullness of life'. St Peter says it means 'sharing in the very being of God'. St Paul calls it 'the strength and power of his spirit in your inner being'. This is the authenticity modern people are desperately seeking. We are seeking to be made 'real'.

Yet so many today feel the loss of the necessary spiritual power. The energy and environmental crisis is an expression of a deeper-rooted sense of the loss of spiritual resources. Both physically and spiritually there is something absurd in this 'crisis'. We speak of the energy crisis and we are the most wasteful, mindlessly over-productive generation ever to walk the earth. We speak of a crisis of faith while we are, each of us, and despite the depersonalizing forces that attack us, a temple of the living Spirit. Still the prevailing fear of imminent chaos is that our sources of power are running down and we are helpless. Below the surface of all our frenetic activity and endless self-distraction lies the fear that this entropy is as true of the spiritual and moral spheres of life as it is of the physical and socio-economic spheres.

And there *is* a complex interdependence between all these spheres. The visible surface of life is more than a reflection of the depths. It is part of the depths because our identity is the integration of everything we are. Moral consciousness is not only a sign of our Godlikeness but an expression of our *oneness* with the power that motivates all morality – the power of love. Christian vision sees surface and depths as they do really correspond. Both personal and collective experience bear this out. We have only to see how the social chaos that follows economic crisis so closely mirrors the moral confusion that follows the loss of spiritual power.

Our sense of an imminent disaster is justified only if we see no chance of affecting the momentum of events through an interior *metanoia* or change of direction. If, as the Christian vision claims, the external is intimately linked to the internal (this is what the Incarnation shows) then a purification of our interior reality should lead to the harmonization of external reality. The social vision of the gospel sees charity, not exploitation, characterizing human relationships, generosity not possessiveness controlling the economy, and freedom not fear shaping the psychological atmosphere. It is a vision, a revolutionary dream that comes true in some Christian communities even if only partially or for short periods of time. But any Christian revolution must be energized by centrifugal forces that radiate from a personal centre outwards not by ideological coercion. An ascending movement of liberation and expansion is the Christian vision of change, not, like most revolutions, a descending movement of aggression and constriction. This centrifugal revolution of the Gospels is conversion, the deep interior shift in the basic orientation of our being from self to what is beyond self.

Conversion is a rediscovery of our *true* self and of our participation in the reality of God which is so much greater than our own limited potential reality. Every conversion (and, as St Benedict understood, our whole life is a conversion, a turning to God) is an ever finer degree of awakening. The intrinsic momentum of human being urges us towards full wakefulness.

Awake, sleeper, rise from the dead
And Christ will shine upon you. (Ephesians 5.14)

To awaken is to expand consciousness. As we open our eyes to what St Benedict called the 'divinizing light' what we see transforms what we are.

Each meditation is a step further into this wakefulness, this state of being-in-light. The more fully we integrate this essential Christian experience into daily life the more awakened we become. Life is then a journey of discovery, an exploration, a constantly renewed miracle of creative vitality. To meditate is to put an end to dullness, to fear, and above all to triviality. We are really on this journey not just thinking or talking about it. A danger for religious people is to believe that they have all the answers sown up. The arrogance of religious egoists is in believing that they have arrived before they have even started. It is easy to read about wakefulness, to have ideas about enlightenment and yet all the while to be fast asleep. The person who is awake knows without doubt he or she is awake. But whoever is dreaming also believes they are awake. In the dream state the pictures of the dream convince us that they are the same realities we know to be real when we are awake. But we enter wakefulness, as the meditator knows, by letting go of the images and by learning to wait for the light of reality. 'Christ will shine upon you.'

This is the essential Christian experience. It is unchanging but also new in every generation, unique for every individual and indeed unique every time we meditate; each time we enter the vitalizing and creative presence of God. Its manifold uniqueness is our common ground and our human unity in God. This is why it is the basis of Christian community, diversity and unity. The dynamic of the experience is always conversion, a turning from self to an *other*, a rediscovering of a realm beyond ourselves in which we have our unique place. The dream image we let go of is of a universe that revolves around us as its centre. The reality revealed – and the burden of illusion lifted – is the revelation that we are in our indispensable place in the universe centred in God and permeated by the divine presence, for this centre is everywhere.

This rediscovery has a particular colouring in every culture and period. In the modern world the rediscovery we need is not primarily a *religious* one. We don't need to recover our identity in a superficial religious sense within religious demarcations – for example, as good Baptists, Anglicans, Catholics or even atheists. What we need is the spiritual experience of depth to touch the surface levels of life with identity, meaning and purpose once again. This experience happens upon contact with our own spiritual nature as it is in our deepest centre, where the Spirit of God in all its fullness dwells in love. From that contact – and the word is 'contact' as much as 'contemplation' – arises a rooted and sane spirituality that will naturally communicate itself across the whole spectrum of religious, social, and interpersonal life.

The universal call today is to become spiritual. To be spiritual we need to leave behind our official religious selves, the Pharisee that lurks inside all of us, because, as Jesus told us, we have to leave our whole self behind. All images of ourselves come out of the fevered consciousness of the ego and have to be renounced and transcended if we are to become ourselves in true relation to God, to each other. That is to become truly human, truly humble. All images of God must also fall away. To be spiritual is to cease to be an idol-worshipper. We find that the images of God fall away as our images of self fall away. This suggests what we probably always guessed anyway, that images of God were really images of ourselves. In this process of coming into the light of Reality and of falling away from illusion, a great silence emerges. From the centre we feel engulfed in the eternal silence of God. We are no longer talking to God (or worse, talking to ourselves). We are learning to be, to be with God, to be in God.

That is why it is so important to learn to be still. In stillness we learn to remain with the energy that arises from our spiritual nature. Much contemporary 'spirituality' is not in fact a pilgrimage to the centre at all, but more like a raid mission that descends suddenly, plunders what can be got by way of spiritual experiences or insights, and then retreats behind the walls of the religious ego. The difference between a pilgrim and a tourist is the same as between reality and illusion. Pilgrims stay on the journey, steadily and selflessly, focused not on emotional or intellectual satisfaction but upon the goal that leads direct to the goal who is Christ. This pilgrimage is Christian conversion, the revolution that Christ first taught and then exemplified in his own person. This is what makes our religious beliefs and institutions credible to ourselves and ourselves credible to others. The steadiness, firmness, 'rootedness' as St Paul describes it, is the ultimate guarantee of our sanity. Our seriousness about the journey is what makes it joyful.

On the spiritual journey it takes more energy to be still than to run. Most people spend their waking hours rushing from one thing to another, often because they are afraid of stillness and silence. An existential panic can overtake us when we first face stillness and approach the state of pure being. If we can find the courage to face this silence and be still, we enter the peace beyond all understanding. It is easier to learn this in a balanced and stable society with respect for spiritual value and a healthy religious life. But even in a turbulent and confused world like ours where there are so many deceptive voices and distractions, it is possible.

The Christian vision is uncompromising in its sanity. It rejects extremism. In its invitation to have the courage to be ourselves and not merely respond to social conditioning or expectations, the Christian vision proclaims that not only is it possible but that the spiritual resources needed to achieve it are given to us in the power placed in our hearts by the redemptive love of Jesus Christ. The Christian message is one of limitless hope because of the limitless generosity of Christ. We need also to recognize that there is a certain austerity and rigour to the message. We hear it again in the Letter to the Hebrews:

> When people have once been enlightened, when they have had a taste of the heavenly gift ... and after all this have fallen away, it is impossible to bring them again to repentance. (6.4, 6)

It is not that God withdraws his gift in pique and anger. The writer of the Letter to the Hebrews means that if we persist in treating ourselves trivially we will mortally damage our capacity in this life to receive the divine gift. Meditation is the cure for triviality. The discipline of daily meditation takes the words of Jesus seriously. We respond seriously by turning, as our first responsibility, to his presence in our hearts each morning and evening of our lives.

We trivialize ourselves whenever we set limits to the energy we can access for this inner journey to our own heart and to the presence of Christ within us, the journey *with* Christ *to* the Father. The power source from which we draw our dynamism for this journey is inexhaustible. It can be measured by nothing less than the power that God exercised in raising Jesus from the dead. This power was exercised in the root of Christ's being, and Christ's presence is found in the root of every human being. The transformation that this power of God brought about – 'the glory of the Resurrection' – was worked in the depth of the collective being of all humanity. In the depth of our soul we have died and been raised to new life in Christ. The basic challenge of existence is to be open to the life of Christ. To be open to it is to become fully alive. Only life can respond to life. Only in the loving attention of our own deep openness to Christ can we recognize that his life is the energy of the whole creation, the energy of the Creator, the energy of love.

This journey could also be described as taking us from self-consciousness (the prismatic distraction and narrowness of the ego) to

self-awareness (the clarified and expansive knowledge of our participation in reality). The Church is meant to be a special sign of this
transformation of consciousness. It is called beyond concern for its
own image, its own success or influence. The Church is only truly itself
when it is aware that it possesses the mind of Christ and that it is the
conscious presence of Christ in this world. This consciousness *is* its
innate transcendent nature that can never be institutionalized. The
Church has and always will be vitalized by men and women who
have trod this way beyond self into the consciousness of Christ. The
tradition that preserves, nurtures and then communicates this awareness of God in Christ is the Spirit present in and enlivening the Church.
All this points to the primacy of the Spirit over the letter. Rules,
dogma, even scripture can only build up into the living Word that the
Church utters to each generation if the contemplative energy of
new life is set free in the depths of our hearts to enliven the letter. As
Christians we must speak a living Word to our contemporaries. It
must be a Word that is authoritative, not authoritarian; a Word that
is not sectarian but truly catholic. We can only speak this Word when
we are alive with the life of Christ. The Church we meet in the New
Testament is a community of the spiritually alive and enlightened,
charged with a life beyond their own arising from the power of the
risen Christ. The writers of the New Testament everywhere call on
Christians to be open to this power. We today, carrying on a tradition
greater than ourselves, must enter the dynamism of the marriage
between God and humanity in Christ. We can only do so when we
ourselves have begun the pilgrimage into this union by our commitment to the selflessness of deep prayer.

In the experience of our meditation we learn that the power for this
pilgrimage is inexhaustible and present. It takes only one step of faith
to know it from our own experience. The important thing to remember is that one real step of faith, however faltering, is worth more than
any number of imaginary journeys. As beginners we need to accept
that there is a gap between what we say and what we are internally. As
we tread the path that unites surface and depth we recognize that we
are limited and that we are sinners. We are only setting out, we have
not yet arrived. Nothing is more arrogant than to imagine that we
have arrived even before we have actually left. Leave we must. When
we reflect on the need today for this commitment to depth in prayer it
illumines both the opportunity and the responsibility we face. Christ

is consciously present in time to the degree that we, his brothers and sisters, open our minds and hearts to him now and commit to be real, to be still, to persevere. When we do embrace this commitment, the Church becomes first of all not a building or institution, not an organization or hierarchy but the Body of Christ filled in every limb with his vital and vitalizing power. Not only filled with his power but – in the way of all conscious life – alive to that life in full self-awareness.

All this remains potential energy – not the kinetic energy which the Resurrection is – until we realize it. Commitment to the reality of Christ is in effect commitment to prayer. Prayer is our empathy with the consciousness of Christ. In that empathy we know that his consciousness is his love for the Father and the Father's infinite love for him. Our openness to this consciousness is the Spirit praying within us and it sweeps us out of and beyond ourselves into the stream of power flowing from the human heart and mind of Christ to the Father, his Father and our Father. Rooted in our human depths this eternal stream of the spirit is also within time. So we return to our times of meditation each day lest amid the cares and concerns of time we forget the supreme reality in which our being is rooted. As, faithfully and simply, we follow the pilgrimage we discover that this stream of love will carry us beyond time, beyond all division and limitation into the *now,* the infinite liberty of God. Until we know the ordinariness of the way of prayer we will fail to know how sublime its goal is. Never forget the importance of the daily return to stillness and silence each morning and each evening.

The essence of the Christian experience is knowing this love even though, as St Paul says, 'it is beyond knowledge'. This means we know it with knowledge greater than our own knowledge. We must know it in the consciousness of Christ himself. This is the essential and also the redemptive Christian experience.

We are invited to be open and available to this experience. There are two elements to this. First, we must hear the Word of the Gospel – and this is not perhaps as easy as it sounds. Today there are many competing voices clamouring for our attention. The Word of the Gospel is a call to sanity and it remains steady and strong in its utterance even in a world gone mad. Once we have become silent and steady, and rooted enough in ourselves really to hear it, the second step is to 'remain within the Revelation'.

For all this we need our humanity balanced and integrated. We need the encouragement of the human love of others. Our deepest need is to be open to the inexhaustible power of the love of Christ, the love of his human consciousness pervaded by the light of God. The miracle of Christianity is that this need is already met. This power dwells within us, so far exceeding our need that contact with it sweeps us out of ourselves into the reality that is the Kingdom and beyond anything we could have imagined or desired. With the very first step we take towards this power, the Kingdom begins to overtake us, to come to birth within us.

With much love,

John Main OSB
(November 1981)

In the autumn, Laurence Freeman conducted a retreat in Buffalo, New York, and another at Queen's University in Kingston, Ontario. He also taught a course on the history and practice of meditation at Marianapolis College in Montreal. We published a pamphlet on how to start a Christian meditation group and listed, as accurately as we could, the weekly groups meeting around the world. Guests continued to enrich the community. Among them was the whole House of Bishops of the Anglican Church in Canada. We received new oblates and heard about new meditation groups formed in New York, Toronto, Montreal, Vermont and England.

20

SELF-WILL AND DIVINE WILL

My Dearest Friends,

At Brother Paul's solemn monastic profession recently I spoke about the Benedictine vision of life. It is a vision that makes life more vital because for St Benedict the principal quality of a truly Christian life is the ongoing spirit of conversion. Whenever this spirit is present there is a continuous turning, beyond the limitations of our isolated and isolating self-will towards the divine will.

If our self-will dominates us we live in the prison the bars of which are desires and disappointments. On the other hand if we turn away from this and are motivated instead by the divine will, we are swept into a liberty without frontiers where everything in our experience is transformed into pure gift marked by endless epiphanies.

For those of us trained in a traditional religious vocabulary it is necessary to remind ourselves of the limitless liberty implied by the phrase the 'divine will'. It is easy to limit it by confusing it with our own needs and desires. The next logical step, but one that leads into absurdity, is to see prayer as influencing the divine will, trying to make the divine will coincide with our will. It illustrates how dangerously illusory any deduction or action becomes, in the spiritual or material sphere, when the ego is the point of departure. Experiencing our potential for egolessness – in meditation – is, therefore, also a powerful way of ordering our perspectives on reality. Only when we begin the journey away from egoism can we construct a religious language that really makes sense. From the experience of spiritual knowledge we know that to speak of the divine is not the same as speaking of what God wants. It is to speak of what God is. Then we also know what Dante meant in his great saying, 'In his will is our peace.' What is the divine will? It is, simply, love.

St Benedict knew this mystery and clearly lived it. His Rule is understood through the harmonious interplay between obedience and love. He saw monastic obedience as immature as long as there remained any trace of fear. We maturely obey because we listen and then respond out of love. This humane vision aligns the whole person – body, spirit, mind and heart – on the divine reality.

The actual experience of love, not the theological idea or emotional dream, transports the life of the monk far beyond a merely intellectual assent to certain propositions and even further from a retreat from reality. Instead, it makes for a lifelong commitment to truth, integrity and wholeness. Each of these ideals is interwoven in the monk's daily life of prayer and work. Because they are fused and balanced in the monk's experience he enjoys the essential gift of the monastic vocation: liberty of spirit grounded in wholeness of vision. He is empowered to commit himself to truth because the experience of love, simultaneously welling up from within and greeting him from without, teaches him that what he is experiencing is the actual structure of reality. 'Happy are the poor in spirit.' The joy of the monk is seeing how wonderfully simple it all is.

Truth, integrity, wholeness. The ancient writers called them 'oneness'. We often fear the power of oneness – and with good cause. It is not less than the power of the living God which no dividedness or disharmony can withstand. We are, all of us, absurdly attached to our disunity and alienation. Monastic detachment renounces this absurdity which underlies all sin and the sadness and isolation that sin causes. This sane commitment to unity requires courage, indeed a kind of passion and recklessness. It requires both the strength and flexibility of genuine humility which is the capacity to learn about oneself, to find oneself through gentleness and rootedness in faith and perseverance in relating to our gentle but uncompromising Lord.

The monk (the word *monos* means one who is *one*) is one with himself because he faces and passes beyond all personal divisions. One with the brethren, he does not seek his own selfish convenience. He constantly turns to the community in his oneness with God and he only fully becomes himself when he is lost in this oneness.

Benedict's understanding of conversion helps not just monks but everyone who wants to lead a vital, expanding Christian life. The practice of daily meditation is an expression of commitment to Benedict's vision of conversion as obedience in love that unites our whole person and harmonizes life. It is hard to convey this in words to someone who has not at least begun to experience meditation. It is one of the most frustrating of all human limitations that spiritual experience cannot adequately be verbalized beyond the community that it creates among those following its path. Nevertheless everyone in that community has to try and the attempt succeeds best when they realize that the experience itself is one of self-communication. It is the experience of God, the self-communication of love. The self-communication of this redemptive experience of love progresses as we are unified by it. To be unified means 'to possess eternal life', as the New Testament puts it. This means too that no part of ourselves, no aspect of our total human sensitivity, is lost or destroyed.

One of the first things we discover when we start to meditate on a daily basis is that the practice has results right across our life. The harmonic sounded within us at the time of meditation sets up sympathetic responses in every area of personality and life. If it were not so – if meditation were practised in a spiritual vacuum – then we would know that it was illusory.

It is good to remind ourselves from time to time that meditation is not just another activity or interest in life. It is so absolutely fundamental and central that we can say that it is both lifegiving and life-transforming. Life involves movement, growth and development. A person or an institution begins to die when their commitment to growth begins to wane. This is why faith is the energy that fuels the journey of meditation and, because it is a journey into God who is the source of life, faithful commitment to meditation is a hopeful commitment to life as a deep, divine movement of infinite growth. The journey, like the gospel itself, as St Paul describes it, 'begins in faith and ends in faith'. Daily commitment to meditation both expresses and renews faith.

Conversion is to the spiritual life what revolution is to political life. It is the free, conscious principle that assures freshness, honesty, creativity. It is all we mean by integrity. The ideal revolution is peaceful. It occurs in a society that recognizes the necessity for change as an indispensable part of life and recognizes the growth principle in life. It also understands that, like the limbs of a body, all the mutually contributing parts of society, all its groups and institutions, need to develop if they are to meet new situations, new technologies and to serve the new aspirations of humanity that arise from its new discoveries. Creative energy activated in one part challenges the response of the whole.

The whole can only respond to a new phase of growth – the new situations created by an eruption of creativity – if it has already achieved some degree of integrity. This means it must have an awakened conscious centre. Unconscious centres are more common than conscious ones such as centres of political powers or of human emotions that operate by repression out of fear rather than by liberation out of love. The truly conscious heart – whether the centre of an individual person or of society – can cope with the new energies of growth, because it has already, up to that moment, harmonized to some degree the diversity of forces at work. The centre is the heart. It is the open space where the paradoxes of being are held in dynamic and wonder-filled suspension. This dynamic suspension of conflict is both the goal of all life-affirming movement and the condition that makes infinite growth possible. Another name for this dynamic suspension of paradox is peace.

The best revolutions are initiated and concluded peacefully. An orderly process of constitutional assimilation and advance is set in motion out of the immense resources of power held in the peaceful heart. The whole body politic is galvanized by this power. The more conservative and the more progressive forces unite maturely in a creative reassessment of the needs of society. The circumferences of society expands because everyone desires it once they are conscious together that their common centre has produced more than can be absorbed by present structures.

True revolution is driven by this instinct to maintain – by expansion – the equilibrium between the centre and the circumference, between the parts and the whole. It is motivated by a *passion for peace*. Like the word love, we use peace loosely. We have not really experienced peace if we think of it as merely the cessation or absence of violence. Peace is really the harmony of all the mighty forces that, when they are disunited, lead to violence. Peace is not so much a consoling interlude or an escape. It is a power in its own right and a rooting principle of reality.

Throughout history the social and political influence of individuals who have understood and realized this, like Gandhi or Martin Luther King, is out of proportion to the material force at their disposal. This should remind us what it was that Jesus bequeathed when he 'breathed on his disciples' and spoke the word 'Shalom', peace, over them. Peace is an aspect of human experience. It is part of the human perceiving of the mystery of the will, the life and the love of God. It is a form of the divine energy. As such it cannot be destroyed but it is capable of infinite transformations. The Holy Spirit is the universality of God's power, God's freedom to take all forms and to remain free, untrapped by any forms. It is therefore both the love we find welling up in our inmost heart and the passion for justice that impels us to struggle for social equity and global peace. It is the power of all true peaceful revolution.

In the spiritual life the same principles apply. We do not approach true conversion of life in a self-dramatizing way. But we need the steady, daily return to that process whereby we alter our angle of vision and become capable of seeing the basic laws of nature at work. Because we are in a state of continuous conversion, we cannot say we have ever turned fully enough towards God. Each phase of growth clarifies and sharpens our vision further. Some teachers have said that conversion is the spiritual law by which we learn to live by the will of God rather than by our own will. In a sense this is true enough. But what I think the practice of daily meditation soon reveals is that conversion is much more a matter of learning to love as God loves.

St Paul tells us that there is a light shining in our hearts. St John tells us that this light is the point of divine consciousness, of infinitely pure love, to be found and worshipped in every person – the light that enlightens everyone who comes into this world. This is what it means to be human: to enshrine this unique and universal divine one-pointedness. St Paul and St John are witnesses to this. But our own experience must also teach us that everything and everyone is en-lightened by this same point of light that we find in ourselves. We must discover others in ourselves and ourselves in others. We must become real selves. Divine love is the originating and sustaining power of all creation and consciousness. Our hopes for peace are not vain hopes because the experience of God, in the Christ-light shining within us, leads peace and unifies us. It harmonizes our interior forces and satisfies our every desire beyond anything we can imagine or desire.

Life is the pursuit of wisdom because wisdom requires that we learn to live out of the resources of this light and energy. To be wise is to be in harmony with it and vitalized by it. To slip out of this harmony is to descend from wisdom to mere cleverness and to begin to slide down the slope that ends in the hell of non-being. This slipping is the reverse process of conversion. Whenever someone is travelling in this reverse direction, they may see everything that a person in conversion sees but they see it in reverse as mirror images of reality. Whereas conversion leads us to love and more life, slipping increases only the egoism which diminishes life. Love is creative; egoism is death-dealing. Conversion is commitment to the creativity of love. But to be turned towards non-love, egoism is to be enthralled by the fascination for death. This is met with in individuals as well as in societies. In both, affluence and power are not the test of true creativity. The only trustworthy measure is the depth of peace flowing from the centre that harmonizes all its parts in love.

Conversion requires significant readjustments in our lifestyle and our ways of seeing. These readjustments can be thought but they cannot be brought about by thinking of them. They can only be realized by the creative power that we find in our centre. That is why we can best understand meditation, not as a process of self-improvement, or as a tool used for desired ends, but rather as a process of learning, of wonder and deepening humility. Above all we learn that God is the centre, the universal centre and source of all that is. Everything begins in God and everything returns to God.

This is obvious enough but it becomes a more challenging truth when we examine our own practice. The light which helps us do this is meditation. Here, as always, the touchstone is the degree to which we are living out the consequences of our meditation. How do we live our lives? How do we make our daily decisions? Isn't it often the case that, in practice, the centre we align ourselves upon is ourselves? Seeing ourselves as the centre of the universe, we take our decisions more or less solely on the basis of how they will advance our own comfort, amusement or self-fulfilment. This self-centredness is a loneliness more terrible than any physical solitary confinement cell in the worst prison.

As we break through egoism we find that we do certainly have a point of centredness, a place of our own but it is not the ego's illusion of being the universal centre. Human destiny is to find our particular insertion point in the universal reality of God's love. Then we are divinized. We can love as God loves because then we can be who we truly are. The power to love is present in those who know or who have begun to know who they are. This self-knowledge is not our achievement or creation. It is a potential for wholeness present in the creative movement of God's love for us – our creation. We exist because we share the divine being. We are capable of loving, which is to say capable of living the divine life because we are loved. The first step in conversion is, therefore, not renunciation, asceticism or an option for suffering. It is allowing ourselves to be loved. If so many people never really begin this journey it is because they have never been able to draw the curtains of their spirit and allow the light of love to illumine their darkened hearts. There is no greater tragedy than to die without ever having escaped from such a curtained, untouched heart.

Once we are stabilized in our insertion point in love the truth sets us free, propelling us always further into the infinite liberty of the children of God. This liberty is the truth about God and about us. It is the universal truth. We can only see this truth of the identity of life and love if we are rooted and grounded in God. Otherwise we see only partially, aspects of things unrelated to their convergent centre. In this egocentric and fractured vision we can never make true meaning from what we see.

Jesus has told us that he is the truth. He is also the way to the truth because in him our vision is healed and focused. In and with and through his life we find our way into the place destined for us by divine love. Meditation is so important because we only come to the truth if we have the confidence to face it and yet this confidence only arises from the encounter with pure love in our own hearts. Meditation familiarizes us with being loved. It teaches the really important thing to know in and for life, that truth is love and that God is love. It may be of some preparatory use also to know that we are sinners. But it is much more necessary to know that our sins are of no account, no real truth. They cannot even exist in the light of God's love because they are entirely blotted out, burned away by God's pure light of truth.

It is very simple. The first task for anyone wanting to respond to their potential is to come into contact with this light in order to be purified and made real. Only in this contact do we discover our divine potential. The term 'enlightenment' is used widely today. For those of us who follow in the footsteps of Christ it is also an important term to understand. For us it means that we see with his light and that what we see transforms who we are. As St John tells us, we become like him because we see him as he really is.

The first lesson to learn is that the coming of Jesus has enlightened and transformed the ordinary. If we see this we can see our spiritual journey and religious practice entirely shot through with the potentiality of Christ's redemptive love. In order to see this clearly we need to understand how ordinary meditation is. Just as breathing is necessary for the life of the body, so meditation is necessary to develop and sustain spiritual life. To say the mantra is a very ordinary thing to do. It is as ordinary as eating, breathing, sleeping. It seems esoteric only to those who have not yet undertaken the journey. To those who have begun, it is as ordinary and as wonderful as daylight. Like the other functions of a balanced, healthy life, meditation requires regular, daily practice. But it is unique among these functions because meditation is the supreme integrating function by which all the others are balanced and aligned on the centre. Achieving the balance is the first step. From there on, we progress steadily into the heart of the divine Mystery.

The Church's vital role in the world is in calling people to this divinizing work. Many of our secular contemporaries are longing to hear this good news. But we can only speak the enlightening word to them if we ourselves are on the way. The Church has an unparalleled spiritual opportunity in this time, but it can rise to it only if it can train enough Christians to take Christ at his word: 'Anyone who wishes to be a follower of mine must leave self behind' (Mark 8.34). This is lived out most authentically in deep prayer and the loving service of others that deep prayer prepares us for.

The faithful saying of our mantra is the Christian meditator's deep and personal response to this call of Jesus. It is the work of God. Above all, meditation is an all-out confronting of egoism, an assault on the life-denying enclaves of isolation and sadness. Meditation is an affirmation of conscious living through the experience of love. The Christian vision needs a community that is created and vitalized by this affirmation. The message this community will then communicate is that it is possible for all to become alive with the life and truth of God. It is not only possible, it is the destiny of each one of us.

The way to this vitalizing Christianity – a Christianity which is a light for the nations, the salt of the world and a power for peace – is the way of prayer. The prayer that is not our prayer because it is the prayer of Jesus himself. Even now as you read, this same prayer is flowing in your heart and my heart. Our meditation is full acceptance of this reality of our being. To meditate is to fully accept the gift of our being as it flows from the being of God fully embodied in Jesus.

With much love,

John Main OSB
(January 1982)

The new year of 1982 started with the simple profession of Paul Geraghty, who was the first monk professed specifically for the Montreal community. As part of his continuing work for Christian unity, Bishop Henry Hill, a resident oblate in the community, was appointed as the delegate of the Archbishop of Canterbury to visit churches in the Middle East.

2 1

A WAY OF VISION

My Dearest Friends,

For our community here Easter was a time of fullness and joy when we united to reflect upon the deepest mysteries of life. We celebrate Easter liturgically over a few days but we discover its meaning throughout a lifetime. Every year I celebrate it I hear these words of St Paul read out during the Vigil service and their meaning becomes sharper and more real, more urgent and also more mysterious.

> By baptism we were buried with him, and lay dead, in order that, as Christ was raised from the dead in the splendour of the Father, so also we might set our feet upon the new path of life. (Romans 6.4)

To know this is what it means to be a Christian, not just a member of a church or sect but a joyful personal disciple. It means knowing that this 'new path of life' is already opened up for us because of the energies set free within all humanity by the Resurrection. From one point of view we may see only the same tired, worn, old paths. But if the Resurrection energy has touched us and if we have touched it in our hearts, the new path stands out brilliantly as a new way of living that transcends all the old ways. As the snows of winter melted in our garden here, a carpet of brown, withered leaves from last fall was exposed. As we raked them away we found that the soil was covered with young green shoots pushing up from the earth with the irrepressible energy of new life. We have to penetrate beyond the surface to make contact with the new life of the Resurrection.

The Resurrection is the eternal sign of our invitation to share in the glory, the complete realization of Christ. But just what does the new Resurrection-life mean? Does it have personal meaning for each of us or is it like a news item that everyone talks about and almost no one feels personally involved in? We find the answer to this in the New

Testament accounts of the Resurrection. They all make it transparent-
ly clear that the risen Jesus could only be seen and recognized with the
eyes of faith.

> She turned around and saw Jesus standing there, but did not recog-
> nize him ... Jesus said, 'Mary'. She turned to him and said,
> 'Rabbuni!' (which is Hebrew for 'My Master'). (John 20.14–16)

In the atmosphere of this encounter, both profoundly real and
symbolic, we witness a marvellously condensed account of the human
response to the Resurrection. We can hear and see the good news but
until that moment when it engages our absolute personal attention, by
name, we fail to recognize it. Then, in recognizing it, all thought of self
evaporates in the overwhelming joy of an experience of reality so
much greater than ourselves that calls us by name into union with
itself. Mary is described as 'turning' twice, in this encounter. For all of
us there is a two-fold conversion that unfolds throughout a lifetime,
the searching and the finding that leads eventually to the total conversion in absolute harmony of mind and heart.

We need clarified vision to *recognize* what we see. Without this new
dimension of faith, that is the vision of the invisible, we fail to see *and*
to recognize the risen Christ within the creation that he now pervades.
Finding the power of vision which allows us to see what is really there
requires the wisdom to penetrate the outer shell of reality and to go
beyond appearances. Yet, this does not mean rejecting the ordinary or
cultivating an esoteric 'essential' spirituality, a false transcendence.
Far from it. To go that route is to stay locked at the most superficial of
all levels of reality which is the vanity of the self-centred consciousness, the egoism of the isolated 'me'. Penetrating through appearance
of things means rediscovering – in a childlike wonder – the divine correspondence between appearance and meaning, between the mortal
and the immortal. In the Christian vision of eternal life – which means
the full realization of all potentiality – nothing is rejected or wasted.
Nothing is condemned. Even the most fragile and ephemeral dimension of our mortal body is 'saved' from the death process that so
frightens us. As St Paul said, our mortal part is absorbed into life
immortal (2 Corinthians 5.4).

We need wisdom to search into the depth dimension. We also need
to deepen our sensitivity to that dimension of reality which can only be
seen by those who *want* to see and who are humble enough to cry out

with the blind beggar of Jericho, 'Lord, that I may see' (Mark 10.51). Only the blindly arrogant claim to see enough. Those who are truly beginning to see are aware of how much more their faith-vision needs to be purified. They know that no one can see God, with their own eyes, and live. The more we see God the further self-consciousness contracts and the ego evaporates. To see God is to be absorbed into God, to see with the divine vision not our own. When the eye of the heart is opened by the process of love we lose our very sense of the 'I' who sees. This is the sensitivity, the selflessness and delicacy of spiritual refinement that we need to see the risen Christ. It is the awful calm that follows the cataclysm of death. It is the spirit of fully selfless love that does not flinch from being transformed into the beloved.

> What we shall be has not yet been disclosed, but we know that when it is disclosed we shall be like him, because we shall see him as he is. (1 John 3.2)

There is an immortal energy, the 'strength' of God, in this sensitivity. And that is why we cannot enter the new vision without finding a harmony with the basic structure of reality, without being sensitive to the truth that the underpinning reality of everything we see already *is* God.

In this sense meditation is rightly called both a way of wisdom and a way of vision. Wisdom is more than the knowledge derived from accumulated experience. Vision is more than the power to visualize. To be wise we must learn to know in an integrated way with the heart. To see we must learn to see beyond the subject-object divide with the eye of the heart – with love.

The only analogy I know that does justice to this way of wisdom and vision is of falling in love. When we have fallen in love – and if we are still falling, still letting go of ourselves – the beloved changes before our eyes while remaining the same in all appearances to others who are not caught up in the vortex of love. Loving the other deeply and unreservedly we see them in a new light (and a new light in them) which burns away (makes us forget) our own self-important isolation. It allows the smallest gesture of theirs to reveal to us what no one else can recognize. That is why falling in love is so important for us because it sweeps us out of ourselves beyond our bonds of fear and pride into the reality of the other. Until we can lose ourselves and find ourselves again in the other I don't believe any of us can ever know what liberty really is.

Profound meditation is of the same order of reality. Silence, stillness and fidelity to the simplicity of the mantra leads us away from an isolated, self-centred view of life. We are only 'realized' or 'fulfilled' in meditation when we have ceased to seek or desire realization or fulfilment. We only learn to be joyful, because we have learned neither to possess nor want to possess. The ordinary discipline of daily meditation progressively shifts the centre of consciousness from ourselves into the limitless mystery of God's love. At first effort is needed to root the practice as a discipline in us rather than it being just a technique or another routine. It needs to be rooted as an interior *and* external discipline so that it will carry through all the changing circumstances of life. Life is in flux. Even monasteries change their timetables! But when the rhythm of the twice-daily meditation becomes rooted in the ground of our being, naturally renewed and self-renewing, then life is transformed from the centre outwards. We learn to see even the surface dimensions of ordinary life, work and relationships with the eye of the heart, the eye of love. As a disciple of Jesus, the Christian is called to see all reality with the eyes of Christ.

We are so used to remaining on the surface level of life, however, without this depth of perception. Rather than penetrating beyond appearances we are enmeshed in the images and it seems fanciful to say that the way to real vision is the transcendence of all images. While we live in spiritual blindness on the surface it seems to us that without images there can be no vision. Then it seems to follow that without thought there is no consciousness. We have then lost touch with the contemplative dimension of life and with the wisdom that flows from it. What takes us beyond this shallowness of unbelief? Firstly perhaps the frustration of shallowness itself, the anxiety of finding that year after year we have penetrated no further into the real experience and meaning of life. In this shallowness there is not the depth needed for hope to flourish. St Paul wrote, 'Your world *was* a world without hope.' This is the dilemma of the modern world. What ultimately makes depth of vision possible is faith: the leap into the unknown, the commitment to a reality we cannot see. Modern as this dilemma is it was well-known to the first teachers of the faith as well:

What is faith? Faith gives substance to our hopes, and makes us certain of realities we do not see. (Hebrews 11.1)

The discovery of the scientific method may be said to be the invention of modernity and it influences our entire way of responding to life. It has persuaded us not to believe in or to commit ourselves to anything until we can *see* the proof of it. As a method it works very well in the verification of scientific theory and the application of this kind of knowledge to the material world. Thank God for it! But it ceases to work in the dimension of reality that lies beyond appearances. There we must commit ourselves *before* we see God because without that love and faith there is no purity of heart, no undivided consciousness, no falling in love. And only the pure of heart can see God. Commitment must be unconditional, innocent of self-interest, childlike: a condition of complete simplicity demanding not less than everything. It requires just a little experience of meditation to understand what Mother Julian means.

Commitment can take years to mature. Between it and the vision there is a hiatus. It is a vital interlude – what some men and women of prayer have called a glowing night – because here happens the loss of self which must precede the unified vision and wisdom which is our human destiny. The waiting period, however, is not time wasted. It is not a delay or postponement as our instant-gratification culture teaches us. It is a time of joyful purification and preparation. It is a time of learning to be ready, ready to be sufficiently disciplined so that, when the gift is given, we will not try to possess it. For us it is a time of learning to say the mantra.

The saddest people that I have met in my life have been those who have, in one way or another, turned back from pursuing this. Unfortunately it is not enough to see the way or even to understand what is demanded. Nor is it enough to become an expert in other people's experience. The only sufficient commitment is that total personal commitment that comes from a childlike heart. As we realize what is involved all of us are tempted to compromise and to seek consolation or evasion in distraction. We look for ways out, ways to turn back, perhaps because we feel we haven't got what it takes to complete the journey to the other shore. This is why it is so important to remember the humility we need: the faith is the faith of Christ. The power to complete the journey flows from him if we can acknowledge our poverty and accept it.

The sign and the medium of this commitment is silence. By becoming genuinely silent, going beyond all images and thoughts, we quite naturally open the eyes of our heart to the infinite light of God. We begin to see reality with a new clarity of vision, with a sharpness and acuity which is startling and with a profundity which is intoxicating. What do we see? We see knowledge. We see, that is, the One who knows that he is. We see oneness everywhere and at all times because we know with this divine knowledge that is the Spirit of God that 'all must be one'. All divisions must be transcended. We see love as the supreme unifying power of creation. We see that all scientific knowledge and worldly wisdom are nothing compared with the all-inclusive reality of the love who is.

When we set out on the path of meditation we all imagine we will soon become spiritually knowledgeable or at least know *more*. A good sense of humour is essential for humility because gradually we see that the desire for knowledge leads nowhere except becoming cleverer. We have to decide then either for cleverness or for wisdom. Rather than becoming more knowledgeable we become more loving because everything is revealed to us through love. To see the world unified and to know ourselves as one means that we are learning to love our neighbour as ourselves and to love God with our whole heart and whole soul. To love is to be one with. The infinite mystery of love, its intoxication and its boundless creativity, is to discover the freedom given us when we love. Then comes the sheer wonder of discovery that we are loved in return. It is the Trinitarian mystery – Father, Son and Spirit – the cosmic mystery of reciprocal love.

We must be wholly committed. We must be *ready*. The revelation takes place in the moment of God's choosing: the co-mingling of the eternal with time that we cannot predict or record. Incarnation as it unfolds in each person's life configures us to the one Incarnation. Resurrection, as it unfolds in each person's life configures us to the one Resurrection. The configuration is the work of love. The only ultimate tragedy in life would be not to be ready for this moment of love, to be distracted at the time when time is transcended.

Meditation and our daily *re*-commitment to it is our preparation for this moment. Day by day we leave egoism behind and shed all divisions. We meditate in deepening silence in the humble acknowledgement that everything we can learn or experience is in the direct gift of God.

Underpinning the journey and the deepening commitment is the simple acknowledgement that God is God and God is one, God is love. The moment of revelation is our entry into the eternal now of God. So the revelation encapsulates, unifies time. It unifies our whole life 'before' and 'after', just as the one Incarnation, the one Crucifixion, and the one Resurrection embraces past and future in the eternal present. At this moment we recognize what we have all along been seeing. We know that we are called – by name, personally – into the ocean of oneness ever closer towards God. We recognize the call because it comes from one of ourselves who has attained this oneness. It comes from our brother, Jesus, our Lord, our Guide.

May his oneness in the power of his Resurrection always inspire strength and guide our pilgrimage.

With much love,

John Main OSB
(April 1982)

Laurence Freeman returned from a six-week visit to Tanzania during January and February, where he gave a series of retreats and work-shops on meditation. He was gladdened by the positive response from both the Africans and the European missionaries. On his way home, he visited Germany, where he conducted a seminar on contemplative prayer at the University of Wurzburg that had been organized by our oblates there. During this early part of 1982, many groups visited the monastery. They ranged from the Knights of Columbus, a lay Catholic organization, to a group from the Church of the Advent. A long-term monk guest, Michael Hall from St Anselm's in Washington, DC, participated in our life and teaching work. We were also visited by Father George Maloney, SJ, author of many books on prayer. We received new oblates in Toronto and Montreal. Rosie Lovat, our first oblate, stayed with us in March.

22

PARTS OF A WHOLE

My Dearest Friends,

I often meet and meditate with people who faithfully follow this extraordinary, wonderful pilgrimage of meditation as they live their ordinary lives day by day. It helps me to see the true nature of this journey we are all making together: a journey of faith, an expanding of the capacity to love and to be loved, and a deepening of our vision of reality. To know this is also to realize that meditation is a way that never ceases to demand more faith. Mountains get steeper the closer you approach the summit and the path narrows as the view gets wider and vaster. The greater the view the more humbling it is and humility is a mighty force that strengthens us for that deeper commitment required for the last stages of the climb.

Our journey is a way of solitude. True, it is the end to loneliness and isolation. Solitude becomes the crucible of integrity, personal wholeness, which the love of God transforms into communion, into belonging and inter-relatedness at every level of our lives. But still it is an *ascesis*. The solitude of the path is a continual purification, a continual refining in the fire of love.

We can best understand the true nature of solitude by meditating regularly with a group. On my recent visit to England and Ireland I meditated with many of the new weekly groups and I was powerfully struck by this relationship between solitude and community. At the heart of this paradox is the mystery of the unique human person. Each one of us is responsible for responding personally and for committing ourselves personally. No one – neither parent, friend or church – can absolve us of the ultimate personal responsibility to accept the gift of our own being. By accepting it personally we bring it to fruition in the mystery of the source and goal of all being, the infinite love of God. Yet, for all that solitude, it is not a journey we make *alone*. The Father of Lies, working through the ego, makes his best converts from the most religious people. As religious people we are prone to self-importance, self-fixation and self-dramatization. We can think of spiritual progress or our vocation self-centredly and so solemnly that the spirit is stifled and the inner pilgrimage becomes an introverted desire for perfection, for happiness or for spiritual success.

Of all the areas which are vulnerable to the ego's subtle ways, the most vulnerable is that point where we choose between solitude and loneliness as the vehicle of the journey. It is a crucial choice that has often to be reaffirmed by the other decisions that life presents, challenging us to self-transcendence and selfless love. So many people – and this is a cause of the desperate sadness of our time – choose to be lonely in the crowd rather than find communion in solitude. The community of faithful friends, the monastery, the meditation group, the spiritual family, each one of these prepares us for this most important of choices. Alone, we can hardly even see it as a choice because, when we are isolated, we cannot see beyond ourselves. This is the terrible delusion of self-centredness. But in communion we awaken to the deeper truth of our being that we are *meant* to see; and so we learn to travel beyond ourselves. This is why meditating regularly, whether daily or weekly, with the same group is such a healthy source of spiritual sustenance to the pilgrimage. We cannot sustain the delusion of being an isolated pilgrim when we are present with others. This physical and spiritual presence leads to deeper commitment to stillness, to silence and to fidelity. The group or community exposes any false heroism and self-dramatization. Being in touch with the ordinary failings and limitations of others puts our own response into perspective. In the presence of others we know ourselves.

The Christian life summons us to loss, not to the destruction or repression, of self. We lose ourselves in our love for others. One of the desert fathers returned from his hermitage to the community speaking about the dangers of spiritual pride when separated from others. Then he added, 'There, when I was alone, whose feet could I wash?' The life of charity, of practical other-centredness, is an experience of Christ. It is the great stabilizing and enriching element in the contemplative dimension to life. The important decisions of life either take us deeper into reality or thrust us further into lonely illusion but they are not about choosing between two extremes. Those are comparatively easy. The life-giving choices are the harder decisions that keep us on the path we are already treading, and make us more centred, more deeply rooted. St James knew this and puts it this way in his letter to new Christians:

> Let endurance perfect its work in you that you may become perfected, sound throughout; lacking in nothing. (James 1.4)

One of the fears people often experience as they face these decisions to go deeper is that their options are diminishing; the ways of escape are getting fewer. The narrowing of the road is actually a cause for joy, though, not fear; because it is a sign we are approaching our goal. I was deeply moved and inspired by the groups I met with in England and Ireland. They taught me how important it is to understand meditation in terms of spiritual health and psychological balance rather than as an esoteric or arcane secret. They reminded me also just how desperately our world needs men and women who are seriously committed to persevering on the simple path to God. The ordinary regularity of the weekly meetings and the simplicity of their format together highlight the sublimity of the pilgrimage.

People probably do not start to meditate because they feel it will help society. Perhaps at first they even see their meditation times as their ration of quality time-for-me separate from what they do for others. But after some time we experience the true nature of meditation. We sense the profound (though silent and initially inconspicuous) change it works in our life, and then the meditator begins to see things differently. Through experience gained in regular practice we see what is meant by saying that 'being is prior to action'. The meaning and quality of what we *do* depends upon our simply being who we *are*. This is only an abstract idea until we meditate but, as with so many other ideas and dogma of our faith, making contact with our own deeper reality transforms theory into practice through the wonder of personal discovery. The more we open to the mystery of being the more clearly we see the meaning of all activity. The same clarifying process transforms our view of the pilgrimage as well.

Everyone begins the pilgrimage with a certain level of egoism seeing everything in relation to ourselves. In effect we see ourselves as the centre of the universe. This affects even our meditation when we begin. But as we progress we reduce this self-centred perception and become more other-centred. Meditation then sets the standard of other-centredness for life as a whole. We become less concerned with ourselves and more centred in the one who is, who was and who always will be with us: our brother, guide and Lord, the Christ whose centre is simultaneously in God *and* in us. His othercentredness becomes our centre.

At one of the meetings in England somebody asked me how daily meditation fits in with the greater vision of humanity in its movement back to God through evolution and through free will. Is the Christian just one of an elect, a tiny minority from among all races and generations who will awaken to God? If so, does it mean that the Christian meditator is one on the inner track among the elect? It is an important question for us to face today.

Every day I am more amazed at the diversity of people who understand the teaching about meditation and who hear it from a deep, perhaps hitherto unsuspected stillness within themselves. I am even more inspired that so many remain faithful to the discipline and the fidelity that then makes their initial breakthrough in understanding truly significant. They are of all ages and backgrounds, educational, social and religious. If they are Christian they have now discovered a deeper and more personal faith through a common centre in the 'mind of Christ' who lives in their hearts and in the heart of all creation.

It would not be easy to generalize about what they have in common. It is certainly nothing as superficial as a personality type, an I.Q. rating or even a religious orientation. For those who form community on the pilgrimage it is essentially their experience of faith that makes their common ground. The wonder is that this faith is so pure, unpredictable, invincible and such pure gift. That much we know; but as to what purpose or with what design the gift is given we are much less clear. The phenomenon of God's self-revelation and embodiment in humanity is the purest of mysteries; knowable but beyond understanding. To know it is, however, to be made real and to be set at peace. To strive to understand it only rationally is vainly to try to go beyond the limits of what is the specifically human reality. Even though this may seem to point towards spiritual elitism in the context of real practice it actually reinforces the solidarity, interdependence and equality of the human family. Precisely because the capacity of faith to hear and respond to this mystery is pure, inexplicable gift, it is not a cause for pride or elitism. And because the giver of the gift is God, it can never be without meaning.

The meaning is this: by hearing and responding, by pursuing the call to poverty of spirit and purity of heart, we discover that in the depth of our being we fulfil a unique part of the divine plan for all humanity. As experience teaches, the mantra is an act of pure, universal love. Anyone who meditates faithfully through their personal storms and challenges begins to know this. They also come to know that they meditate through the crises and tragedies of the world. The further they go on this path, the closer they feel themselves to be to the whole which is greater than the sum of all its parts. The Spirit moves us all into transcendent wholeness giving us that completion that is redemption and that is also the centre of God's design. The communion we find in the solitude of our hearing and responding is not only harmony within ourselves. That is the first sign – a deeper personal harmony and freedom. But it goes beyond this, to the communion we share with all men and women, with all the dead and all the living and the yet unborn. With all we share the mysterious gift of life – in the flesh and in the spirit. As we awaken to this deeper sense of wholeness we sense the transcendent communion which contains all this and of which these are epiphanies. The communion we have with God and the communion within God – this is the great truth we encounter. All we can say in the end is what we said at the beginning – that the meaning of life is the mystery of love.

Because our incorporation in the whole has both material and spiritual dimensions every experience in the human family influences the whole. St Paul calls the early Christians 'to weep with those who weep and to rejoice with those who rejoice'. Violence, injustice, and any suffering within the Body of Christ affects and implicates us all. The reality is that we are not isolated. We are one with the One. We are one with all. Yet we are more than component cells in a huge organism. We are each of us given a unique and essential place within the infinite mystery of God. Each of us has a personal call to hear and to respond. And if *we* fail then the whole is impoverished.

In breaking through the walls of egoism and fear that encase our hearts the light is a universal beam. The mystery of love is that we become what we delight to gaze upon and so, when we have opened our hearts to this light, we become a beam of light. We are still ourselves because God does not remove the gift of personal being and we are being continuously renewed in the divine eternal present. But we are transfigured. We burn with a light brighter than ourselves and, however dark the world may be, this light cannot be extinguished.

To judge only by appearances we might be tempted to say that the Body of Christ is being broken down in our world. But it is in fact being built up – in very human, ordinary ways and incarnations that testify to a power beyond themselves, beyond appearances and beyond materialistic ideas of success. I felt this very strongly when I was meeting with the meditators in England and Ireland. Their individual fidelity and collective witness seemed to me like open doors for the light of the transfigured Christ to enter homes, schools, factories, offices and hospitals. In all these places the human consciousness of Christ appears through the consciousness of those who seek him daily in love, service and humility. In London and in Dublin where our groups met for a day together, many came up to me afterwards and said how extraordinarily happy and peaceful the day had been, and what a power of love they had felt flowing around them. We are, all of us, moving towards this love and the light is moving towards us. But we can, none of us, possess the light for ourselves. It is 'the' light rather than 'my' light. There is only one enlightenment – the opening of the human consciousness of Jesus to the light of God. Because he is incorporate in our humanity, we are, all of us, affected by that enlightenment. Indeed his light is what we call our redemption. We are redeemed in the light of his love.

To try to define this in exclusive terms *would* lead to pride or arrogance. To know it through the fidelity of our daily pilgrimage is to be made humble by the sheer wonder of it. Each of us has a unique and urgent responsibility to know it. Once we hear, we must respond as generously as we can. When the light of the kingdom dawns in our hearts it touches all we touch. We need not fear the dawn because the light *must* dawn and *must* expand and burst in our hearts until it becomes the full dawn of the Resurrection.

With much love,

John Main OSB
(June 1982)

The Abbot Primate of the Benedictine Confederation visited our small monastery on his North American tour. He spoke at Mass and then met many of our friends who had supported and accompanied us since we arrived. John Main discussed with him the possibility of a new Benedictine contemplative congregation, which the Primate viewed with enthusiasm. (If it had not been for John Main's death within a year of this discussion, this new branch of Benedictinism might have become a reality.) Bishop Henry Hill left to visit Orthodox churches in the Middle East. In June, John Main enjoyed an encouraging visit with our groups in London where Rosie Lovat and Sister Madeleine Simon organized a general meeting of the meditation groups. He went on to Liverpool and Manchester and then to Ireland, where he visited the Benedictine nuns at Kylemore and gave a day of retreat to the Dublin meditation groups.

23

BEYOND MEMORY

I gave a talk recently in Montreal to the International Conference on Palliative Care – the care of the dying. I tried to say that meditation is a way of living, and a way of growth and development. It is a major way of growth because through meditation we are growing into life itself, making us more affirming of life and therefore more fully alive. Although meditation also resembles other ways of growth and development (for example, the pain that accompanies all growth), it is of a different order from all other experiences because it synthesizes them all. Many of life's experiences challenge us with their contradictoriness and can confuse or complicate us. But meditation is continuous growth into greater unity and simplicity.

Unity is freedom. Simplicity is truth. Whoever realizes his or her own essentially simple oneness can perceive their unity with others. Realizing this oneness is the *raison d'être* of all consciousness. Unless we are on the way towards this realization life forfeits meaning and we live as if life were a battle against discontent rather than a celebration of joy in the fact of being. The ultimate tragedy of life would be never to realize any degree of this oneness and so to remain trapped in and by our limitations. The only significant limitations in life are those which retard our entry into full unity. From a materialistic perspective we regard limitations as being whatever conditions restrict freedom of action – illness, poverty, accidents, mortality, misunderstandings. Naturally these are limiting imperfections which need to be confronted by our commitment to life and an innate trust in goodness. But we can be ill, poor, misunderstood and still be free. We can suffer from many forms of external limitation and remain still flowing with joy in the gift of being. We can be restricted in our ability to move and touch and even to communicate and yet still be in communion, in unity. The really dangerous limitations are not physical but those that arise from our egoism, our preference for isolation, our habits of self-centredness, the *reification* of self, others – and God.

Meditation is a gentle way of growing into a freedom beyond all egocentric limitation. It is not magical. It is not instantaneous. Meditation does however surely restore us to a deeper harmony of body and spirit and so it is an essentially spiritual growth. We cannot measure it therefore. But we can recognize it. All growth is a kind of healing. Not only a retrospective healing of past wounds but a making-whole that propels the person-in-healing we all are now into a fuller life, a greater wholeness, the holy health that gives life meaning because it is what we are created for. And so we can say that meditation is growth beyond all the limitations that prevent us from being whole, entire, in 'divine health'.

Once we have passed a limitation that previously held us back we discover that we are free from it forever. We are no longer dominated by the fear or the narrowness that limitations impose on us and which seem, while we are still in their power, to be immovable. Time is so precious because we have to use the opportunity time gives us to grow as much as we can beyond all limitations. Time used for liberation prepares us to enter into eternity – fullness of being – as persons who are essentially free to be fully alive. What we call eternal life is the state of perfect oneness. It demands that all those who enter this unity are free to do so because they are free of self-consciousness, free to love, free to commit ourselves without reserve.

The process of growing into this freedom involves us in the divine dimension of human life and consciousness. God is infinite growth, boundless and perfect freedom. God is the one who is complete. As I have suggested in these letters before, divine perfection is not a stationary stillness, a merely static achievement. This is why we cannot contemplate it as a fixed object within our own horizons. To meet God is to be swept beyond our limitations. God is quite different from the monolithic mental image we so often construct. God is Person. To be personally complete is to be simple and free from all the limitations that impede expansion. God is the infinite expansion who is perpetually centred in the divine self. God is centred in each human consciousness through the medium (the mediation) of the unique human consciousness of Jesus. God is complete and is completeness itself. The state of completeness is always *present*. It is never future or past. God is always now. Meditation is always another step into this *present moment* of God and its degree of growth is the degree to which we allow ourselves to take this step unconditionally. Each meditation is another step into the eternal now of God. Every time we meditate we take one more step into the divine life that heals and enlivens us and brings us to fullness. Whoever turns from self opens his or her self to this new life. The paradox we find by taking this step day by day is the divine paradox, the union of opposites. A life which is grounded in the present, wholly free of reverie and daydream, in which everything is whole and yet always expanding in self-transcendence, is a life of love. The divine paradox is love.

Like all growth, entering the divinizing experience of the present moment involves pain. It is the pain inherent in all maturing. It hurts because of the necessity of leaving behind all earlier stages of development. All that we have been is let go in favour of what we are to become. Growth is the transition from time to eternity and so it is continuous. Every moment is a dying to the past and a rising to a new present in which the past is not rejected but enfolded. We are who we have become through the experiences of a lifetime in which memory is allowed to crumble back into the dust from which it was formed. No memories survive the transition from the condition of incompleteness to the state of fulfilment. All limitations are created and sustained through memory. We have to forget, to un-know everything we have been if we are to come to completeness. The pain of overcoming the limitations of memory is that we have to learn to let go of not just part of ourselves but of all self-consciousness. We are only fully present to the now of the divine moment when we leave the past behind totally.

We resist this complete loss of self. We try to maintain observation points, base camps along the paths of our development. Each of these little camps is an outpost of the ego's central command. Each is a link in the chain of command that stretches down from the ego HQ into every corner of our life. Limitations serve the ego's attempt to bring all of life within its sway and to cast its net over all consciousness. At each of these observation points we are tempted to hang on to part of ourselves just as we reach the brink of a new stage of growth. If we opt for this, instead of our life becoming an experience of growth we find ourselves contracting. Instead of finding that there is more and more space of consciousness to fill within which we accept the gift of Being and love, we find the net of self-consciousness tightening around us like a noose, persuading us there is less and less space to expand into. Our life gets ever more deeply entrenched in a cul-de-sac rather than being a bridge to the further shore.

At each stage of growth we are meant to leave all of ourselves behind and then go forward as a new creation. But it is not enough just to accept this as a theory of life. Believing is not enough. How arid a state we are in when we have the right theories but still do not have the right practice. It was about this state that Jesus was speaking when he said that to those who have, more will be given, and to those who have not even what they think they have will be taken away. It is one of his hard sayings but it is a recognizable truth.

Harder to recognize is where we are now. To *have* means to be a follower of the Way, our feet really touching the pilgrim path at each step. Not to have is to be sustained along the path only by theories of the pilgrimage, treading air, marking time, losing time. It is hard to see that we may have fallen among the *have nots*. Our theories can deceive us. They can make us sound convincing while making us impotent and self-important, like people proud of their car manual but no car. We don't like to admit that we may not have been really making the pilgrimage at all up to this moment of truth. Yet the humility to accept this might be the case and then to make a new beginning is demanded (and re-demanded) of us if our feet are ever to touch the ground. Without the humility of the beginner's mind even what we *think* we have – all our theories – are inadequate to express but a small part of the whole mystery and will be swept away from us when reality dawns. It will dawn for all of us, whether we are ready or not, when death removes the camouflaged superstructure of limitations that we mistake for reality.

We need to pass through theory into experience and this is just what we do each time we meditate. Everything we have been and everything we have done up to that moment is abandoned as we sit down to meditate. The more fully the past is truly abandoned, the more completely renewed we are as we get up and return to the work of our day. Meditation is a continuous breakthrough into the present moment of God. We understand this process of growth in the perspective of our whole life. The person who meditates *is* the person we are, the person we become from birth to death – the whole person. We see that we are not the isolated self we identify with as we weave in and out of the situations and phases of life.

Our growth in and through meditation cannot therefore be restricted to isolated experiences. Being concerned for what we are experiencing in meditation from day to day defeats the purpose. Spiritual growth is growth into union which means moving beyond self-consciousness. If we incarnate this principle of reality in daily fidelity to meditation we find ourselves in the happy position of enjoying the humble yet absolute confidence of St Paul: the Christian 'gifted with the Spirit (who) can judge the worth of everything'. Rooted in this real pilgrimage we know what advances or retards growth towards completeness in Christ. Does it make us think more often about ourselves or does it lead us beyond egoism? That is the Christian touchstone.

Analysing and monitoring our spiritual experiences is an attempt to fix God in time and so to stifle the divine expansion in us that is the work of the Spirit. As soon as we do this we experience not God but our ego-made image of God. To be accurate, meditation does not give us any 'experience of God'. Experiences of the kind we mean by the word require an observer or witness. 'No one can see God and live.' God does not even experience himself; rather, God knows and is the ground of all knowing, all consciousness and all being. For God to experience himself suggests a divided consciousness, a limitation to divine boundlessness and freedom. The knowledge God has of himself is one with God. God's self-knowledge is love.

Meditation takes us into the self-knowledge which is the life of God. It is full with the knowledge of self born from self-transcendence. Meditation is entry into divinization through Jesus. Through union with him we pass beyond the limitations of division to become one with God in God. Through Jesus we utterly transcend ourselves, eventually leaving our whole self behind and becoming a new creation in him. Meditation is the process of self-transcendence. To the degree that we are transcending self we are becoming divine because we are becoming one with the power of love.

Spiritual growth is more than the accumulating of experiences; rather it is the transcendence of all experiences. What we so often call a memorable experience is first and foremost a memory. But in the eternal act of creation which is the life of the Trinitarian God everything is now.

We must try not to become self-important about self-transcendence. It is easy to so completely inhabit the centre of an imaginary universe that we think the rest of the world would fall apart if we left our position at its centre. Of course the only world that does fall apart is the world of the ego. The *real* world then comes into being and we become a new creation.

Small though the relative cosmic impact of our self-transcendence may be it still has an absolute value. The completion and liberation of a single human consciousness express the mysterious meaning of all creation. Each of us, by our own little liberation, is empowered to become one with God. We must not forget this if we want to remain rooted in the expansion of the divine life, if we are to grow on the pilgrimage of daily life. Each time we sit down to meditate we enter into the oneness of God who is now and who is love.

We can barely begin really to understand this vocation to total, integral unity. It is too much for the mind alone to hold or imagine except in fragments. But we can sit down and say our mantra. To do this with humility, fidelity and absolute trust in the goodness of God leads us beyond limitations to become 'like him'. Jesus calls us, such is the marvel of the Christian revelation, to expand into the divine boundlessness.

The more we contemplate the wonder of the human vocation the humbler we become and the poorer in spirit. Humility is self-knowledge. Poverty of spirit is freedom from possessions. As meditators we see how we become humble and poor by fidelity to the mantra. At first it may seem that as we make progress we won't have to say the mantra quite so faithfully in the future. But as we actually progress, in experience not theory, we see that we enter more and more completely into the poverty and fidelity which is the gift of saying the mantra continuously.

With much love,

John Main OSB
(October 1982)

The highlight of the 1982 summer was a holiday we had as a community in Nova Scotia. We were lent a house by the sisters of the Congregation of Notre Dame, on Iona, a remote peninsular of the Bras d'Or Lakes. On his way home, John Main was struck by pain in the lower spine that was to mark the beginning of his terminal period. At this time, three new groups started in New York City and New

Jersey. We received new oblates from Toronto, Los Angeles, Boston, Calgary and Montreal. At our next oblate meeting, we were surprised to discover that the Montreal oblates had organized a fifth anniversary party for us and invited a large number of old and new friends. Early in October, John Main spoke to the Palliative Care International Conference organized by Dr Balfour Mount, his own physician and the founder of palliative care in Canada. There were over a thousand participants whose work was to care for the terminally ill. It was an opportunity to speak to a large group of sensitive and caring people on the importance of meditation. It was in these autumn weeks that John Main became aware of his own impending death.

24

THE OCEANS OF GOD

My Dearest Friends,

In monastic life as indeed in all kinds of Christian life we become even more aware during Christmas of the mysterious blend of the ordinary and the sublime. We can see that it *is* a blend not an opposition.

It is tempting to treat the birth of Christ in a romantic or sentimental way as if it were outside the full meaning of his life. That is what often makes Christmas festivities seem pre or post-Christian. Even in the richly symbolic, beautiful Gospel stories of his birth we can be tempted to see them as consoling fantasies. But it is part of the human mystery that nothing is outside the Mystery. The story of the birth tells us about the life that follows. In the Incarnation God accepted this inclusive aspect of the human condition. The birth and childhood of Christ are part of the whole mystery of his life that culminated on the cross and reached a transcendent completion in the Resurrection and Ascension.

Meditation teaches us this inclusiveness. It shows how fully every part of us has to be involved in the radical conversion of life. It teaches us how we have to put our whole heart into this work of the Spirit. If we are fully to respond to the call to leave the shallows and enter the deep, direct knowledge of a life lived in the mystery of God, then everything in life must be seen in the depth dimension of divine Presence. It is foolish to look for 'signs' on the way – 'signs and wonders' are a form of spiritual materialism that Jesus rebuked – because *if* we are on the way, in the bright cloud of God's presence, then life is wondrous and all things are signs. Everything mediates the love of God.

There is literary art in the infancy narratives of the Gospels of Luke and Matthew. But it does not mean that the details of the birth were not charged with wonder and mystery for all those involved in it. We are told that Mary and Joseph, the parents of Jesus, 'wondered at what was being said about him'. Mary shows us how this experience of wonder can be assimilated by 'treasuring these things in her heart': a deep interior reading or 'lectio' of life. The 'heart' is that focal point in our being where we can simply rest in the Mystery without trying to explain or dissect it. A mystery analysed becomes merely another problem. It must be apprehended whole and entire and so we, the readers of our own book of life, must ourselves be made one in heart and mind.

The mystery surrounding Jesus was perceptible from the beginning of his life. Not until his death and resurrection, however, could it be fully apprehended, fully known, because not until then was it complete. Our life does not come to full unity until it transcends itself and all limitations by passing through death. This is why we do not fully comprehend the mystery of Christ, through which we enter the mystery of God, until our own life is complete. We begin to enter it as soon as consciousness stirs into perception and learns the laws of reality by learning to love and be loved. But in this life we are always learning, always preparing for the fullness that eventually comes to us all. Until the life of Jesus passed through death and returned in the Resurrection this completion of life was a source of terror or despair when the human mind looked deeply at it. Now it has been transformed. What seemed a dead-end has now been revealed to the eyes of faith as a bridge. This is the hidden significance of the birth of Jesus, his growth through infancy and manhood and his supreme sacrifice of self on the Cross. In our beginning our end is always present. And in the birth of Jesus death had already begun to be transformed. The intuitions shared by those involved in his birth and his upbringing were fulfilled in his teaching and his final paschal mystery. His life, like every human life, had a hidden, mysterious unity. End and beginning are two ends of the string of life held in the mystery of God and joined together in the mystery of Christ's oneness with God and humanity.

Our life is a unity because what is real in it is centred in the mystery of God. But to know its unity we have to see beyond ourselves with a perspective greater than when self-interest dominates. Only when we turn from self-interest and self-consciousness does this larger perspective begin to open.

Another way of saying that our vision expands is to say that we come to see beyond mere appearances, into the depth and interconnected meanings of things. Not just the depth and significance in relation to ourselves is involved, but depth in relation to the whole to which we belong. This is the way of self-knowledge and it is why true self-knowledge is identical with true humility. Meditation opens up for us this precious form of knowledge. It is what enables us to pass beyond mere objectivity – merely looking at the mystery of God as observers – and to enter the mystery itself. Knowledge becomes wisdom when we enter the silence, the 'cloud' of the mystery and when we know, no longer by mental analysis and definition, but by direct participation in the heart in the spirit of Christ.

We learn by the path of meditation what cannot be learned otherwise and what is unknowable as long as we hesitate to become pilgrims of the spirit. Following this path of personal experience is a basic requirement of Christian life which must be a life lived at depth rather than in the shallows. This is why Christian discipleship completes the human condition. Human beings always seeks the *complete* action, something that will call forth all our powers simultaneously, focus and unify all the dimensions of our being. Until we have performed this action we are restless, always mastered by distraction or by the desire that masquerades as reality.

Naturally, if we are in touch with our own humanity, we know that this action is love. Only when we live in love do we know that miraculous harmony and integration of our whole being which is what makes us fully human. This is practical rather than idyllic. I mean that the human condition is made up of frailties, accidents and imperfections, either of personality, conditioning or environment. The Incarnation of God in the human condition, however, absorbs all these in such a way that they no longer prevent us from experiencing the fullness of love. The saint is not super-human but fully human.

Every part of us, including our faults and failures, must be included in the commitment we make to the pilgrimage to this fullness. Nothing real is excluded from the kingdom of heaven. Nothing that is natural is against it. Human wholeness is the accumulative result of staying on the pilgrimage. Gradually the separate compartments of life coalesce. The room dividers are taken down and we find that our heart is not a prison made up of a thousand individual cells but a great chamber filled with the light of God whose walls are constantly being pushed back.

Meditation expands our knowledge of God because, in leading us into self-knowledge, it propels us beyond self-centred consciousness. We know God to the degree that we forget ourselves. This is the paradox and the risk of prayer. It is not enough to study the paradox because, like love, it can only be known when it is lived firsthand. Once we begin to live it we read the great testimonies of the spirit – the Scriptures and the spiritual classics – from within the same experience in which they were written. Until that point we are merely observers waiting to begin.

It is never an easy paradox to grasp. How can one grasp the spirit? It helps us to see and touch this paradox to reflect on the purely human manifestation of this dynamic of reality: loving others and being loved by them. To love another person involves more than thinking about them, more than just enjoying their company and more even than sacrificing oneself for them. It involves allowing ourselves to be loved by them. This is the most moving and awe-inspiring mystery of the Incarnation. In becoming human God allows himself to be loved within the human range of love, as ordinarily as any infant, child, adolescent or adult.

The humility of God in allowing himself to be loved in the man Jesus is the cue for recognizing the basic structure of reality. Our first step in loving God is to allow ourselves to be loved. The grammar of language is misleading here because this sounds passive: being loved. But there is nothing passive about allowing ourselves to be loved. Just as there is nothing passive about turning the attention off ourselves, nothing passive about saying the mantra: these are ways we allow ourselves to be loved in any human or divine relationship.

Meditation leads us into the basic relationship of our life. It does this because it leads us into the intimacy with God that arises out of the eternal reality of God's loving and knowing us. In loving us God creates us, calls us into being. Human existence itself witnesses to the hunger inherent in God's love and knowledge of us. It is the demand that we love and know God in return. Yet we can only know God, not as an object of our thought or imagination, but by sharing in God's own self-knowledge, which is the divine life, the Holy Spirit. Thus we are led back to the point of creating, the starting point of our being, God's love and knowledge of us. We come to know and love God because we allow God to know and love us. We allow the divine self-knowledge to become our self-knowledge. This is the alchemy of love.

This kind of knowledge is certain and unshakeable. 'Be rooted and founded in love,' wrote St Paul. Just as the roots of trees hold the soil firm and stop erosion, so it is the roots of love that hold the ground of our being together. They provide the context in which we live and grow. And they each trace back to God as the root of all being. The roots of love in our life bring us into contact with him, with ourselves and with each other. They show us that to *be* is to *be in relationship*, each contributing to the other.

Sanity and balance mean knowing the context in which we live. This kind of knowledge makes us sensitive to the presence of God in all our surroundings. Meditation teaches us, in the only certain way, by experience, that God's presence is not external to us. It is interior because it is the presence that constitutes and holds together the deepest ground of our being. Feeling this we no longer look for God's presence just in the externals of our life or in transcendent ways. We see and recognize God in them too, however, because our inward eyes are opened interiorly to the indwelling Spirit. But we no longer try to possess or manipulate God. Instead we are grasped *by* his presence, interiorly and exteriorly, because we know that the presence is all pervasive, the ground of all that is.

To be possessed by God in this way is the only true freedom. The tyranny of love is the only true relationship. Inevitably we fear this as it develops and emerges during our pilgrimage because our initial sense of freedom is so different. It is naively imagined as the freedom to choose what to do rather than to be. But if we have the courage to be simple and humble enough to enter real freedom we discover within ourselves the power of a faith that is unshakeable. Christian confidence is the discovery of this unshakeability and this confidence empowers the gift of self and therefore also underlies compassion, tolerance and acceptance. We are made wonderfully secure in our own existence by this discovery and in this security we are empowered to drop our defenses and to go out to the other. Our faith is unshakeable, not rigid, because it is one with the ever-living ground of being. Through Christ's union with his disciples his faith becomes their faith and their faith is not a part or an adjunct of their being. It is the breath of life.

So, deepening our commitment to this pilgrimage means deepening the knowledge that faith gives birth to in the soul. As Christ is formed in us, as we ourselves live no longer for ourselves but for him and as his spirit breathes the new life of faith into our mortal bodies, we do truly come to 'know Christ' more personally and more deeply. Maybe it sounds arrogant to claim that we come to know Christ in this way by persevering in meditation. But the truth is not less than this. We come to know what it is to live each moment, every decision, joy or difficulty, from within his presence and touching the infinite resources of his power of love and compassion.

How do we enter this presence? How can we acquire this 'knowledge that is beyond knowledge'? Because it is the knowledge of unknowing, it is the presence that forms when we allow ourselves to go beyond being present merely to ourselves and instead become present to God – to be known and loved into full being. As we are unformed in meditation's work of attention Christ is formed in us. We learn to forget ourselves. Nothing is simpler to do. It is ultimately the condition of full simplicity. Yet nothing – or so it seems – is more difficult. It is easy in theory to accept this. But in practice it is supremely difficult to live and love by placing our centre in the other person as if the other were really more important than ourselves, or as if our first loyalty were really not to the ego but to the other.

The greatest difficulty is to begin, to take the first step and launch out into the depth reality of God revealed in Christ. Once we have left the shore of our self we soon pick up the currents of reality that give us our direction and momentum. The more still and attentive we are, the more sensitively we respond to these currents. And so the more absolute and truly spiritual our faith becomes. By stillness in the spirit we move in the ocean of God. If we have the courage to push off from the shore we will not fail to find this direction and energy. The further out we travel the stronger the current becomes, and the deeper our faith. For a while faith is challenged by the paradox that the horizon of our destination seems to be always receding. Where are we going with this deeper faith? When will we arrive? Then, gradually we recognize the meaning of the current that guides us and see that the ocean is infinite.

Leaving the shore is the first big challenge, but it is only necessary to begin to face it. Even though later the challenges may become even greater, we are assured that we shall be given everything we need to face them. We begin by saying the mantra. Saying the mantra is always to be beginning, to be returning to the first step. We learn in time that there is only this one step between us and God.

Opening our hearts to the spirit of Christ is the only way into the certain knowledge that that step has already been taken. Christ has taken it in himself. He himself *is* the step between God and man because he is God and man. The language we use to express this greatest universal mystery of the human race and of all time, is pathetically inadequate – as theological controversies down the centuries have shown. No word, image or language concept could adequately express the mystery of Christ, because Christ is the *full* embodiment of God and there is no adequate expression of God except God's own self-expression. The only way to know Christ is to enter his personal mystery, in the silence of love, leaving ideas and words behind us. We leave them behind so that we can enter fully the love to which life, death and meditation is leading each of us.

With much love,

John Main OSB
(December 1982)

A few weeks before John Main's death on 30 December 1982, a weekend seminar was held at the monastery in which artists, poets, sculptors and musicians who meditate shared their work and discussed the spiritual value of art. This was repeated in subsequent years and evolved into the John Main seminar. In London, Sister Madeleine Simon, a Sacred Heart nun, started the first 'Christian Meditation Centre', where daily meditation and teaching were shared widely and from which the network of meditation groups in England was served. A collection of the first 12 of John Main's spiritual newsletters was published as Letters from the Heart. *In his last months, he continued to welcome many guests. A Benedictine nun from Stanbrook Abbey enlivened the community with her stories about monastic life on both sides of the Atlantic. Long-term guests from Canada and overseas also came. The renowned international journal* Monastic Studies *was entrusted to the monastery and a new issue was published. This last letter of John Main expresses his final teaching on the meaning of meditation within the whole mysterious paradox of human life.*

Part 3

POSTSCRIPT

At about 8.45 am on 30 December 1982 John Main took the last step of his pilgrimage. He died peacefully in the monastery, several of us beside him. He was buried at Mount Saviour Monastery on Monday 3 January 1983 and a Memorial Mass was held in Montreal on 15 January at the Ascension of Our Lord Parish where he and I had stayed on our arrival in Montreal five years before. Bishop Leonard Crowley who had invited and supported the adventure was the principal concelebrant and monks from nearby monasteries, including Weston Priory and Mount Saviour joined the meditators and representatives of many denominations from the community of Montreal.

Over the previous few months there had been a powerful surge of witness to the profound and enduring effect that John Main had on a widening circle of lives through the simplicity and depth of his teaching. Those who had been open to it were changed by it. His teaching was rooted in the living tradition and in the mystery itself. So it shares in the life and surprising patterns of the mystery. His new life in the Kingdom means new life for the work he began.

We strive to be faithful to the gift of his life and teaching.

Laurence Freeman OSB

A THEOLOGY OF EXPERIENCE

Laurence Freeman OSB

I once received a letter from a Carthusian monastery – one of the most silent and intense forms of contemplative life in the Christian world – asking for more of the books of John Main. Their interest had been aroused by reading his *Word into Silence*. A few weeks later they wrote again saying what a joyful discovery his teaching had been to them – and how practical and useful for their life of prayer.

It reminded me of an incident John Main recounted about the response to a talk on prayer he had given to a Trappist monastery in Ireland. The abbot had made an impromptu request for an hour's conference on contemplative prayer and led him into a stark church lined with two choirs of silent, hooded monks. He spoke from his heart about meditation. At the end of the conference the monks filed out silently, showing no response, but, at the end of the line, one of the oldest monks stopped by him and whispered a question: 'What was the mantra?' Father John told him, 'Maranatha'. The old man absorbed it for a few moments. Then, as he moved away, he looked at Father John and said, 'You know, I have been waiting 40 years to hear this.'

To those who heard him pass on the tradition of Christian meditation, John Main's personal presence and authority could be life-changing. His words were a powerful restatement of an ancient teaching brought alive in a fresh and challenging way. To John Main himself, an incident such as that awakening of the old monk testified to the authority of the teaching itself – the message rather than the messenger. For him, the medium of communication was not essentially a human personality but the Holy Spirit, who is equally present in speaker and hearer and in the living Word that connects them. He spoke and wrote with the authority of one who had been led directly into the living heart of the tradition and who had thoroughly appropriated it personally, but it was the living tradition, not just his private experience, that he meant to communicate.

'In your own experience' is a phrase often found in St Paul that John Main also used often in both his oral and written teaching. He had confidence in the teaching itself to do the work of persuading through experience. The Buddha delivered his dharma with personal authority but told his disciples to test it for themselves in their own experience. Christian *kerygma* (teaching), similarly, insists on faith (*pistis*) developing into knowledge (*gnosis*). John Cassian's *experientia magistra* ('experience is the teacher') expresses a profoundly Christian truth: that Christ is the teaching and the teacher and, if we can faithfully meet the time-tested spiritual conditions – silence, stillness and simplicity – we will be led into experiential understanding of this unity. So, as John Main would say, the first task of the human teacher is to 'phase himself out as quickly as possible' and lead people to see Christ as the 'teacher'.

There is a strong emphasis on experience in John Main's teaching. Meditation for him is a way of experience in faith not of belief alone. Only in the contemplative experience is this really understood. He did not develop a systematic theology or a teaching that depended on always finding something new to say. His imagination and intelligence might have led him to follow this path, but it was in fact his own experience – based on his daily meditation – that was so real it did not let him forget his own discovery that Christian prayer is about participatory *knowledge*, not *thought*: 'By thought you will never know Him, only by love' (*Cloud of Unknowing*).

Yet, seeking experiences for their own sake is not the way beyond thought. In the confused, often superficial eclecticism of the marketplace of modern spirituality, John Main saw the danger of hunting for experience for its own sake. Prayer, he taught, was more than inflated self-consciousness: 'If anything happens during your meditation,' he would say, 'ignore it. Continue to say your mantra.' This simple and down-to-earth discipline came from both his study and his own experience of the tradition.

In the Christian meditation tradition that he first learned from the desert monks, this discipline shines out as faith in practice. Ultimately, it derives its authority from the Gospel: 'You cannot tell by observation when the Kingdom of Heaven will come. You cannot say look here it is or there it is', says Jesus (Luke 17.20–21). John Main's emphasis on experience avoids the spiritual perils of the two extremes of the new gnosticism and the old dualistic pietism. Experience for John Main always needs to be grounded in faith. However, faith means more than belief or cognitive knowledge. It is not about conforming to opinion, but conforming to reality. It is an entire dimension of consciousness, an inclusive, participatory way of knowing and seeing. Faith is therefore itself a kind of experience: 'Faith gives substance to our hopes and convinces us of realities we do not see' (Hebrews 11.1). By itself, experience could lead one astray into spiritual subjectivism, but experience *attended to in faith and active in love* forms us as citizens of the Kingdom in true discipleship.

John Main, as one of his theological commentators has remarked, was not a systematic theologian,[1] but he was a theologian in the sense of Evagrius' definition: 'If you are a theologian you truly pray. If you truly pray you are a theologian' (Chapters on Prayer 60). In this sense, theology means more than mind games. It denotes a system by means of which both the experience and its meaning can be expressed or evoked in ways useful and intelligible to others. Reading John Main's letters and listening to his recorded talks in their deep coherence and consistent simplicity have for 30 years led people into more authentic personal experience. What precisely are this simplicity, depth and coherence? By reading these letters you may find out. Truth is discovery; it is uncovered rather than delivered. Being given the answer is not the same as finding it for yourself. This is a recurrent theme of his letters and it suggests the way we should read them.

Having said this, it is difficult not to indicate a pattern that I see in these quarterly epistles sent to a growing global community of Christian meditators. Certain themes recur and recombine throughout John Main's writings, from his first book, *Word into Silence*, through his letters and in his other teachings. His writing attempted to communicate through words the way to an experience beyond words. Sometimes his books took shape from talks and they deliberately retain as much of an intimacy of the spoken word as print permits, but the letters were written and meant to be read rather than listened to. In the 24 letters he sent from the new kind of Benedictine monastery he led in Montreal between 1977 and his death in 1982, there is a variety

---

1 F. Gerard, 'John Main: A Trinitarian Mystic', in *Monastic Studies*, No. 15, Montreal, 1984.

of themes. There is also news about the day-to-day growth of the community, which also helped this teaching to find expression because it had become the human context, the family of faith, in which the silent experience unfolded. This news section is here placed separately at the end of each letter. It can be skipped, but it can also be read as a kind of parallel commentary on the spiritual teaching. Each letter is a contemporary form of an ancient tradition among Christians of writing to each other about both the mystical experience and the community of discipleship in which this experience finds its crucible of faith. St Paul's letters to the first small Christian communities are the great model of this epistolary tradition. Much of early Christian theology first saw the light in the same medium. Where faith and experience unite in community, the best theology 'makes sense' in every sense of the word. Letters are the most personal form of written communication: the experience is personal and yet the personal is always communal; the personal experience is communicated through community.

So, the very form of these letters carries a teaching: experience can be shared, it cannot be cloned and it must be shared in order to become fully conscious. The very word 'consciousness' means 'knowing with'. The sharing of experience creates a community of faith. This sharing community continuously growing through the marriage of faith and experience becomes Church. John Main loved the Church, even in its institutional form, but he saw the Church essentially as a spiritual and communal event, both personal and organic. For him, this event is tradition, the direct passing on of the Good News, the transmission of the timeless Spirit, which will continue until the 'end of time'. Everything that comes from and serves to advance this transmission is 'traditional'. However novel something may seem at first, if it is 'of God', time will show it to be a contemporary restatement in a new form of a timeless reality.

As the Montreal community developed, we witnessed the emergence of a new form of monasticism. As our identity as a community developed with its own internal traditions and customs, we felt new energy released in both form and spirit. Curiously perhaps, because of our urban location, it seemed that the spirit of our community was closer to primitive than medieval or nineteenth-century revivalist monasticism. This reinforced John Main's belief in the contemporary relevance of Christian desert spirituality. He saw it as a force for today and as a sign that the root tradition can inspire the most radical innovation. It restores conscious contact with the source. John Main's guide back to this source was John Cassian, a fifth-century monk whose 24 *Conferences* shaped St Benedict and had a formative influence on all of Western spirituality. In Cassian and the *Sayings* of the desert monks he found the best commentary on what we as modern monks are doing. The rediscovery and refreshing of a tradition is invigorating. Tradition does not live in libraries. It is not more baggage to carry or a legalistic test of 'orthodoxy'. It is the rails on which we run the straightest course from past to future.

John Main's quarterly letters soon became a little tradition of their own. From the first two-page letter written at Christmas 1977, to his last profound teaching on death before his own death in December 1982, he used a simple format of news and teaching. The teaching section usually followed the news. It was often related to one of the news items – a meeting, development in the community, new member joining or one leaving. He decided against a magazine format for the newsletter. Each letter was typed and photocopied. He wrote the salutation 'My Dearest Friends' and signed it 'with much love'. Circulation was about 3000 at the time of his last letter. As we laboriously stuffed envelopes and sent them out, we were encouraged by knowing that every addressee had asked to be on the mailing list.

Tradition and personal experience, Church and society, meditation and prayer – these are the themes you will find weaving in and out of these letters. At the centre is the experience of awakening, of spiritual vision, but it is not described as just one experience among others – it is the central experience that encompasses and unifies all the rest. John Main does not try to describe 'what it is like'. For him, the experience of the Kingdom, like leaven in the dough, permeates every dimension of living – solitary and relational. It is *like* life lived to the full. The pervasive presence of the experience he speaks about in these letters is a vision of the 'new creation' of Christ, full of hope and prophetic encouragement. The collection of his letters, here re-edited in one volume, shows how his theology grew in his vision of 'Christ in all' and of Christ as the unity of all.

Monastic communities, like other types of family, are aware of themselves passing through time. They have the human instinct to record their growth and development and protect their most significant experiences from distortion or oblivion. The early experiences of a young family, however mundane, are also significant for its entire later history. Meaning often seems most intense at the beginning, so even the early letters and their news of the first days of a small community, which was to grow into a global community now spread through 113 countries, are part of the overall message.

One family photograph album may be much like another but, if you know the family or even if you became part of it later, you are interested to see its uniqueness developing. So, the news items gathered in this edition as the monastic chronicle of the Benedictine Community of Montreal will introduce you to its successor, The World Community for Christian Meditation, which grew out of these salad days. Many of the first recipients of the letters wrote to express their appreciation of the news. Perhaps it was because they felt helped in their own daily discipline by news about the ordinary life of a community trying to do the same – house repairs and decoration, guests' comings and goings, talks and tours, new members of the community. This was not just community gossip but also Christian realism. Meditation as a daily practice led to community as an incarnational spirituality.

In his Introduction to *Letters from the Heart* – the collection of the first 12 letters – John Main describes the genesis of the community. After five years as principal of an American Benedictine high school, he returned to his monastery in London to start a lay community based on meditation. He took this unusual step because of a deepening sense of how hard it was for monastic schools (most monasteries in Britain and America run schools as their principal work) to provide an enduring spiritual preparation for life. They sent out well-educated young people who were better equipped than most for the competitive world of work, but the concern remained, 'Would they know life in the dimension of Spirit, as a mystery rooted in the joy of being? Or would their contact with life be restricted to the sense of a struggle for success to which the fading memory of their monastic schooling would become increasingly irrelevant?'

When he wrote those words, John Main was thinking of the spiritual and social role played by Buddhist monasticism in many countries in Asia. During his years in the East, he had seen how the young people often spent a period of spiritual training in a monastery before starting off in the world. Significantly, right at the beginning of his experiment in the 'new monasticism', John Main was thinking of the young – the focus of hope in any society. He sensed a great potential for monasticism in modern Western society if it could pay attention to the spiritual formation of the young. The particular kind of attention he had in mind was training in contemplative prayer.

At first, he tried to draw a new monastic vision out of the conventional forms. The lay community he started at his monastery in London shared the daily prayer and inhouse work of the monks. Its members lived in a separate house in a serious but relaxed spirit of mindfulness. There was no television and meditation took place three times a day. Out of this small community of six laymen living together for six months under John Main's direction there soon developed the first weekly Christian meditation groups that met at the house on the monastery grounds. These groups drew in all kinds of people and generated the need for teaching material in book and tape form. When news of this reached Bishop Leonard Crowley in Montreal, he invited John Main to start a similar venture there. John Main and the London monastic community considered it carefully. It offered an opportunity to try out in a free way John Main's monastic vision of a contemplative community forming a revitalizing force in the local and universal Church. The stages by which this eventually happened are described in the first section of this edition.

In April 1976, John Main was teaching at the Abbey of Gethsemane, Thomas Merton's monastery in Kentucky. He had been invited to give three conferences to the community on 'Prayer in the Tradition of John Cassian'. The transcripts of these talks became his first published teaching on meditation, *Christian Meditation: The Gethsemane Talks* (Medio Media). While at Gethsemane, he spent a few days in Merton's hermitage and wrote from there to a friend, 'I have just celebrated the most loving Mass of my life in Merton's little chapel. My purpose in coming here was to talk to the community about prayer, but in fact I have learnt so much myself while I have been here.'[2] He had learned a new and risky direction for his monastic adventure. It was a turning point in his life and a moment of convergence between tradition and personal experience. Where Merton had first taught how the contemplative tradition was necessary to secular, technological society, John Main began to teach a way to connect them. He made the most momentous decision of his varied life when he decided to go to Montreal and start a new form of monastic life. It led him to see what

---

2 The chapters of *Moment of Christ* are drawn from these talks.

everything in his life had been the preparation for. He went directly from Kentucky to Montreal and met with Bishop Crowley and knew that here was the place to begin. The abbot and community of Ealing were on the whole reluctant to lose John Main but agreed to a trial period of three years.

In September 1977, John Main and I flew to Montreal to establish what was to be its first monastic community. We found that a small meditation group was already meeting weekly at a Jesuit church in the city using tapes of Father John's talks. So, although we were otherwise unknown there, at least his voice had been heard. After some delay, we moved into a house on Avenue de Vendôme, which the bishop had acquired for us just before Christmas. By then, two of the London lay community had come over to join us. The groups started to meet at the house almost immediately and soon multiplied. Many people asked us why we had come to French-speaking Quebec just when so many anglophone Canadians were leaving. That time of social turmoil was certainly a challenge to our faith in the venture, but many other new spiritual enterprises had also grown up in hard times and difficult places. Even the *Cloud of Unknowing* – one of our core texts – came from a period of war and plague. The social crisis actually strengthened our sense of calling to Quebec, but guests also came from far away – many of them from the growing community of oblates and meditation groups. In retrospect, Montreal seemed an ideal place to begin this global spiritual family. It is a lively and culturally conscious city that is large enough to be international, small enough, in its two cultural groupings, to be human. It is French and English, European and Anglo-Saxon and influenced, but not dominated by, its American neighbour. As a meeting-point of the old and new worlds, it made an ideal place to start to renew an old tradition.

From the time of our arrival in Montreal we felt the need for more room to grow. The lay community rented an apartment nearby. Women guests had to stay in a neighbouring convent. We were receiving an increasing number of long-term guests, including monks and, later, monastic candidates. Every new site we looked at turned out to be either unavailable or too expensive. Then, out of the blue, one of our regular meditators, who had heard of our search, told us of a house his family owned in the heart of the city that might suit us. At first, we were doubtful because we needed space and silence, so we had been looking outside the city. However, when he showed us the house, we realized that the Spirit was guiding us. It was an 18-bedroom house with a coach house, set in 3 acres of garden on the slopes of Mount Royal Park, a few minutes from the city centre and yet secluded and silent. By the time of my ordination in June 1980, the house, along with its contents, had been formally offered to us as a gift by the McConnell family, whose home it had been.

My ordination took place in the motherhouse of the Congregation of Notre Dame, who had been very helpful to us in our early days. Their large chapel was filled with oblates and friends of the community, priests of the diocese and Benedictine and Trappist monks from neighbouring monasteries. It was a symbol of the roots we had already sunk and a sign of hope. Our contact with missionary orders was also increasing during this time. John Main had been to Ireland in the summer of 1980 to give retreats to missionaries, Benedictines and Dominicans and, later, gave retreats to monks in the United States. His retreats were a theological and practical introduction to meditation, with retreatants meditating together for two or three half-hour periods.

Shortly before we left our first small home on Avenue de Vendôme on 3 November 1979, we welcomed the Dalai Lama at the monastery for the midday Office, meditation and lunch. A few days before, John Main had greeted him as a fellow monk at an interfaith service in the cathedral presided over by the Archbishop of Montreal. In the simpler surroundings of the Vendôme house we shared deep silence and a sense of unity that grew into a lasting friendship with the Christian Meditation Community worldwide.

I was a shy junior monk when the Dalai Lama visited and I waited downstairs while he and John Main shared their vision of the spiritual needs of the modern world. However, when I introduced the Dalai Lama at the John Main Seminar in London in 1994, 'The Good Heart', this visit came strongly to my mind, together with a strong sense of John Main's continuing presence in the work he had begun.

There was symmetry to the visit of this great Buddhist spiritual leader. Thirty years earlier John Main had learned to meditate, as a Christian, with an Indian teacher in Malaya. When he became a monk, he was advised to give up what understandably seemed to his novice master then an 'Eastern' practice. Some years later, after enduring the 'spiritual desert' that ensued, he rediscovered the mantra at the Conferences of John Cassian and saw it embedded in his own Western

Christian tradition. Because of the transparent sanctity of his first teacher, John Main had never felt threatened by the great spiritual traditions of the East. His own rootedness in the Christian faith was so deep that it could only be deepened further by encountering the self-revelation of God in other religions. So often when Eastern religious leaders come to meditate with Westerners, the method followed is taught from the Hindu or Buddhist faith. Here, a Buddhist leader had come to share in the depth and silence of a Christian contemplative path, and the unity-in-diversity that this opened held rich promise for the renewal of religion.

Our larger home allowed the expansion of the regular Monday (introductory) and Tuesday (ongoing) evening groups.[3] There were always guests and many returned home to start small meditation groups on the model of those they had participated in at the priory. The simple format of the meeting – talk, meditation, discussion – lends itself to being used in a meditation group meeting in any parish, college, community or home. Most meditators come to feel the need for the support and encouragement of others on this faith-demanding pilgrimage. It is from this spiritual need that groups have come into being in many parts of the world and, in their development, have provided an inspiring model of the Church. These groups were not always directly initiated as a result of contact with the priory, but they looked to it as a focal point of the spiritual family to which they now felt they belonged. As groups grow, through their experience of the faith-filled presence of their silence, they become other-centred and generative of new communities. The laypeople and monks who came to form the Montreal community also discovered that community is created in doing the work of silence together. Such a community becomes a hologram of the Body of Christ: a part of it, but, in that part, containing the whole presence. Contemplative community revitalizes its members' sense of what it means to be 'in the Church'. Each group, each community, is a cell of Christian teaching and a pulse of the life of the Spirit; it enters into the presence of the teacher, consolidates and its members develop each other's faith.

In Montreal, the community integrated four daily periods of meditation with the Divine Office and Mass. In preparing for the times of

---

3 See my article, 'John Main's Monastic Adventure', in *Monastic Studies*, No. 15, Montreal, 1984.

meditation – Cassian's 'pure prayer' – with the Office, we recovered an ancient practice that saw the Office as a communal *Lectio* (spiritual reading) rather than a formal obligation. When we had younger visitors who had little or no religious formation, it impressed us how enthusiastically they responded to the Office, as many priests and religious find it a burden rather than refreshment. Similarly with the Eucharist. By celebrating Mass four times a week rather than daily, we avoided mechanical repetition, deepened our reverence for the Mass and also experienced better the meaning of the indwelling Christ. However deep or reverent one's faith, ritual can become mechanical and diminish the mystery that makes liturgy worshipful and formative. Now, everyone looked forward to the Eucharist (which means literally 'thanksgiving') with an appreciation of it as gift. The half-hour of meditation after Communion not only helped a reverent celebration but also clarified the mystery of the Mass as sacrament – an outward sign of an inward reality.

Many of the meditation groups around the world have been started by Benedictine oblates of The World Community for Christian Meditation – the monastery without walls that succeeded the Montreal priory after it closed in 1990 – but the oblate community itself began during the very early days of the Montreal project. As a form of association with a monastic community, oblation is as old as Christian monasticism. From the days of our first oblates, we realized that this form of lay association with our monastery was significant because of the depth of the spiritual bond created in meditation. Our oblates associated themselves with us for personal reasons related to their spiritual life. They shared the pilgrimage with us and, by communicating it to others, they shared, and still do, in the community's work of teaching meditation. In Europe, North and South America, Australia, Africa and Asia, this fellowship of oblates brings together 18- and 80-year-olds, conservatives and liberals, laity and clergy.

The World Community's work with the spiritual life of children – teaching them to meditate from about the age of seven – also began in the Montreal period. For several years, on Saturday mornings, a group of children met at the priory. This taught us that meditation is indeed practicable 'for everyone' and the problems associated with learning to meditate would be very much reduced if we were taught how when we were young. Children have a natural capacity for meditation, yet this is easily lost as we pass through the ordeals of competitive education and the pressures of consumerism. Many teachers who meditate begin their classes with a few minutes of contemplative silence. This is very popular with the children and, if the teacher omits the silent time, the children ask for it. Encouraged by this, we have recently begun a project to develop a contemplative Christian religious education programme that includes an introduction to and experience of the prayer of the heart. This has been pioneered especially in Australia and, in particular, the religious education office of the Catholic diocese of Townsville, Queensland. By giving children the simple discipline of how to meditate, we hope to help them retain conscious contact with their innate capacity for contemplation. Even if they don't keep up the daily discipline through the turbulence of adolescence – and some can – when in early maturity they begin to seek this inner path, at least they will remember where to begin.

Although most of the teaching at the Montreal monastery took place at the weekly groups and in the liturgy, there were also visits from special groups. Among these were groups of theology students, who often expressed their concern about the lack of spiritual training in their studies. John Main was once asked to give a series of meditation group meetings at the Faculty of Religious Studies at McGill University. I remember that, in one session, an ambulance siren sounded during the meditation period. The theology professor who had come with his class asked, 'During this time of prayer, shouldn't we stop saying the mantra and instead pray for the person being taken to hospital?' John Main's response was that we were already doing this by saying the mantra, because we were praying in the Spirit, joining the prayer of Jesus, who is the one mediator for all. The practical simplicity of meditation opens up a mystical theology of social significance.

At the heart of the community that meditation has created – united by the *Communitas* tapes and other materials in book and video, the quarterly newsletters, website, John Main seminar, school, an international schedule of retreats and seminars and personal visits – is the monastic spirit of the Christian desert. The form by which this has been communicated in the West has traditionally been the Rule of St Benedict, but there are many ways of living it. When we began in Montreal, coming from a good, traditional English Benedictine monastery, we started off with a conventional structure. At first, in the small house on Avenue de Vendôme, in the Notre Dame de Grâce district of Montreal, we did not wear a monastic habit. We kept the monastic timetable and integrated meditation periods with the Divine Office. As young people came and expressed interest in the life, we helped them to try it – as any monastery will. Living the life is the best way to discern if you are meant to live it. Once we had moved to the mansion on Pine Avenue, we began to wear the habit again and have a stricter cloistered area. We received our first novices. By the time of John Main's death, we had a small monastic community, of whom only Paul Geraghty, who had come from London, and I had at that time professed our vows. Even before Father John died, however, we had begun to feel that the conventional forms of monastic life were inadequate for a community so deeply based on meditation.

Meditation is a great democratizer. It redefines the distinctions of status that human organizations create. There are many good reasons for wearing the monastic habit, but it inevitably creates a formal separation from the 'layperson'. Such separations are less helpful when laypeople are sharing in the communal life at the depth of unity that meditation opens up. There are, of course, differences in the degree and length of commitment to a community and, indeed, to the spiritual path itself. Some will stay on for years or for life, while others will move on after a short time.

Before – and increasingly after – Father John's death, the idea that every novice could be programmed to maintain a lifelong commitment through a standard series of training exercises and stages of admission became much more doubtful. There are, as St Benedict says, many kinds of monks. I am sure that the more structured classical form of monastic life – which has much to recommend it and is based largely on the communal celebration of the Divine Office and Eucharist and a common life and work – will probably endure in a smaller number of smaller communities, but new forms, based on a communal contemplative practice and less standardized in their approach to formation and works, have already been developing for some years, both within and on the margins of the institution. In Montreal, we learned the hard way that our monastic commitment to meditation – as both the grounding prayer practice and the teaching work of the community – was a new wine. As such, it needed new wine skins, but the old had to burst before we could see what shape this new form of spiritual container might take.

Father John faithfully continued to speak to the Monday and

Tuesday night groups until about six weeks before his death on 30 December 1982. His last teaching letter, of 8 December, and the short foreword to *Moment of Christ*, which he wrote during those weeks, had an authority and clarity for which his life seemed the preparation. He used to say that we must live well as a preparation for dying well. To be with him as he died, during those months, was to watch the transformation of flesh into spirit. In the expansion of the community and the work into which he breathed his spirit, Father John lives more fully than ever. He lives no longer, but Christ lives in him.

Soon after Father John's death, the two novices left. At this stage, there were only two monks: myself, professed and ordained for just two years, and Brother Paul Geraghty, still in simple vows. Others joined, too, including the former Anglican bishop of Ontario who had become a resident ecumenical oblate. We were able to run the house because of the generous gifts of time and themselves donated by external oblates such as the Schofield and Jass families and friends of the likes of the Mounts, Kaufmans and many others, including the long- and short-term guests who we put to manual work as soon as they arrived. It was a hard but exhilarating time. Shortly before he died, I asked Father John what I should do. He paused a few moments and looked at me with a mixture of sadness and humour and said, 'You'll do what you have to do.' At the time, this did not seem very instructive or consoling, but, as time passed, I realized the wisdom of his not telling me more specifically what I had to do. We carried on. We just did the next thing that needed to be done.

Before long we were receiving requests from men to enter as monks. A women's community also formed that eventually also took on monastic status via a sponsoring women's monastery in the USA. The outline of these and later days is recorded in the monastic chronicle in my own two collections of newsletters, *Web of Silence* and *Common Ground*. In the face of this gratifying growth, we also struggled with the grave problem of how to give adequate formation to the new monastics. I tried to poach some older monks from other monasteries, but, not surprisingly, few monasteries were willing to send their best teachers away to a fragile new foundation, as we were. We took help from wherever we could – the occasional visit from a monk of St Benoît du Lac, near Montreal, or from the much-loved Father Jean Leclercq, the renowned Benedictine peripatetic scholar, and later from Father Bede Griffiths, who would visit us during his American tours.

He above all was the monk who supported and encouraged us most warmly as he himself knew from his experience of his community – Shantivanam in India – that new monastic initiatives are built with blood and tears as well as love and joy. For the rest, we simply trusted that the deepening process of the daily meditation would make up for what was lacking in our monastic resources. I warned new members that we were not a fully equipped monastery and a quicker and deeper monastic maturity would be needed to make a go of it.

At the same time, we had a constant and growing stream of visitors from the expanding meditation community around the world. These stimulated and spiritually enriched us but also became a severe strain on the resources of the new monastic community. Maybe we were not so unlike some of the desert monks of the fourth century who were visited and idealized too much for their own peace of mind. To add to the strain, there was my increasing amount of travel in response to requests from many parts of the world to share the teaching of meditation with them. The Montreal community was at once strengthened but also strained by all this and, as prior, my frequent absences were not good for the community. Shortly before the priory closed as a monastery, I resigned as its prior, but it was unsuccessful. As a community, we tried several ways to keep going. In the end we failed. We had to face the disappointing fact that we could not combine this form of monastic life with the kind of open and increasingly global contemplative community that we were founded to be.

It was, like all deaths, painful. Because it was death, it seemed at the time terminal – perhaps the end of everything. Personally, I was greatly supported by Father Bede Griffiths and then received a warm invitation to join the Olivetan Benedictine monastery at Cockfosters, London, which has remained my monastic home during the extensive travels I have been doing in recent years. Very soon after the closure of the priory, and even before the psychological dust had begun to settle, I realized that its death was, like all deaths, transitional, not terminal.

There was personal suffering for many of those within and associated with the community, but it was also clear that those committed to John Main's vision of a community of love and to all it had achieved in the previous 13 years were determined to help it continue. In 1990, for the first time, the John Main seminar was held outside Montreal and this was led by Bede Griffiths in New Harmony, Indiana. It was our Pentecost and the birth of the World Community for Christian

Meditation, which has become a monastery without walls with members in more than 100 countries. It continues to surprise us with its growth. As I write this, we are preparing for a meeting of national coordinators from more than 30 countries. The monastery that the letters in this book describe has remained true to its vision. It has leapt over its own walls, which I believe the real St Benedict and John Main would have approved of.

International Centre
The World Community for Christian Meditation
London

BIOGRAPHY OF JOHN MAIN

John Main, one of the spiritual masters of our time, was born into an Irish family in England in 1926. He served briefly in the Royal Corps of Signals at the end of the World War Two and then embarked on a period of training in religious life. Deciding it was not the time for vows he studied law in Ireland and then joined the British Diplomatic Service. Posted to Malaya he was introduced to meditation and began to integrate its practice into his Christian prayer. He returned to Europe and became Professor of International law at Trinity College, Dublin. In 1958 he became a Benedictine monk at Ealing Abbey in London and was advised to give up his practice of meditation, which he did before returning to it, as he said in his autobiographical *The Gethsemani Conferences*, 'on God's terms not my own' some years later. He studied in Rome during the heady years of the Second Vatican Council and then returned to teach at the monastery's school in London. In 1969 he was sent to St Anselm's Abbey in Washington DC and here he reconnected, through John Cassian and the Christian monastic desert tradition, to the path of meditation. Increasingly conscious of the importance of this tradition of contemplative prayer for modern Christianity and the world, at his monastery in London he formed a small lay community committed to its practice in community and integrated with traditional Benedictine monastic life. At the invitation of the Archbishop of Montreal in 1977 he formed a new kind of Benedictine community of monks and lay people based on the practice of Christian meditation, and committed to teaching it as its primary work. His talks and retreats during the next period of his life formed the basis of his enduring influence on the spiritual life of contemporary Christianity. In *Word into Silence* he wrote a powerful and concise explanation of the meaning of Christian prayer in contemporary terms true to the theological and mystical traditions and yet able to connect with the spiritual questions and searching of his time. His letters to the growing worldwide community of Christian meditators (*Monastery Without Walls*) opened up new dimensions of spiritual meaning within the tradition and in dialogue with other faiths. Through the spoken word in particular, such as his weekly talks at the monastery, recorded as the *Communitas* series, his influence is still powerful in the formation of Christian meditation groups worldwide. He died in Montreal on 30 December 1982.

BIBLIOGRAPHY

Books

Awakening, London, Medio Media/Arthur James, 1997

Christian Meditation: The Gethsemani Talks, The World Community for Christian Meditation 1977; Medio Media, 1999

Community of Love, London, Darton, Longman & Todd, 1990; New York, Continuum, 1999

Daily Readings with John Main – Silence and Stillness in Every Season, Paul Harris, Darton, Longman & Todd, 1997

John Main – A biography in Text and Photos, Paul Harris editor, Medio Media, 2001

John Main – Essential Writings, Laurence Freeman, Orbis Books, 2002

Joy of Being: Daily Readings with John Main, London, Darton Longman & Todd, 1987; USA, Templegate

Letters from the Heart, New York, Crossroad, 1982

Moment of Christ, London, Darton, Longman & Todd, 1984; New York, Crossroad, 1984

The Heart of Creation, London, Darton, Longman & Todd, 1988; New York, Crossroad, 1988

The Present Christ, London, Darton, Longman & Todd, 1985; New York, Crossroad, 1985

The Way of Unknowing, London, Darton, Longman & Todd, 1989; New York, Crossroad, 1989

Word into Silence, London, Darton, Longman & Todd, 1980; New York, Paulist Press, 1981; Norwich, Canterbury Press, 2006

Word made Flesh, London, Darton, Longman & Todd, 1993; New York, Continuum, 1998

CDs/cassette tapes

Being on the Way, Medio Media, 1991

Christian Meditation: The Essential Teaching, Medio Media, 1991

Communitas, Volumes 1,2,3,4,5, Medio Media, 1991

Fully Alive, Medio Media, 1991

In the Beginning, Medio Media, 1991

The Christian Mysteries, Medio Media, 1991

Bibliography

The Door to Silence, Medio Media, 1991
The Last Conferences, Medio Media, 1991
The Life and Teachings of John Main, Laurence Freeman OSB, Medio Media, 2002
Word made Flesh, Medio Media, 1991

THE WORLD COMMUNITY FOR CHRISTIAN MEDITATION: CENTRES/CONTACTS WORLDWIDE

For countries not listed contact International Centre.

International Centre
WCCM
St Mark's
Myddelton Square
London EC1R 1XX
UK
Tel: +44 20 7278 2070
Fax: +44 20 7713 6346
Email: mail@wccm.org
www.wccm.org

Australia
Australian Christian Meditation
   Community
PO Box 246
Uralla
New South Wales 2358
Australia
Tel: +61 2 9904 4638
Email: palmy@ozemail.com.au
www.christianmeditationaus-
tralia.org

Belgium
Christelijk Meditatie Centrum
Beiaardlaan 1
B-1850 Grimbergen
Belgium
Tel/Fax: +32 2 305 7513
Email:ccm@pandora.be
www.christmed.be

Brazil
Comunidade de Meditacao Crista
Caixa postal 62559
CEP 22252 Rio de Janeiro
Brasil
Tel: +55 21 2523 5125
Email: ana.fonseca@umusic.com
www.wccm.com.br

Canada

Christian Meditation Community
Canadian National Resource
   Centre
P.O. Box 552, Station NDG
Montreal
Quebec H4A 3P9
Canada
Tel: +1 514 485 7928
Email:
ChristianMeditation@bellnet.ca
www.meditatio.ca

Méditation Chretiénne du Québec
7400 boul. St Laurent, Suite 513
Montréal
Québec H2R 2Y1
Canada
Tel: +1 514 525 4649
Fax: +1 514 525 8110
Email: medchre@bellnet.ca
www.meditatio.ca

France

Communauté Mondiale de
   Méditants Chrétiens
126 rue Pelleport
75020 Paris
France
Tel: +33 1 40 31 89 73
Email: cmmc@wanadoo.fr
www.meditationchretienne.org

Germany

Zentrum für Christliche
   Meditation
Untere Leiten 12d
82065 Baierbrunn
Germany
Tel: +49 0 89680 20914
Email: Mariya@wccm.de
www.wccm.de

India

Christian Meditation Centre
Kripa Foundation
Mt Carmel Church
81/A Chapel Road
Bandra (W)
Mumbai 400050
India
Tel: +91 22 640 5411
Fax: + 91 22 643 9296
Email: frjoe@bom5.vsnl.net.in

Ireland

Christian Meditation Centre
4 Eblana Avenue
Dun Laoghaire
Co. Dublin
Ireland
Tel: +353 1 280 1505
Fax: +353 1 280 8720
Email: mclougf@hotmail.com
www.wccmireland.org

Italy
Comunità Mondiale per la
  Meditazione Cristiana
Via Marche, 2/a
25125 Brescia
Italy
Tel: +39 030 224549
Email: wccmitalia@virgilio.it
www.meditazionecristiana.org

Mexico
La Communidad Mundial de
  Meditacion Cristiana
Paseo de Golondrinas Closter
  11-401
C.P. 40880
Ixtapa, Guerrero
Mexico
Ubifone: 800-1320 1320
Tel: +52 755 55 3 01 20
Email: lucia_gayon@yahoo.com
www.meditacioncristiana.com

New Zealand
Christian Meditation Community
PO Box 15-402
Tauranga
New Zealand
Tel: +64 7 544 7955
Email: stanman@xtra.co.nz

Singapore
Christian Meditation Centre
Church of the Holy Family
6 Chapel Road
Singapore 429509
Tel: +65 67376279
Email: daulet@pacific.net.sg
Tel: +65 64458062
Email: rebeccalim@pacific.net.sg
www.wccm.org/singapor.html

United Kingdom
London Christian Meditation
  Centre
St Mark's
Myddelton Square
London EC1R 1XX
UK
Tel: +44 20 7833 9615
Fax: +44 20 7713 6346
Email: uk@wccm.org
www.christian-meditation.org.uk

USA
WCCM-US National Information
  Center
627 N 6th Avenue
Tucson
Arizona 85705-8330
USA
Tel: +1 800 324 8305 / +1 520
882 0290
Fax: +1 520 882 0311
E-mail:
meditate@mediomedia.com
www.wccm-usa.org

ABOUT THE WORLD COMMUNITY
FOR CHRISTIAN MEDITATION

The World Community for Christian Meditation took form in 1991. It continues John Main's legacy in teaching Christian meditation and his work of restoring the contemplation dimension of Christian faith in the life of the church.

The Community is now directed by Laurence Freeman OSB, a student of John Main and a Benedictine monk of the Olivetan Congregation. The World Community has its International Centre and a retreat centre in London. There are a number of centres in other parts of the world. The Community is thus a 'monastery without walls', a family of national communities and emerging communities in over a hundred countries. The foundation of this Community is the local meditation group, which meets weekly in homes, parishes, offices, hospitals, prisons and colleges. The World Community works closely with many Christian churches.

Annually it runs the John Main Seminar and The Way of Peace. It also sponsors retreats, schools for the training of teachers of meditation seminars, lectures and other programmes. It contributes to interfaith dialogues, and in recent years particularly with Buddhists and Muslims. A quarterly spiritual letter with news of the community is mailed and also available online. Weekly readings can be sent direct by email. Information on current programmes, connections to national co-ordinators and the location of meditation groups can be found on the Community website www.wccm.org, which also offers a range of online audio talks. This site is the hub of a growing internet family: the websites of national communities and special interests such as the teaching of meditation to children and the contemporary spirituality of priests.

Medio Media is the communication and publishing arm of The World Community and offers a wide range of books, audio material and videos to support the practice of meditation. The online bookstore is at www.mediomedia.org.